VISUAL
ENCYCLOPEDIA
OF ANIMALS

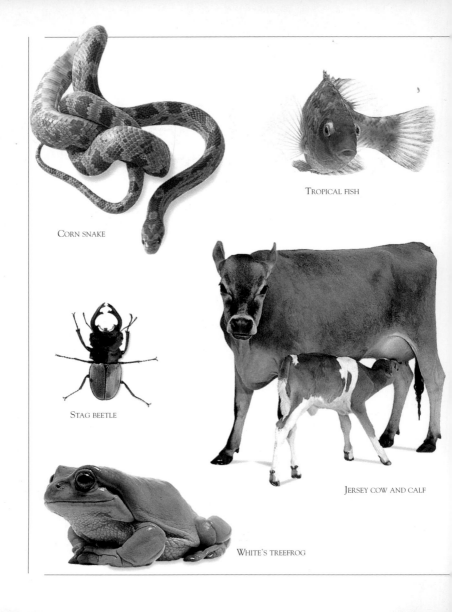

CORN SNAKE

TROPICAL FISH

STAG BEETLE

JERSEY COW AND CALF

WHITE'S TREEFROG

VISUAL
ENCYCLOPEDIA
OF ANIMALS

AMMONITE

CRESTED WATER
DRAGON

LESSER
FLAMINGO

DK

A Dorling Kindersley Book

Dorling Kindersley

LONDON, NEW YORK, SYDNEY, DELHI,
PARIS, MUNICH and JOHANNESBURG

Writers and consultants:
David Alderton, Steve Brooks, Dr. Barry Clarke,
John Farndon, Mark Lambert, Laurence Mound, Scarlett O'Hara,
Barbara Taylor, Steve Parker, Joyce Pope, David Taylor

Originally produced for Dorling Kindersley as
Pockets Animals of the World by PAGE*One*,
Cairn House, Elgiva Lane, Chesham,
Buckinghamshire, HP5 2JD

2001 Edition
Managing Editor Punita Singh
Managing Art Editor Rachana Bhattacharya
Senior Editor Sheema Mookherjee
Senior Designer Sabyasaachi Kundu
Designer Sukanto Bhattacharya
DTP Coordinator Jacob Joshua
DTP Designer Umesh Aggarwal
DTP Operator Sunil Sharma

Second American Edition, 2001

00 01 02 03 04 05 10 9 8 7 6 5 4 3 2 1

Copyright © 2001 Dorling Kindersley Limited

A CIP record is available from the Library of Congress.

ISBN 0-7894-7871-4

Color reproduction by Colorscan, Singapore
Printed and bound in Italy by Printer Trento Srl

See our complete catalog at
www.dk.com

CONTENTS

BIRDWING
BUTTERFLY

GREEN MANTELLA

Tawny owl

MAMMALS 366

ARMADILLO

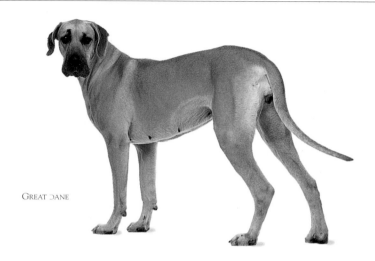
GREAT DANE

DOMESTIC MAMMALS 438

HOW TO USE THIS BOOK

These pages show you how to use the *Visual Encyclopedia of Animals*. The book is divided into seven sections about the animal kingdom. There is also an introductory section about the origins of animal life, and how animals are classified. At the back of the book, there is a comprehensive index.

HEADING AND INTRODUCTION
Every spread has a subject heading. This is followed by the introduction, which outlines the subject and gives a clear idea of what these pages are about.

Label

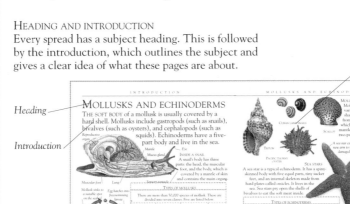

Heading

Introduction

Data box

Fact box

DATA BOX
Some pages have data boxes, which contain detailed numerical information. This box gives data about types of mollusk.

FACT BOXES
Many pages have fact boxes. The information in these is related to the main topic on the page.

LABELS

For clarity, some pictures have labels. These give extra information about the picture, or provide clearer identification.

SECTION NAMES

Down the sides of the pages there are section names. The lefthand page gives the section, the righthand the subject.

SIZE INDICATORS

In some sections of this book, you will find clear symbols next to photography. These indicate the average size of an animal.

Size indicator

REPTILES

REAR-FANGED SNAKES
SNAKES WITH FANGS in the back of their mouth are found in both the Old and New Worlds, and, as with other groups of snakes, they vary greatly in color, size, and habitat. They are not as efficient as front-fanged snakes at injecting venom, and so most species are harmless to humans. Large rear-fanged snakes, however, can be dangerous.

CORAL SNAKE
The false coral snake preys on lizards, small mammals, and other small snakes. It is found in the forests of Central America, from Venezuela to Costa Rica.

Colors resemble those of a

FALSE CORAL SNAKE

This snake often feeds on eggs laid on leaves by frogs

SNAKES

LIZARD HUNTER
The blunt-headed tree snake is found in trees and shrubs from northern Mexico to Bolivia and Paraguay. It is active by night and feeds mostly on lizards such as anoles and geckos.

BLUNT-HEADED TREE SNAKE

Gaping mouth has warning coloration

IDLE THREAT
When threatened, a parrot snake opens its head and opens its mouth, but rarely strikes. Slender and well camouflaged, it hunts lizards and amphibians in the dense foliage of the rain forests of Central and South America.

Camouflaged for life in the treetops

GREEN PARROT SNAKE

IN THE TREETOPS

HIGH UP IN THE RAINFOREST CANOPY it is light and warm and there is plenty of food, especially fruits, seeds, and insect life. Bird life includes large bird predators such as eagles which patrol the treetops looking for prey. Canopy birds, such as parrots and toucans, climb well and have strong feet for grasping branches.

HARPY EAGLE
The huge harpy eagle is one of the most powerful birds of prey. It swoops into the canopy to seize monkeys (like this capuchin), birds, sloths, and reptiles. It can fly very fast through the branches.

Bare, "booted" yellow face and bill

LADY ROSS'S TURACO
This African turaco lives in small, noisy groups, usually high in the canopy. Although clumsy fliers, turacos are good at running along tree branches. They make a great variety of cackling and croaking calls.

MANGROVE SNAKE
In the mangrove swamps of the Malay Peninsula the long snake - as this tree snake - is common... it... towers to 6 ft (2 m). It preys on a wide variety of small mammals. There are subspecies of mangrove snake have different numbers...

TOCO TOUCAN
This is the largest toucan, with a bill up to 7½ in (19 cm) long. The bill is hollow with supporting struts, so it is not as heavy as it looks. The colors help it to recognize other toucans and find a mate.

ORANGE-BELLIED LEAFBIRD
This Asian leafbird helps to pollinate the forest trees as it feeds on nectar. It also spreads the seeds of plants in the mistletoe family by eating the berries.

This leafbird is good at mimicking other birds' songs

The cocque is a thin layer of skin and bone over a honeycomb structure

GREAT HORNBILL
The hornbills of Southeast Asia and Africa look like the toucans of South America because they live and feed in a similar way. They are named for the horny casques on their bills. No-one knows how these horny growths are used.

Annotation

ANNOTATION

Pictures often have extra information around them, which picks out features. This text appears in *italics*, and uses leader lines to point to details.

Caption

INDEX

There is an index at the back of the book that alphabetically lists every subject. By referring to the index, information on particular topics can be found quickly.

CAPTIONS

Each illustration in the book is accompanied by a detailed, explanatory caption.

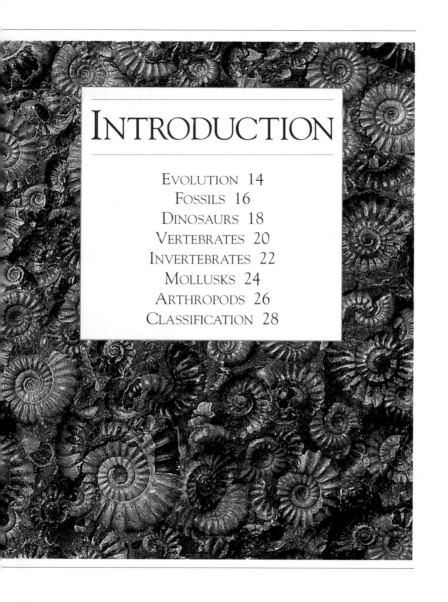

INTRODUCTION

INTRODUCTION

EVOLUTION

SINCE LIFE appeared 3.8 billion years ago, millions of different creatures have come and gone. As habitats changed, some species survived by adapting, while others died out quickly. This gradual turnover of species is called evolution.

PORPOISE'S
FRONT
FLIPPER

"Finger"
bones form a
powerful flipper
for swimming

Two sets of short
"arm" bones

Two sets of long
bones make up
the arm

ADAPTATION

Evolution works by slowly adapting existing features to suit different purposes. Although they look very different, humans and porpoises both have two "arm" bones and five "finger" bones.

Five sets of finger
bones make up
hand

HUMAN
ARM

LIFE-FORMS
THROUGH THE AGES

By working out when certain rocks formed, and then studying the fossils found in them, paleontologists – who study the life-forms of the past – have built up a remarkable picture of the way species have changed since the dawn of the Cambrian period 590 million years ago (mya). Little is known of Precambrian life forms as very few fossils remain.

PRECAMBRIAN	PALEOZOIC	
	Cambrian	Ordovician

4600–590 mya
Single-celled life-forms such as bacteria and algae appear, then soft multi-celled life-forms, like worms and jellyfish.

590–505 mya
No life on land. Invertebrates flourish in the seas. First mollusks and trilobites.

505–438 mya
First crustaceans and early jawless fish appear. Coral reefs form. Sahara glaciated.

HOW EVOLUTION WORKS

According to Darwin's theory of evolution, animals and plants developed over millions of years, surviving according to their ability to adapt to a changing environment. Until the mid-19th-century, people believed that life-forms did not change since their creation by an omnipotent deity.

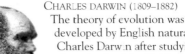

CHARLES DARWIN (1809–1882)

The theory of evolution was developed by English naturalist Charles Darwin after studying the animals of the Galápagos Islands. He published his findings in 1859 in his book *On the Origin of Species.*

EVOLUTION OF THE HORSE

Eohippus
This hare-sized creature browsed in woodlands.

Mesohippus
Over millions of years, Eohippus evolved into a larger grazing animal.

Merychippus
As early horses adapted to the grasslands, they developed longer limbs to escape from predators.

Modern horse
The horses of today are highly developed grazers; they have long legs for running and sharp senses.

Silurian	Devonian	Carboniferous	Permian

438–408 mya
First jawed fish. Huge sea scorpions hunt in the sea. Small land plants colonize the shore.

408–355 mya
Age of sharks and fish. Insects and amphibians appear on land. Giant ferns form forests.

355–290 mya
Warm swampy forests leave remains that will turn to coal. First reptiles.

290–250 mya
Reptiles diversify, conifers replace tree ferns. Mass extinction as Earth turns cold.

FOSSILS

THE REMAINS of living things preserved naturally, often for many millions of years, are called fossils. Most fossils are formed in rocks; however, remains can also be preserved in ice, tar, peat, and amber. Fossils tell us nearly all we know about the history of life on Earth.

Spider trapped inside resin

SPIDER IN AMBER
Amber is fossilized tree resin that may also preserve trapped insects.

AMMONITES
BECAME
EXTINCT 65 MYA

Fossilized shell

KINDS OF FOSSILS
Most fossils form on the seabed, so shells and sea creatures are the most common. Fossils of land animals and plants are rarer. Footprints, burrows, or droppings may also be preserved.

MESOZOIC			CENOZOIC	
Triassic	Jurassic	Cretaceous	Tertiary	
			Palaeocene	Eocene
250–205 mya Mammals and dinosaurs appear. The climate warms and seed-bearing plants dominate.	205–135 mya The age of the dinosaurs. The first known bird, Archaeopteryx, appears.	135–66 mya First flowering plants. Period ends with a mass extinction that wipes out dinosaurs.	66–53 mya Warm, humid climate. Mammals, insects, and flowering plants flourish.	53–36 mya Mammals grow larger and diversify. Primates evolve.

16

1 ANIMAL DIES
The body of a dead animal lies decaying on the surface of the land.

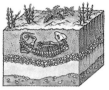

2 REMAINS SINK
Gradually, the body becomes covered with sand or mud.

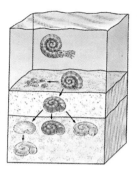

FOSSILIZATION AT SEA
Dead organisms sink to the seabed and are buried. As the sediment turns to rock, their remains are either chemically altered or dissolve to leave a cavity, which may fill with minerals to form a cast.

3 BONES ALTER
Over time, the bones are altered, and the sand and mud turn to rock.

4 FOSSIL IS EXPOSED
Eventually, weather and erosion expose the fossil at the surface.

| | | | Quaternary | |
| Oligocene | Miocene | Pliocene | Pleistocene | Holocene |

36–23 mya First humanlike creatures appear. Hunting birds thrive. Some mammals die out.	23–6.3 mya Climate cools, and forests shrink. Deerlike hoofed mammals flourish. First hominids.	6.3–1.6 mya Cold and dry. Mammals reach maximum diversity. Many modern mammals appear.	1.6m–10,000 ya Ice Ages. Homo sapiens evolves. Mammoths and saber-toothed tigers die out.	10,000 ya to present Humans develop agriculture and technology. Human activity threatens many species.

17

DINOSAURS

FOR 150 MILLION YEARS, Earth was dominated by giant reptiles called dinosaurs, including *Seismosaurus*, the largest creature ever to walk on land. Then, 65 million years ago, all the dinosaurs mysteriously died out.

Light bones for flying

Wings of skin

Furry body

PTEROSAUR
While dinosaurs ruled the land, giant reptiles, like Pterosaur, flew in the air.

DINOSAUR GROUPS

Scientists divide dinosaurs into two orders according to the arrangement of their hipbones. Saurischians have lizardlike hips and include both plant and meateaters. Ornithischians have bird-like hips and are all plant eaters. The two orders are divided into five subgroups.

Muscular tail balanced the front of the body

Long neck for browsing in treetops

Ruff

SALTASAURUS

Horn

STYRACOSAURUS

Sauropods (Saurischians) were huge, long-necked four-legged planteaters.

Marginocephalians (Saurischians) had a bony ruff and horns for self-defense.

TYRANNOSAURUS

STEGOSAURUS

CORYTHOSAURU

Thyreophorans (Ornithischians) were spiny-backed planteaters.

Theropods (Saurischians) were two-legged meateaters.

Ornithopods (Ornithischians) had a horny beak and birdlike feet

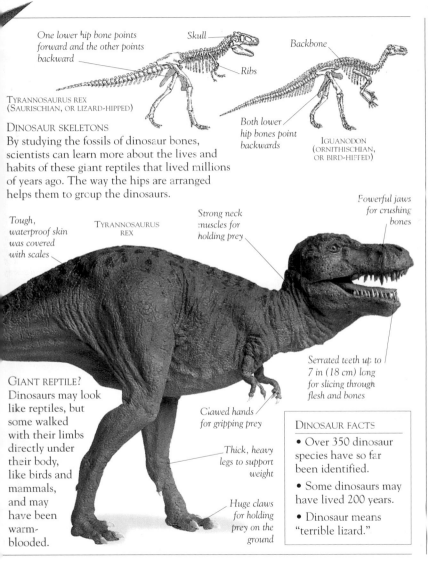

One lower hip bone points
forward and the other points
backward

Skull

Backbone

Ribs

TYRANNOSAURUS REX
(SAURISCHIAN, OR LIZARD-HIPPED)

Both lower
hip bones point
backwards

IGUANODON
(ORNITHISCHIAN,
OR BIRD-HIPPED)

DINOSAUR SKELETONS

By studying the fossils of dinosaur bones,
scientists can learn more about the lives and
habits of these giant reptiles that lived millions
of years ago. The way the hips are arranged
helps them to group the dinosaurs.

Tough,
waterproof skin
was covered
with scales

TYRANNOSAURUS
REX

Strong neck
muscles for
holding prey

Powerful jaws
for crushing
bones

GIANT REPTILE?

Dinosaurs may look
like reptiles, but
some walked
with their limbs
directly under
their body,
like birds and
mammals,
and may
have been
warm-
blooded.

Clawed hands
for gripping prey

Thick, heavy
legs to support
weight

Huge claws
for holding
prey on the
ground

Serrated teeth up to
7 in (18 cm) long
for slicing through
flesh and bones

DINOSAUR FACTS

• Over 350 dinosaur
species have so far
been identified.

• Some dinosaurs may
have lived 200 years.

• Dinosaur means
"terrible lizard."

19

INTRODUCTION

VERTEBRATES

ONLY ABOUT three percent of all animals have backbones, and these are called vertebrates. There are more than 40,000 different species of vertebrates, divided into classes of mammals, birds, fish, reptiles, and amphibians. Their sense organs and nervous systems are well developed, and they have adapted to almost every habitat.

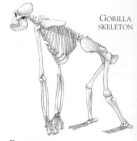

GORILLA
SKELETON

BACKBONE
Vertebrates have a skeleton of bone, with a backbone, two pairs of limbs, and a skull that protects the brain. Inside are the heart, lungs, and other organs.

REPTILES
Lizards, snakes, crocodiles, and geckos are reptiles. They all have a tough, scaly skin. Young reptiles hatch from eggs, and look like tiny versions of their parents. This chameleon is a type of lizard.

Spines along backbone give protection from attack

Scaly skin

Female frog lays eggs, called frogspawn

MADAGASCAN
CHAMELEON

Male fertilizes spawn

ANIMAL REPRODUCTION
In vertebrates, offspring are created when males and females come together and the male's sperm join the female's eggs. This is called sexual reproduction, and usually involves mating. A few animals are neither male nor female, and they reproduce asexually.

Prehensile tail for holding onto branches

SENSES

Mammals and other vertebrate animals have senses to help them find their way, locate food, and avoid enemies. For land animals, such as this caracal, sight, hearing, and smell are the most important senses. Sea creatures rely more on smell and taste to escape danger and find food.

Sharp eyesight for hunting, even at night

Long, sensitive ears pick up even the faintest sounds

Strong sense of smell

Sharp teeth

CARACAL

FISH

With streamlined bodies covered in slippery scales, these vertebrates are perfectly suited to life in the water.

TWINSPOT WRASSE

Scales covered in slimy mucus

BIRDS

The only animals that have feathers are birds, and most of them are powerful fliers. Birds have a beak, or bill, instead of teeth, and all reproduce by laying eggs.

COUNT RAGGI'S BIRD OF PARADISE

AMPHIBIANS

Frogs, toads, newts, and salamanders are amphibians. These vertebrates spend part of their lives in water and part on land. They all reproduce by laying eggs.

RED-EYED TREE FROG

Large eyes spot prey

Long legs for jumping

MAMMAL

A mammal is usually covered by fur or hair. It gives birth to live young, which it feeds with milk.

Fur helps keep body warm

PORCUPINE

Spiny quills protect body

21

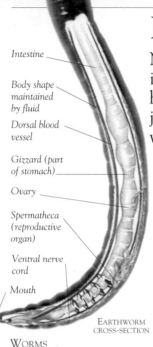

Intestine

Body shape maintained by fluid

Dorsal blood vessel

Gizzard (part of stomach)

Ovary

Spermatheca (reproductive organ)

Ventral nerve cord

Mouth

EARTHWORM CROSS-SECTION

INVERTEBRATES

NINE-TENTHS of all animals are invertebrates, which means they have no backbone. They include jellyfish, sponges, starfish, coral, worms, crabs, spiders, and insects.

Hard shell to protect soft body

Soft body

Eyes on stalks

MOLLUSKS

These soft-bodied invertebrates are often protected by a hard shell. Most mollusks, such as squid and octopuses, clams, mussels, and scallops, live in water, but some, like snails and slugs, live on land.

WORMS

A worm is an animal with a long soft body and no legs. There are many different kinds, including flatworms, tapeworms, earthworms, roundworms, and leeches.

STARFISH AND URCHINS

Starfish, sea urchins, and sea cucumbers are all of echinoderms. All are predators, and most have sucker-tipped "tube feet" through which they pump water to move along and feed. The five broad arms of a starfish can wrench open a shellfish to suck out the contents.

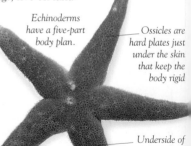

Echinoderms have a five-part body plan.

Ossicles are hard plates just under the skin that keep the body rigid

Underside of arm is covered with fluid-filled tube feet for moving and feeding

Arm

LIFE CYCLE
Each invertebrate has its own life cycle, but most species lay eggs. Some go through several larval stages; others hatch as miniature adults.

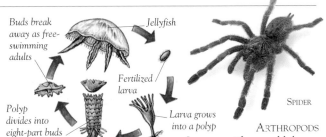

Buds break away as free-swimming adults

Jellyfish

Fertilized larva

Polyp divides into eight-part buds

Larva grows into a polyp

SPIDER

ARTHROPODS
Insects, spiders, and lobsters are all arthropods. They have jointed limbs and a tough external skeleton.

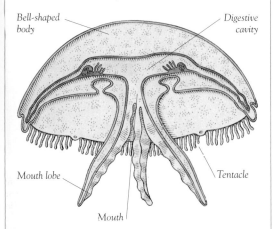

CROSS SECTION OF A JELLYFISH

Bell-shaped body

Digestive cavity

Mouth lobe

Tentacle

Mouth

SPONGES
These primitive sea creatures feed by drawing water into the holes in their soft bodies and filtering out any food.

Jellyfish, anemones, and coral are all kinds of coelenterates – sea creatures with a mouth surrounded by tentacles. These tentacles usually carry a stinger to stun or kill prey. Some coelenterates, called polyps, always attach to a solid object, such as a rock; others, called medusas, move by contracting their bell-shaped bodies.

INVERTEBRATE FACTS

• Up to 500 million hookworms may be found in a single human.

• Roundworms are probably the most numerous animals on Earth.

MOLLUSKS AND ECHINODERMS

THE SOFT BODY of a mollusk is usually covered by a hard shell. Mollusks include gastropods (such as snails), bivalves (such as oysters), and cephalopods (such as squids). Echinoderms have a five-part body and live in the sea.

Reproductive organ

Mantle

Mucus gland

Eye

INSIDE A SNAIL
A snail's body has three parts: the head, the muscular foot, and the body, which is covered by a mantle of skin and contains the main organs.

Muscular foot *Lung* *Sensory tentacle*

Mollusk sinks to a suitable spot on the seabed

Egg hatches into freeswimming larvae

Sperm cells fertilize egg cells outside the adult's body

This is the veliger larvae stage

Shell forms

LIFE CYCLE OF AN OYSTER
Mollusks usually lay eggs that hatch into larvae. As a larva grows, its shell develops. The young adult then settles on the seabed. Some snails hatch out as miniature adults.

TYPES OF MOLLUSKS			
There are more than 50,000 species of mollusk. These are divided into seven classes. Five are listed below.			
MOLLUSK	NAME OF CLASS	FEATURES	NUMBER OF SPECIES
	Bivalves (clams and relatives)	Shells in two parts, which hinge together	8,000
	Polyplacophorans (chitons)	Shell made of several plates	500
	Gastropods (slugs, snails, and relatives)	Mollusks with a muscular sucker-like foot	35,000
	Scaphopods (tusk shells)	Mollusks with tapering tubular shells	350
	Cephalopods (octopus, squid, cuttlefish)	Mollusks with a head and ring of tentacles	600

CUBAN LAND SNAILS

SCALLOP

TRITON

PACIFIC THORNY
OYSTER

SEA STARS

MOLLUSK SHELLS

Mollusk shells have a huge variety of colors and shapes. They are formed from calcium carbonate, which is secreted by the mantle. Bivalves have a two-part shell with a hinge.

A sea star can grow a new arm to replace a damaged limb

SCARLET
SEA STAR

A sea star is a typical echinoderm. It has a spiny-skinned body with five equal parts, tiny sucker feet, and an internal skeleton made from hard plates called ossicles. It lives in the sea. Sea stars pry open the shells of bivalves to eat the soft meat inside.

TYPES OF ECHINODERMS

Echinoderms are a distinctive group of invertebrates that live in the sea. There are 6,500 species in six classes (four listed here).

ECHINODERM	NAME OF CLASS	FEATURES	NUMBER OF SPECIES
	Asteroids (sea stars)	Central mouth surrounded by arms	1,500
	Echinoids (sea urchins)	Body surrounded by a case bearing spines	1,000
	Crinoids (feather stars)	Mouth surrounded by feathery arms	600
	Holothuroidea (sea cucumbers)	Wormlike body with feeding tentacles	1,100

MOLLUSK FACTS

• The world's most venomous gastropod is the geographer cone in the Pacific Ocean. Its venom can kill a human.

• The largest land snail is the giant African land snail *Achatina achatina*. It can grow up to 15.4 in (39 cm) from head to tail.

25

ARTHROPODS

ARACHNIDS, CRUSTACEANS, and insects are part of the arthropod group of invertebrates. Insects are by far the largest of these three groups. All arthropods have a jointed body with a tough body case. The case is shed as the animal grows.

The egg is laid in a silk sac to protect it

Spiderlings resemble the adult spider

Spiderling molts

LIFE CYCLE OF A SPIDER
Arachnids such as spiders lay eggs that hatch into tiny versions of adults. They molt several times before they are mature.

IMPERIAL SCORPION

Poison gland
Sting
Heart
Intestine
Cephalothorax
Pedipalps – a pair of pincers for feeding
Abdomen
Spiracle – air hole

INSIDE AN ARACHNID
The body of an arachnid is divided into a front and middle part (cephalothorax) and a rear part (abdomen). Arachnids have four pairs of walking legs.

TYPES OF ARACHNIDS

The class Arachnida includes spiders, mites, and scorpions. It contains 73,000 species, which are grouped into ten orders. Six orders are listed below.

ARACHNID	NAME OF ORDER	NUMBER OF SPECIES	ARACHNID	NAME OF ORDER	NUMBER OF SPECIES
	Scorpiones (scorpions)	2,000		Uropygi (whip scorpions)	60
	Solifugae (camel spiders)	900		Opiliones (harvestmen)	4,500
	Acari (mites and ticks)	30,000		Araneae (spiders)	40,000

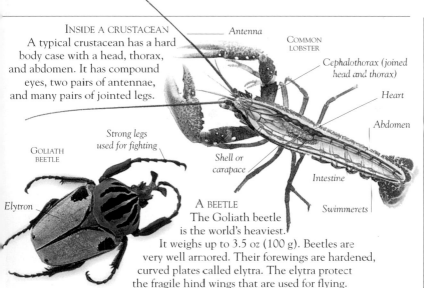

INSIDE A CRUSTACEAN

A typical crustacean has a hard body case with a head, thorax, and abdomen. It has compound eyes, two pairs of antennae, and many pairs of jointed legs.

Antenna

COMMON LOBSTER

Cephalothorax (joined head and thorax)

Heart

Abdomen

GOLIATH BEETLE

Strong legs used for fighting

Shell or carapace

Intestine

Elytron

Swimmerets

A BEETLE

The Goliath beetle is the world's heaviest. It weighs up to 3.5 oz (100 g). Beetles are very well armored. Their forewings are hardened, curved plates called elytra. The elytra protect the fragile hind wings that are used for flying.

TYPES OF CRUSTACEANS

There are more than 55,000 species of crustaceans divided into eight classes. These include the four classes below.

CRUSTACEAN	NAME OF CLASS	FEATURES	NUMBER OF SPECIES
	Branchiopods (fairy shrimp, water fleas)	Small animals of freshwater and salty lakes	1,000
	Cirripedia (barnacles)	Immobile animals with a boxlike case	1,220
	Copepods (cyclopoids and relatives)	Small animals often found in plankton	13,000
	Malacostracans (shrimp, crabs, lobsters)	Many-legged animals, often with pincers	30,000

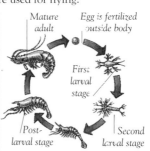

Mature adult

Egg is fertilized outside body

First larval stage

Post-larval stage

Second larval stage

LIFE CYCLE OF A SHRIMP

Crustaceans usually lay their eggs in water. Once hatched, the egg begins its first larval stage. After two more larval stages, there is a final post-larval stage before adulthood.

CLASSIFICATION

BIOLOGISTS HAVE identified
and classified most species of
vertebrates (animals with
backbones), although it is
likely that new species of fish
await discovery. Invertebrates
have not been so well
documented and there may be
many species to be identified.

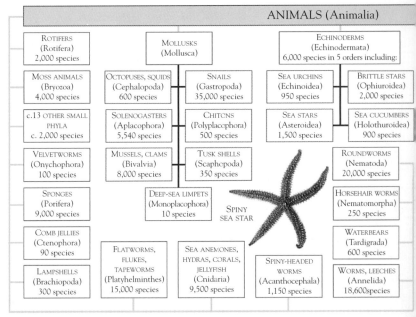

Springtails	Lice
Bristletails	Thrips
Diplurans	Booklice
Silverfish	Zorapterans
Mayflies	Bugs
Stoneflies	Beetles
Webspinners	Ants, bees, wasps
Dragonflies	Lacewings and
Grasshoppers,	antlions
crickets	Scorpionflies
Stick and leaf insects	Stylopids
Grylloblattids	Caddisflies
Earwigs	Butterflies and moths
Cockroaches	Flies
Praying mantids	Fleas
Termites	

INSECTS
(Insecta)
1,000,000 species

ANIMALS (Animalia)

ROTIFERS
(Rotifera)
2,000 species

MOSS ANIMALS
(Bryozoa)
4,000 species

c.13 OTHER SMALL
PHYLA
c. 2,000 species

VELVETWORMS
(Onychophora)
100 species

SPONGES
(Porifera)
9,000 species

COMB JELLIES
(Ctenophora)
90 species

LAMPSHELLS
(Brachiopoda)
300 species

MOLLUSKS
(Mollusca)

OCTOPUSES, SQUIDS
(Cephalopoda)
600 species

SOLENOGASTERS
(Aplacophora)
5,540 species

MUSSELS, CLAMS
(Bivalvia)
8,000 species

DEEP-SEA LIMPETS
(Monoplacophora)
10 species

FLATWORMS,
FLUKES,
TAPEWORMS
(Platyhelminthes)
15,000 species

SNAILS
(Gastropoda)
35,000 species

CHITONS
(Polyplacophora)
500 species

TUSK SHELLS
(Scaphopoda)
350 species

SPINY
SEA STAR

SEA ANEMONES,
HYDRAS, CORALS,
JELLYFISH
(Cnidaria)
9,500 species

ECHINODERMS
(Echinodermata)
6,000 species in 5 orders including:

SEA URCHINS
(Echinoidea)
950 species

BRITTLE STARS
(Ophiuroidea)
2,000 species

SEA STARS
(Asteroidea)
1,500 species

SEA CUCUMBERS
(Holothuroidea)
900 species

ROUNDWORMS
(Nematoda)
20,000 species

HORSEHAIR WORMS
(Nematomorpha)
250 species

WATERBEARS
(Tardigrada)
600 species

SPINY-HEADED
WORMS
(Acanthocephala)
1,150 species

WORMS, LEECHES
(Annelida)
18,600species

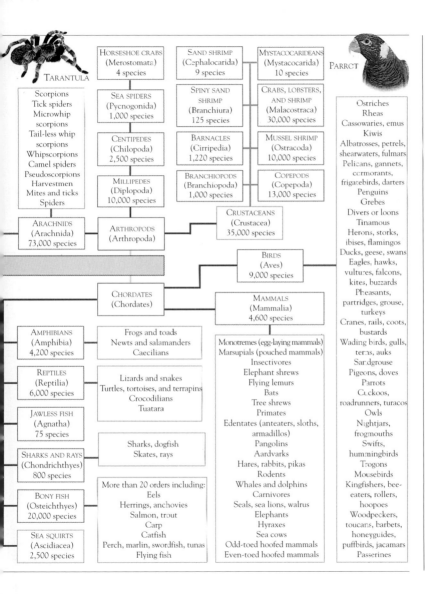

TARANTULA

PARROT

HORSESHOE CRABS (Merostomata) 4 species	**SAND SHRIMP** (Cephalocarida) 9 species
	MYSTACOCARIDEANS (Mystacocarida) 10 species

Scorpions
Tick spiders
Microwhip scorpions
Tail-less whip scorpions
Whipscorpions
Camel spiders
Pseudoscorpions
Harvestmen
Mites and ticks
Spiders

SEA SPIDERS (Pycnogonida) 1,000 species

SPINY SAND SHRIMP (Branchiura) 125 species

CRABS, LOBSTERS, AND SHRIMP (Malacostraca) 30,000 species

CENTIPEDES (Chilopoda) 2,500 species

BARNACLES (Cirripedia) 1,220 species

MUSSEL SHRIMP (Ostracoda) 10,000 species

MILLIPEDES (Diplopoda) 10,000 species

BRANCHIOPODS (Branchiopoda) 1,000 species

COPEPODS (Copepoda) 13,000 species

ARACHNIDS (Arachnida) 73,000 species

ARTHROPODS (Arthropoda)

CRUSTACEANS (Crustacea) 35,000 species

BIRDS (Aves) 9,000 species

CHORDATES (Chordates)

MAMMALS (Mammalia) 4,600 species

Ostriches
Rheas
Cassowaries, emus
Kiwis
Albatrosses, petrels, shearwaters, fulmars
Pelicans, gannets, cormorants, frigatebirds, darters
Penguins
Grebes
Divers or loons
Tinamous
Herons, storks, ibises, flamingos
Ducks, geese, swans
Eagles, hawks, vultures, falcons, kites, buzzards
Pheasants, partridges, grouse, turkeys
Cranes, rails, coots, bustards
Wading birds, gulls, terns, auks
Sandgrouse
Pigeons, doves
Parrots
Cuckoos, roadrunners, turacos
Owls
Nightjars, frogmouths
Swifts, hummingbirds
Trogons
Mousebirds
Kingfishers, bee-eaters, rollers, hoopoes
Woodpeckers, toucans, barbets, honeyguides, puffbirds, jacamars
Passerines

AMPHIBIANS (Amphibia) 4,200 species

Frogs and toads
Newts and salamanders
Caecilians

REPTILES (Reptilia) 6,000 species

Lizards and snakes
Turtles, tortoises, and terrapins
Crocodilians
Tuatara

JAWLESS FISH (Agnatha) 75 species

SHARKS AND RAYS (Chondrichthyes) 800 species

Sharks, dogfish
Skates, rays

BONY FISH (Osteichthyes) 20,000 species

More than 20 orders including:
Eels
Herrings, anchovies
Salmon, trout
Carp
Catfish
Perch, marlin, swordfish, tunas
Flying fish

SEA SQUIRTS (Ascidiacea) 2,500 species

Monotremes (egg-laying mammals)
Marsupials (pouched mammals)
Insectivores
Elephant shrews
Flying lemurs
Bats
Tree shrews
Primates
Edentates (anteaters, sloths, armadillos)
Pangolins
Aardvarks
Hares, rabbits, pikas
Rodents
Whales and dolphins
Carnivores
Seals, sea lions, walrus
Elephants
Hyraxes
Sea cows
Odd-toed hoofed mammals
Even-toed hoofed mammals

29

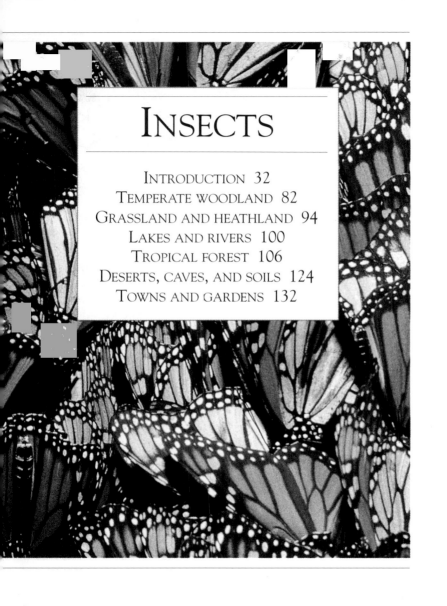

INSECTS

INSECTS

WHAT IS AN INSECT?

THERE ARE AT LEAST one million named insect species – they are the most abundant animals on earth. All insects have six legs, and their skeleton is on the outside of their body. This outer skeleton forms a hard, protective armor around the soft internal organs.

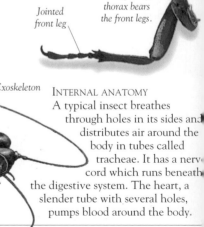

The antennae of insects can sense smells and vibrations in the air.

DISSECTED BEETLE

Eye

First part of thorax bears the front legs.

Jointed front leg

SHEDDING SKIN
An immature insect is called a nymph. As each nymph feeds and grows, it must shed its hard outer skin, which is also called an exoskeleton. When it grows too big for its skin, the skin splits, revealing a new, larger skin underneath.

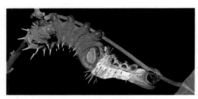

Heart

Digestive system

Exoskeleton

Nerve cord

Trachea

Antenna

INTERNAL ANATOMY
A typical insect breathes through holes in its sides and distributes air around the body in tubes called tracheae. It has a nerve cord which runs beneath the digestive system. The heart, a slender tube with several holes, pumps blood around the body.

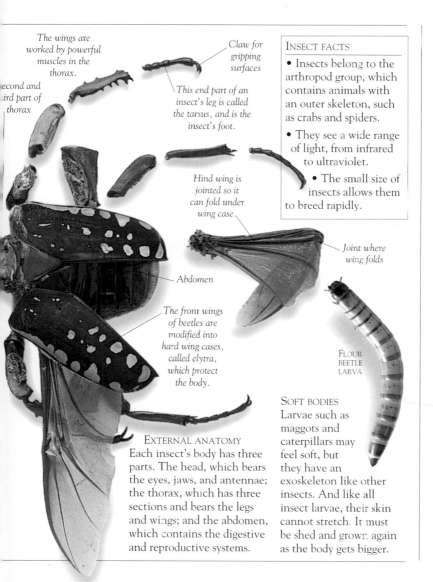

The wings are worked by powerful muscles in the thorax.

Claw for gripping surfaces

Second and third part of thorax

This end part of an insect's leg is called the tarsus, and is the insect's foot.

Hind wing is jointed so it can fold under wing case.

INSECT FACTS

• Insects belong to the arthropod group, which contains animals with an outer skeleton, such as crabs and spiders.

• They see a wide range of light, from infrared to ultraviolet.

• The small size of insects allows them to breed rapidly.

Joint where wing folds

Abdomen

The front wings of beetles are modified into hard wing cases, called elytra, which protect the body.

FLOUR BEETLE LARVA

SOFT BODIES
Larvae such as maggots and caterpillars may feel soft, but they have an exoskeleton like other insects. And like all insect larvae, their skin cannot stretch. It must be shed and grown again as the body gets bigger.

EXTERNAL ANATOMY
Each insect's body has three parts. The head, which bears the eyes, jaws, and antennae; the thorax, which has three sections and bears the legs and wings; and the abdomen, which contains the digestive and reproductive systems.

33

THE FIRST INSECTS

INSECTS WERE the first animals to fly. They appeared 300 million years ago – long before humans, and even before the dinosaurs. The ancient insect species are now extinct, but some were similar to modern dragonflies and cockroaches.

INSECT IN AMBER

Amber is the fossilized tree resin which came from pine trees over 40 million years ago. Well-preserved ancient insects are sometimes found in amber. This bee is in copal, which is similar to amber but not as old.

FLOWER FOOD

When flowering plants evolved 100 million years ago, insects gained two important new foods – pollen and nectar. Insects thrived on these foods. They pollinated the flowers, and many new species of plants and insects evolved together.

FIRST INSECT FACTS

• The oldest known fossil insect is a springtail that lived 400 million years ago.

• Some of the earliest insects seem to have had three pairs of wings.

• The oldest known butterfly or moth is known from England 190 million years ago.

MODERN
EARWIG

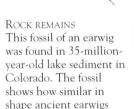

ROCK REMAINS

This fossil of an earwig was found in 35-million-year-old lake sediment in Colorado. The fossil shows how similar in shape ancient earwigs were to modern ones.

Fossil earwig

FOSSIL DRAGONFLY
Dragonflies were one of the first types of insect. Fossils show that they have not changed very much in appearance over millions of years. Some ancient dragonflies were very large and may have had wingspans of over 2 ft (60 cm). This dragonfly fossil, found in southern England, is of a small species. The intricate wing veins can be seen clearly.

Wing laced with veins

End of abdomen

Large eye

Wing veins

MODERN DRAGONFLY
One of the largest present-day dragonflies is this species from Borneo, with a wingspan of 6¼ in (16 cm). Although the larvae of modern dragonflies live in water, we cannot be sure that this was true of prehistoric dragonflies.

AGILE FLIERS
Modern dragonflies are fast, agile fliers, and ancient dragonflies were probably the same. A prehistoric flying reptile would have had greater trouble catching a dragonfly than this fanciful engraving suggests.

35

TYPES OF INSECT

WE DO NOT KNOW exactly how many species, or types, of insect there are, since scientists constantly discover new insects. There are about one million different named species. Each belongs to one of about 28 groups, or orders, which are defined according to body structure and larval development.

Beetles, wasps, bees, and ants

About 350,000 species of beetles are described – they are the largest order of insects. Wasps, bees, and ants form the second largest order of insects, made up of about 125,000 species. The common feature in this order is a narrow "waist."

Jaws

STAG
BEETLE

*Hard wing
cases meet
midline.*

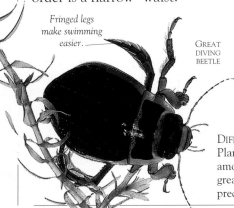

*Fringed legs
make swimming
easier.*

GREAT
DIVING
BEETLE

BEETLES

WINGS AND JAWS
The front pair of wings in beetles is hardened and forms a strong shield over the folded hind wings. Some beetles, such as stag beetles, have greatly enlarged jaws that look like horns.

DIFFERENT FOODS
Plants, fungi, insects, and dead animals are among the wide variety of beetle foods. The great diving beetle lives in ponds. It is a fierce predator which hunts tadpoles and small fish.

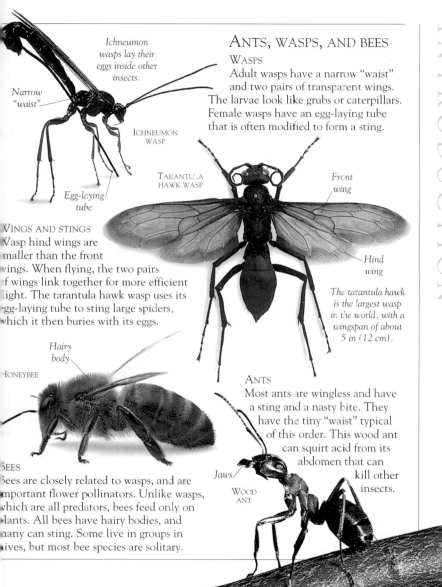

Ichneumon wasps lay their eggs inside other insects.

Narrow "waist"

ICHNEUMON WASP

Egg-laying tube

ANTS, WASPS, AND BEES

WASPS

Adult wasps have a narrow "waist" and two pairs of transparent wings. The larvae look like grubs or caterpillars. Female wasps have an egg-laying tube that is often modified to form a sting.

TARANTULA HAWK WASP

Front wing

Hind wing

The tarantula hawk is the largest wasp in the world, with a wingspan of about 5 in (12 cm).

WINGS AND STINGS
Wasp hind wings are smaller than the front wings. When flying, the two pairs of wings link together for more efficient flight. The tarantula hawk wasp uses its egg-laying tube to sting large spiders, which it then buries with its eggs.

Hairy body

HONEYBEE

ANTS
Most ants are wingless and have a sting and a nasty bite. They have the tiny "waist" typical of this order. This wood ant can squirt acid from its abdomen that can kill other insects.

Jaws

WOOD ANT

BEES
Bees are closely related to wasps, and are important flower pollinators. Unlike wasps, which are all predators, bees feed only on plants. All bees have hairy bodies, and many can sting. Some live in groups in hives, but most bee species are solitary.

Butterflies, moths, and flies

Two common insect orders are the two-winged flies and the butterflies and moths. Flies are distinctive because their second pair of wings is converted into balancing organs that look like drumsticks. Their young stages are maggots. Butterflies and moths have a coiled feeding tube, and their wings are covered in minute flattened scales. Butterfly and moth larvae are called caterpillars.

BUTTERFLIES AND MOTHS

CATERPILLARS

Although caterpillars' bodies are soft, they have an exoskeleton like other insects. Caterpillars grow at a very fast rate. They feed on leaves and have sharp jaws for slicing vegetation.

Leaf-green coloring

Feathery antenna

POLYPHEMUS
MOTH

MOTHS

There are 150,000 species of moth. Most moth species fly only at night. They are usually dull in color and they often have feathery antennae. There are also many day-flying species, and some of these are brightly colored.

Club-tipped antenna

BUTTERFLIES

There are 15,000 species of butterfly. Most butterflies fly by day, have club-tipped antennae, and are brightly colored. The scales that cover moths and butterflies sometimes produce colors by iridescence, which is the effect of sunlight shining on them to produce a display of many different colors.

SWALLOWTAIL
BUTTERFLY

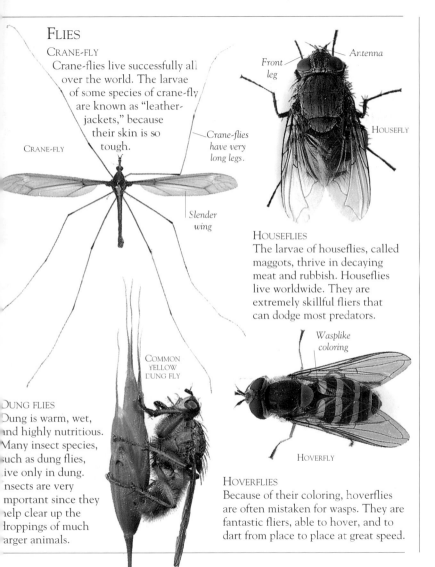

FLIES

CRANE-FLY
Crane-flies live successfully all over the world. The larvae of some species of crane-fly are known as "leather-jackets," because their skin is so tough.

CRANE-FLY

Crane-flies have very long legs.

Slender wing

Front leg

Antenna

HOUSEFLY

HOUSEFLIES
The larvae of houseflies, called maggots, thrive in decaying meat and rubbish. Houseflies live worldwide. They are extremely skillful fliers that can dodge most predators.

Wasplike coloring

COMMON YELLOW DUNG FLY

DUNG FLIES
Dung is warm, wet, and highly nutritious. Many insect species, such as dung flies, live only in dung. Insects are very important since they help clear up the droppings of much larger animals.

HOVERFLY

HOVERFLIES
Because of their coloring, hoverflies are often mistaken for wasps. They are fantastic fliers, able to hover, and to dart from place to place at great speed.

39

Bugs and other types

There are about 67,500 species of bug, the fifth-largest order of insects. Bugs have a feeding tube folded back between the legs, and most of them eat plant food. The other orders of insects contain fewer species. Some of these orders are well known, such as fleas, cockroaches, dragonflies, and locusts.

BUGS

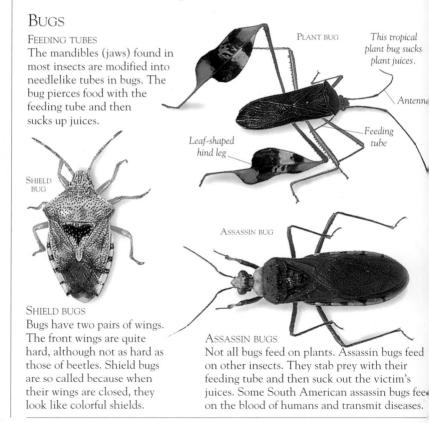

FEEDING TUBES
The mandibles (jaws) found in most insects are modified into needlelike tubes in bugs. The bug pierces food with the feeding tube and then sucks up juices.

PLANT BUG

This tropical plant bug sucks plant juices.

Antenna

Feeding tube

Leaf-shaped hind leg

SHIELD BUG

ASSASSIN BUG

SHIELD BUGS
Bugs have two pairs of wings. The front wings are quite hard, although not as hard as those of beetles. Shield bugs are so called because when their wings are closed, they look like colorful shields.

ASSASSIN BUGS
Not all bugs feed on plants. Assassin bugs feed on other insects. They stab prey with their feeding tube and then suck out the victim's juices. Some South American assassin bugs feed on the blood of humans and transmit diseases.

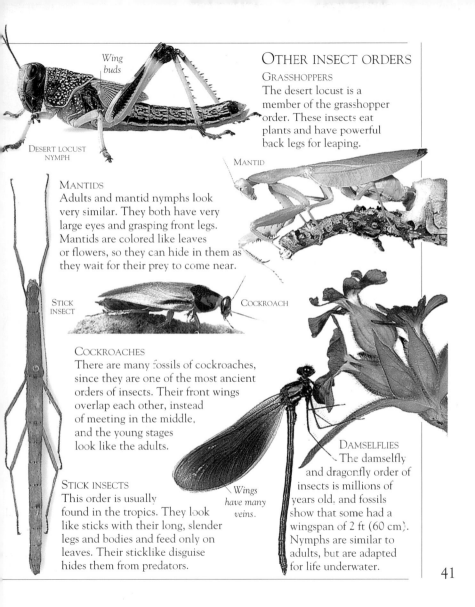

OTHER INSECT ORDERS

GRASSHOPPERS
The desert locust is a member of the grasshopper order. These insects eat plants and have powerful back legs for leaping.

Wing buds

DESERT LOCUST NYMPH

MANTID

MANTIDS
Adults and mantid nymphs look very similar. They both have very large eyes and grasping front legs. Mantids are colored like leaves or flowers, so they can hide in them as they wait for their prey to come near.

STICK INSECT

COCKROACH

COCKROACHES
There are many fossils of cockroaches, since they are one of the most ancient orders of insects. Their front wings overlap each other, instead of meeting in the middle, and the young stages look like the adults.

DAMSELFLIES
The damselfly and dragonfly order of insects is millions of years old, and fossils show that some had a wingspan of 2 ft (60 cm). Nymphs are similar to adults, but are adapted for life underwater.

Wings have many veins.

STICK INSECTS
This order is usually found in the tropics. They look like sticks with their long, slender legs and bodies and feed only on leaves. Their sticklike disguise hides them from predators.

METAMORPHOSIS

INSECTS GO THROUGH several stages of growth before
they become adults. This growing process is called
metamorphosis. There are two types of metamorphosis
complete and incomplete. Complete metamorphosis
has four growth stages – egg, larva, pupa, and adult.
Incomplete metamorphosis involves three stages – egg
nymph, and adult.

Incomplete metamorphosis

This growing process is a
gradual transformation. The
insects hatch from their
eggs looking like miniature
adults. These young insects
are called nymphs. As they
grow, they shed their skin
several times before they
reach the adult stage.

*Clawed feet
hook onto
stem.*

*Wing
buds*

*Adult
head*

*Adult
head and
thorax
emerge*

1 DAMSELFLY NYMPH
A damselfly nymph
lives underwater. Paddle-
like plates on its tail help it
swim and breathe. It sheds
its skin several times as it
grows toward adulthood.

2 HOLDING ON
When the nymph is
ready to change into an
adult it crawls out of the
water up a plant stem.

3 BREAKING OUT
The skin along the
back splits open and
the adult head and
thorax start to emerge.

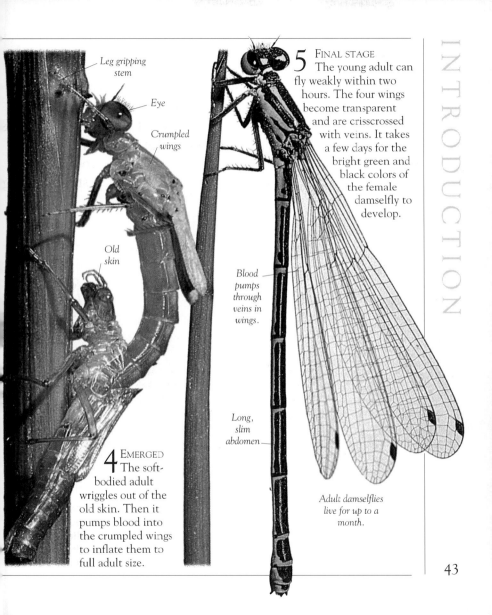

Leg gripping stem

Eye

Crumpled wings

Old skin

Blood pumps through veins in wings.

Long, slim abdomen

4 EMERGED
The soft-bodied adult wriggles out of the old skin. Then it pumps blood into the crumpled wings to inflate them to full adult size.

5 FINAL STAGE
The young adult can fly weakly within two hours. The four wings become transparent and are crisscrossed with veins. It takes a few days for the bright green and black colors of the female damselfly to develop.

Adult damselflies live for up to a month.

INSECTS

Complete metamorphosis

The four growth stages in a complete metamorphosis are egg,
larva, pupa, and adult. The larva bears no resemblance to the
adult it will become. During the pupa stage the larva makes the
amazing transformation into an adult. Insects such as wasps,
butterflies, beetles, and flies undergo complete metamorphosis.

1 LAYING EGGS
Butterflies lay eggs
near leaves that
caterpillars can
eat when they
hatch. Newly
hatched
caterpillars are
too small to
walk far to feed.

Eggshell

Egg

2 THE FIRST MEAL
When a caterpillar
emerges, the first meal it
eats is usually its own
eggshell. The eggshell
provides the caterpillar with
valuable nutrients before it
begins its diet of leaves.

*Strong
jaws slice
food.*

*A caterpillar
can increase its
body weight by
about 100 times in
a few weeks.*

3 GROWING
The caterpillar
chews up leaves and
grows much bigger, shedding
its skin several times. This growth
prepares the caterpillar for the pupal
stage of its life.

A pupa is also known as a chrysalis.

Silk thread holds pupa in place.

A chrysalis often looks like a leaf for camouflage.

4 CHRYSALIS ACTIVITY
A pupa is like a busy factory. From the outside it looks still, but inside there is a great deal of activity. The caterpillar's organs turn into a milky liquid, and new butterfly organs grow rapidly in their place.

5 CHANGE COMPLETED
Once the metamorphosis is complete, the butterfly emerges from its pupa. It stretches its wet, crumpled wings. Before the butterfly is ready to fly, it must wait a couple of hours for its wings to expand and harden.

Empty pupa

Antenna

Wet, crumpled wings

Blood is pumped into the veins in the wings to expand them.

SWALLOWTAIL BUTTERFLY

It takes about eight weeks for this swallowtail butterfly to grow from egg to adult.

6 BUTTERFLY
The fully developed butterfly leads a totally different life from the caterpillar. While caterpillars eat leaves in order to grow, butterflies spend their time sipping nectar from flowers and seeking a mate.

HOW INSECTS MOVE

INSECTS MOVE using muscles which are attached to the inner surfaces of their hard outer skeleton. Many insects walk, but some larvae have no legs and have to crawl. Some insects swim, others jump, but most adult insects can fly and in this way they may travel long distances.

Legs

Insects use their legs for walking, running, jumping, and swimming. Many insects have legs modified for a number of other purposes. These include catching prey, holding a female when mating, producing songs, digging, fighting, and camouflage.

LEGS FOR SWIMMING
The water boatman has long, oar-shaped back legs, allowing the insect to "row" rapidly through water. The legs have flattened ends and a fringe of thick hairs. The front legs are short to grasp prey on the water surface.

LEG FACTS
• Fairy flies, which live as parasites on the eggs of water insects, can "fly" underwater.

• Many butterflies walk on four legs; the front pair is used for tasting.

• The legless larvae of some parasitic wasps hitch a ride on a passing ant in order to enter an ant's nest.

1 PREPARING TO JUMP
The back legs of locusts are swollen and packed with strong muscles for jumping. Before leaping, a locust holds its back legs tightly under its body, near its center of gravity. This is the best position for the legs to propel the insect high into the air.

Long back legs

Wing

Shorter front legs

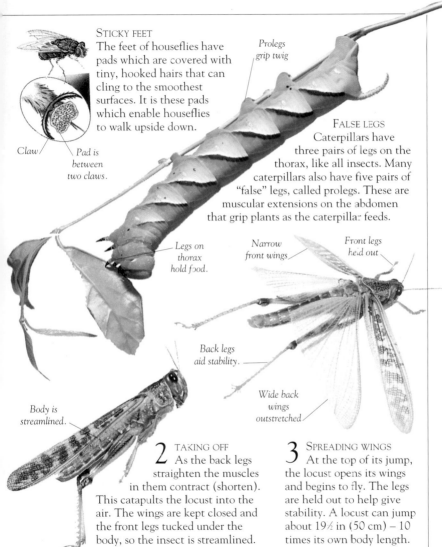

STICKY FEET
The feet of houseflies have pads which are covered with tiny, hooked hairs that can cling to the smoothest surfaces. It is these pads which enable houseflies to walk upside down.

Claw

Pad is between two claws.

Prolegs grip twig

FALSE LEGS
Caterpillars have three pairs of legs on the thorax, like all insects. Many caterpillars also have five pairs of "false" legs, called prolegs. These are muscular extensions on the abdomen that grip plants as the caterpillar feeds.

Legs on thorax hold food.

Narrow front wings

Front legs held out

Back legs aid stability.

Wide back wings outstretched

Body is streamlined.

2 TAKING OFF
As the back legs straighten the muscles in them contract (shorten). This catapults the locust into the air. The wings are kept closed and the front legs tucked under the body, so the insect is streamlined.

3 SPREADING WINGS
At the top of its jump, the locust opens its wings and begins to fly. The legs are held out to help give stability. A locust can jump about 19½ in (50 cm) – 10 times its own body length.

47

Wings and scales

Insect wings are a wide variety of shapes
and sizes. They are used not just for flying,
but also for attracting a mate or hiding
from predators. Most insects have two
pairs of wings, each with a network
of veins to give strength. Flies
have only one pair of wings – the
second pair is modified into small
balancing organs called halteres.
Small insects have few wing veins
since their wings are so tiny.

EXPERT FLIERS
Dragonflies are among the
most accomplished fliers in
the insect world. They can
hover, fly fast or slow, change
direction rapidly, and even
fly backward. As they
maneuver, their two pairs
of wings beat independently
of each other.

WING FACTS

• The scales of
butterflies and moths
contain waste products
from the pupal stage.

• There is a hearing
organ in one of the
wing veins of green
lacewings for hearing
the shrieks of bats.

• Many species of
island insects are
wingless because of the
risk of being blown
out to sea.

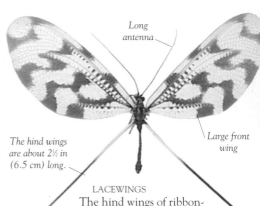

*Long
antenna*

*The hind wings
are about 2½ in
(6.5 cm) long.*

*Large front
wing*

LACEWINGS
The hind wings of ribbon-
tail lacewings are modified into
long graceful streamers. Scientists are
not sure what these are for, but they may
act as stabilizers in flight, or even divert
predators from attacking the lacewing's body.
The lacewing's mottled patterns probably help to
conceal it in the dry, sandy places where it lives.

Eyespot on
front wing

Antenna

Large
wings

Eyespot on
hind wing

PEACOCK
BUTTERFLY

PUTTERFLY

CRANE-FLY

Balancing
organ called
a haltere

WASP

Hind wings are
slightly smaller
than front wings.

BEETLE

EYESPOTS

Insects sometimes use their wings to play tricks on their enemies. Many butterflies and moths have eyespots on their wings. These are probably used to startle predators when flashed suddenly. This gives the butterfly or moth a little more time to escape.

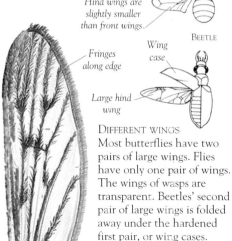

SCALES

The wings of moths and butterflies are covered in over-lapping scales. The scales are formed from specially flattened and ridged hairs.

Fringes
along edge

Wing
case

Large hind
wing

FRINGED WINGS

Tiny insects have difficulty in flying since air is very dense for them. To increase the size of their wings and so improve lift, they often have fringes of hairs around the edges of the wings.

DIFFERENT WINGS

Most butterflies have two pairs of large wings. Flies have only one pair of wings. The wings of wasps are transparent. Beetles' second pair of large wings is folded away under the hardened first pair, or wing cases.

Flight

The ability to fly is one of the main reasons insects have survived for millions of years, and continue to flourish. Flight helps insects escape from danger. It also makes it easier to find food and new places to live. Sometimes insects fly thousands of miles to reach fresh food or warmer weather.

FLYING GROUPS
This African grasshopper has broad hind wings which allow it to glide for long distances. Locusts are a type of grasshopper that fly in huge groups when they need new food. Sometimes as many as 100 million locusts fly together for hundreds of miles.

WARMING UP
An insect's flight muscles must be warm before the wings can be moved fast enough for flight. On cool mornings, insects like this shield bug shiver, vibrating their wings to warm themselves up.

Vibrating wings

Elytra protect body.

1 PREPARING TO FLY
This cockchafer beetle prepares for flight by climbing to the top of a plant and facing into the wind. It may open and shut its elytra (wing cases) several times while warming up.

2 OPENING THE WINGS
The hardened elytra, which protect the fragile hind wings, begin to open. The antennae are spread so the beetle can monitor the wind direction.

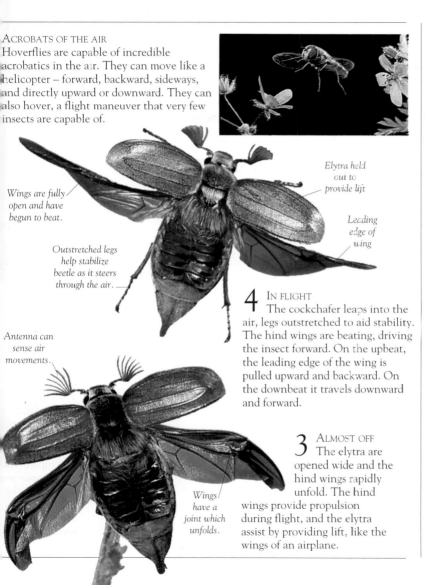

ACROBATS OF THE AIR

Hoverflies are capable of incredible acrobatics in the air. They can move like a helicopter – forward, backward, sideways, and directly upward or downward. They can also hover, a flight maneuver that very few insects are capable of.

Elytra held out to provide lift

Leading edge of wing

Wings are fully open and have begun to beat.

Outstretched legs help stabilize beetle as it steers through the air.

4 IN FLIGHT
The cockchafer leaps into the air, legs outstretched to aid stability. The hind wings are beating, driving the insect forward. On the upbeat, the leading edge of the wing is pulled upward and backward. On the downbeat it travels downward and forward.

Antenna can sense air movements.

Wings have a joint which unfolds.

3 ALMOST OFF
The elytra are opened wide and the hind wings rapidly unfold. The hind wings provide propulsion during flight, and the elytra assist by providing lift, like the wings of an airplane.

51

INSECT SENSES

INSECTS NEED to be fully aware of the world around them in order to survive. Although insects are tiny, some have keener senses than many larger animals. They can see colors and hear sounds that are undetectable to humans, as well as being able to detect smells from many miles away.

Sight

There are two types of insect eyes – simple and compound. Simple eyes can probably detect only light and shade. Compound eyes have hundreds of lenses, giving their owner excellent vision.

HEAD OF COMMON
DARTER DRAGONFLY

SIMPLE EYES
Caterpillars never need to look far for their plant food – they are constantly surrounded by it. Because of this, they do not need sharp eyesight. They can manage perfectly well with a group of simple eyes.

GOOD VISION
The eyes of dragonflies take up most of their head. This allows them to see what's in front, above, below, and behind them all at the same time. Dragonflies use their excellent sight and agile flight to catch prey.

Simple eyes

COMMON DARTER
DRAGONFLY

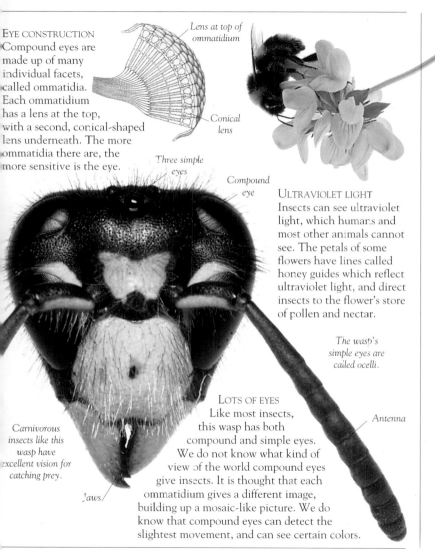

EYE CONSTRUCTION
Compound eyes are
made up of many
individual facets,
called ommatidia.
Each ommatidium
has a lens at the top,
with a second, conical-shaped
lens underneath. The more
ommatidia there are, the
more sensitive is the eye.

Lens at top of ommatidium

Conical lens

Three simple eyes

Compound eye

ULTRAVIOLET LIGHT
Insects can see ultraviolet
light, which humans and
most other animals cannot
see. The petals of some
flowers have lines called
honey guides which reflect
ultraviolet light, and direct
insects to the flower's store
of pollen and nectar.

The wasp's simple eyes are called ocelli.

Carnivorous insects like this wasp have excellent vision for catching prey.

Jaws

Antenna

LOTS OF EYES
Like most insects,
this wasp has both
compound and simple eyes.
We do not know what kind of
view of the world compound eyes
give insects. It is thought that each
ommatidium gives a different image,
building up a mosaic-like picture. We do
know that compound eyes can detect the
slightest movement, and can see certain colors.

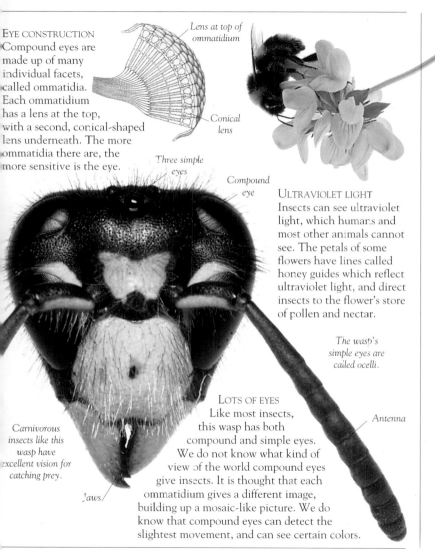

53

Smelling, hearing, and touching

The bodies of insects are covered in short hairs which are connected to the nervous system. These hairs can feel, or "hear," vibrations in the air due to either sound or movement. Some hairs are modified to detect smells and flavors. Sensory hairs are often found on the antennae, but also occur on the feet and mouthparts.

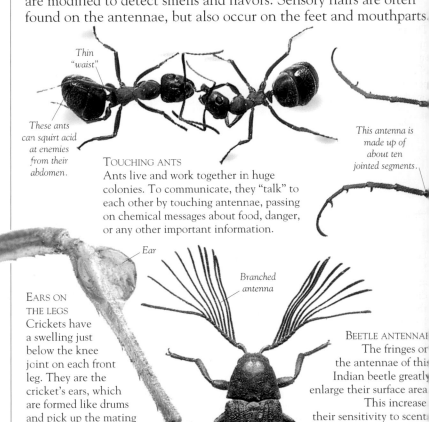

Thin "waist"

These ants can squirt acid at enemies from their abdomen.

This antenna is made up of about ten jointed segments.

TOUCHING ANTS

Ants live and work together in huge colonies. To communicate, they "talk" to each other by touching antennae, passing on chemical messages about food, danger, or any other important information.

Ear

Branched antenna

EARS ON THE LEGS

Crickets have a swelling just below the knee joint on each front leg. They are the cricket's ears, which are formed like drums and pick up the mating songs of other crickets.

BEETLE ANTENNAE

The fringes on the antennae of this Indian beetle greatly enlarge their surface area. This increases their sensitivity to scent carried in the wind.

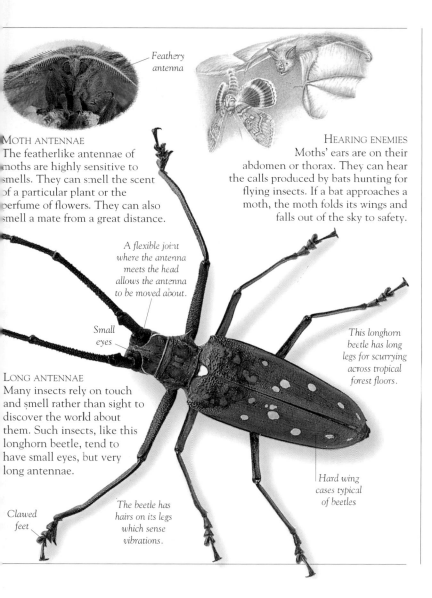

Feathery antenna

MOTH ANTENNAE
The featherlike antennae of moths are highly sensitive to smells. They can smell the scent of a particular plant or the perfume of flowers. They can also smell a mate from a great distance.

HEARING ENEMIES
Moths' ears are on their abdomen or thorax. They can hear the calls produced by bats hunting for flying insects. If a bat approaches a moth, the moth folds its wings and falls out of the sky to safety.

A flexible joint where the antenna meets the head allows the antenna to be moved about.

Small eyes

This longhorn beetle has long legs for scurrying across tropical forest floors.

LONG ANTENNAE
Many insects rely on touch and smell rather than sight to discover the world about them. Such insects, like this longhorn beetle, tend to have small eyes, but very long antennae.

Clawed feet

The beetle has hairs on its legs which sense vibrations.

Hard wing cases typical of beetles

55

Jaws chew leaf.

Caterpillar holds leaf with its legs.

HOW INSECTS FEED

INSECTS HAVE complex mouthparts. The insects that chew their food have a pair of strong jaws for chopping, a smaller pair of jaws for holding food, and two pairs of sensory organs, called palps, for tasting. Some insects drink only liquid food and have special tubular mouthparts like a straw.

Chewing

Predatory, chewing insects need sharp, pointed jaws for stabbing, holding, and chopping up their struggling prey. Insects that chew plants have blunter jaws for grinding their food.

PLANT CHEWER
A caterpillar needs powerful jaws to bite into plant material. Their jaws are armed with teeth that overlap when they close. Some caterpillars' jaws are modified into grinding plates for mashing up the toughest leaves.

THRUSTING JAWS
Dragonfly larvae have pincers at the end of a hinged plate folded under the head. When catching prey, the plate unfolds, shoots forward, and the pincers grab the prey. Toothed jaws in the head reduce the victim to mincemeat.

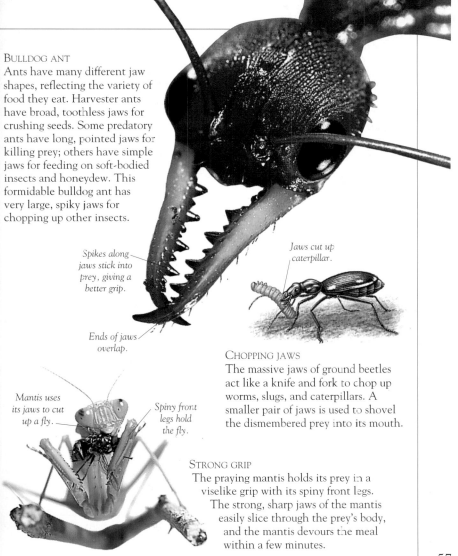

BULLDOG ANT
Ants have many different jaw shapes, reflecting the variety of food they eat. Harvester ants have broad, toothless jaws for crushing seeds. Some predatory ants have long, pointed jaws for killing prey; others have simple jaws for feeding on soft-bodied insects and honeydew. This formidable bulldog ant has very large, spiky jaws for chopping up other insects.

Spikes along jaws stick into prey, giving a better grip.

Ends of jaws overlap.

Jaws cut up caterpillar.

Mantis uses its jaws to cut up a fly.

Spiny front legs hold the fly.

CHOPPING JAWS
The massive jaws of ground beetles act like a knife and fork to chop up worms, slugs, and caterpillars. A smaller pair of jaws is used to shovel the dismembered prey into its mouth.

STRONG GRIP
The praying mantis holds its prey in a viselike grip with its spiny front legs. The strong, sharp jaws of the mantis easily slice through the prey's body, and the mantis devours the meal within a few minutes.

57

Drinking

For many insects, the main way of feeding is by drinking. The most nutritious foods to drink are nectar and blood. Nectar is rich in sugar, and blood is packed with proteins. Some insects drink by sucking through strawlike mouthparts. Others have spongelike mouthparts with which they mop up liquids.

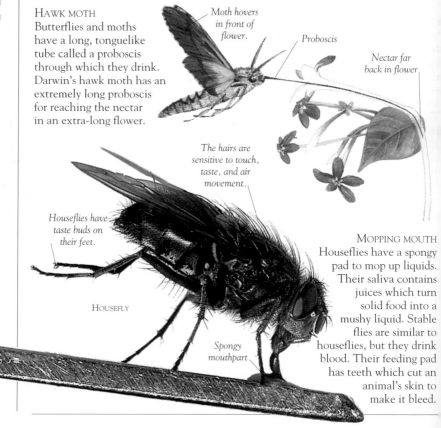

HAWK MOTH
Butterflies and moths have a long, tonguelike tube called a proboscis through which they drink. Darwin's hawk moth has an extremely long proboscis for reaching the nectar in an extra-long flower.

Moth hovers in front of flower.

Proboscis

Nectar far back in flower

The hairs are sensitive to touch, taste, and air movement.

Houseflies have taste buds on their feet.

HOUSEFLY

Spongy mouthpart

MOPPING MOUTH
Houseflies have a spongy pad to mop up liquids. Their saliva contains juices which turn solid food into a mushy liquid. Stable flies are similar to houseflies, but they drink blood. Their feeding pad has teeth which cut an animal's skin to make it bleed.

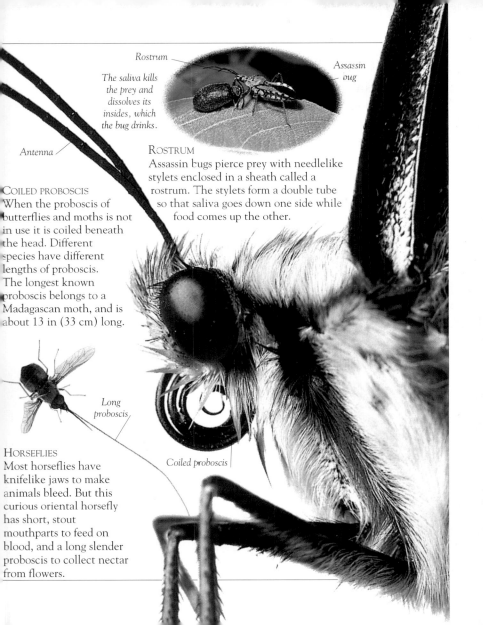

The saliva kills the prey and dissolves its insides, which the bug drinks.

Rostrum

Assassin bug

Antenna

ROSTRUM
Assassin bugs pierce prey with needlelike stylets enclosed in a sheath called a rostrum. The stylets form a double tube so that saliva goes down one side while food comes up the other.

COILED PROBOSCIS
When the proboscis of butterflies and moths is not in use it is coiled beneath the head. Different species have different lengths of proboscis. The longest known proboscis belongs to a Madagascan moth, and is about 13 in (33 cm) long.

Long proboscis

Coiled proboscis

HORSEFLIES
Most horseflies have knifelike jaws to make animals bleed. But this curious oriental horsefly has short, stout mouthparts to feed on blood, and a long slender proboscis to collect nectar from flowers.

COURTSHIP, BIRTH, AND GROWTH

REPRODUCTION is hazardous for insects. A female must first mate with a male of her own species and lay eggs where the newly hatched young can feed. The larvae must shed their skin several times as they grow. All this time the insects must avoid being eaten.

Courtship and mating

Males and females use special signals to ensure that their chosen mate is the right species. Courtship usually involves using scents, but may include color displays, dancing, caressing, and even gifts.

The light is produced by a chemical reaction.

GUIDING LIGHT
Glowworms are the wingless females of certain beetle species. They attract males by producing a light near the tip of their abdomen. Some species flash a distinctive code to attract the correct males.

COURTSHIP FLIGHTS
Butterflies may recognize their own species by sight, but scent is more reliable. Butterfly courtship involves dancing flights with an exchange of scented chemical signals specific to each species.

Butterflies find the scented chemicals, called pheromones, very attractive.

MATING DANGER
Mating between some insect species may last for several hours, with the male gripping the female's abdomen with claspers. This keeps other males away, but the pair are vulnerable to predators at this time.

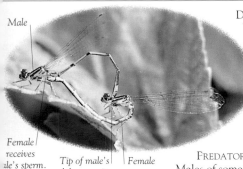

Male

Female receives male's sperm.

Tip of male's abdomen grips female.

Female

DAMSELFLIES
When mating, a male damselfly grips a female's neck with the tip of his abdomen. She receives a packet of sperm from a pouch near his legs; he continues to hold her neck while she lays eggs. This prevents other males from mating with her.

PREDATORS MATING
Males of some predatory species, such as empid flies, give the female a meal of a dead insect when mating so they are not eaten themselves. Some males trick the female. They give an empty parcel, and mate while the female opens it.

Female

MATING ASIAN
SWALLOWTAIL
BUTTERFLIES

UNNATURAL BEHAVIOR
It is often said that a female mantis eats the male while he is mating with her. But this probably happens only when the mantises are in captivity and their behavior is not natural.

Male

61

Eggs and egg-laying

Insects use up a lot of energy producing eggs. To make sure this energy is not wasted, insects have many ways of protecting their eggs from predators. A few species of insect stay with their eggs to protect them until the larvae hatch. Some insects lay their eggs underground with a supply of food waiting for the newly hatched larvae. Most insects lay their eggs either in or near food, so the young larvae do not have to travel far to eat.

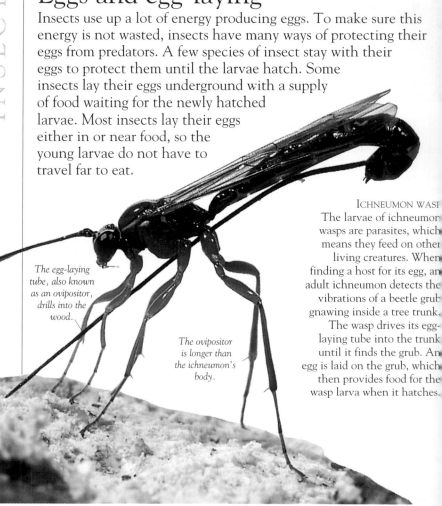

The egg-laying tube, also known as an ovipositor, drills into the wood.

The ovipositor is longer than the ichneumon's body.

ICHNEUMON WASP
The larvae of ichneumon wasps are parasites, which means they feed on other living creatures. When finding a host for its egg, an adult ichneumon detects the vibrations of a beetle grub gnawing inside a tree trunk. The wasp drives its egg-laying tube into the trunk until it finds the grub. An egg is laid on the grub, which then provides food for the wasp larva when it hatches.

SUITABLE FOOD

Butterflies desert their eggs once they are laid. Different butterflies lay their eggs on different plants, depending on what the larvae eat. The Malay lacewing lays its eggs on vine tendrils.

Wasp carrying beetle to nest

Beetles are stored in underground nest.

CARING EARWIGS

[A f]emale earwig looks [after] her eggs, licking [th]em regularly to [ke]ep them clean. [Whe]n the nymphs [ha]tch, she feeds [th]em until they [are] big enough to [l]eave the nest.

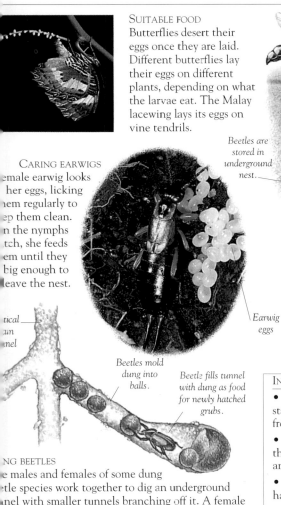

Earwig eggs

[ver]tical [m]ain [tun]nel

Beetles mold dung into balls.

Beetle fills tunnel with dung as food for newly hatched grubs.

HUNTING WASPS

Most species of hunting wasp collect soft-bodied prey, such as caterpillars or spiders, for their grubs. But the weevil-hunting wasp collects adult beetles, which it stings and then stores in a tunnel as food for its larvae.

[DU]NG BEETLES

[Th]e males and females of some dung [bee]tle species work together to dig an underground [tun]nel with smaller tunnels branching off it. A female [lay]s an egg in each of the smaller tunnels and fills them [wit]h animal dung, which the beetle grubs will feed on.

INSECT EGG FACTS

• Whitefly eggs have stalks that extract water from leaves.

• Tsetse flies develop their eggs internally and lay mature larvae.

• Green lacewing eggs have long stalks, making them difficult for predators to eat.

Birth and growth

As an insect grows from egg to adult it sheds its skin several times to produce a larger exoskeleton. While this new skin hardens the insect is soft and vulnerable. Insects have many life-cycle adaptations to protect their soft young stages.

Newborn aphid

EGGS   LARVA   PUPA   ADULT LADYBUG

LADYBUG GROWTH
Ladybugs and all other beetles go through a complete metamorphosis. An adult ladybug lays its eggs on a plant where small insects called aphids feed. Ladybug larvae eat aphids and shed their skin three times as they grow. The colorful adult emerges from the dull resting stage, or pupa.

APHIDS
Female aphids can reproduce without mating. They give birth to live young rather than lay eggs and each female may have about 100 offspring. The newborn aphids can give birth after only a few days.

FROTHY PROTECTION
Spittlebugs are soft-bodied bugs like aphids. A spittlebug nymph produces a frothy liquid from its anus. The froth protects the nymph from drying out, and also hides it from predators.

Frothy hideaway

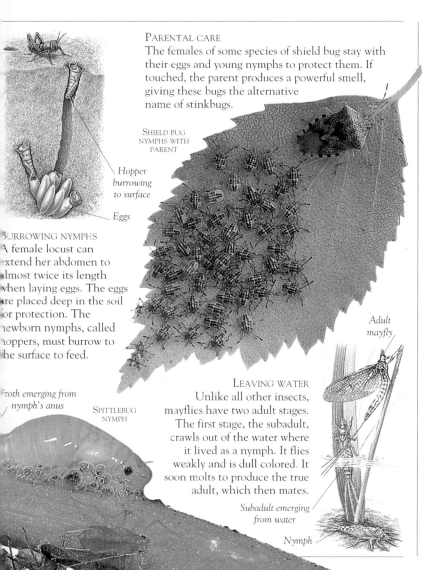

PARENTAL CARE
The females of some species of shield bug stay with
their eggs and young nymphs to protect them. If
touched, the parent produces a powerful smell,
giving these bugs the alternative
name of stinkbugs.

SHIELD BUG
NYMPHS WITH
PARENT

Hopper
burrowing
to surface

Eggs

BURROWING NYMPHS
A female locust can
extend her abdomen to
almost twice its length
when laying eggs. The eggs
are placed deep in the soil
for protection. The
newborn nymphs, called
hoppers, must burrow to
the surface to feed.

Froth emerging from
nymph's anus

SPITTLEBUG
NYMPH

Adult
mayfly

LEAVING WATER
Unlike all other insects,
mayflies have two adult stages.
The first stage, the subadult,
crawls out of the water where
it lived as a nymph. It flies
weakly and is dull colored. It
soon molts to produce the true
adult, which then mates.

Subadult emerging
from water

Nymph

65

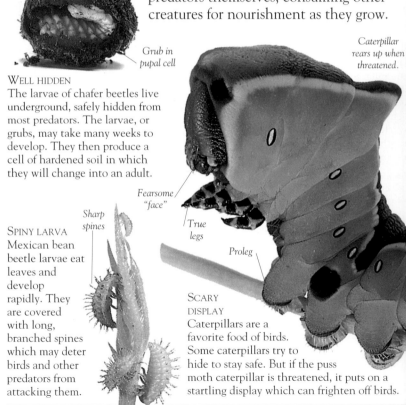

Survival of the young

Predators eagerly hunt insect larvae since many are slow-moving, soft, and nutritious. To ensure survival, most insect species produc large numbers of young which grow rapidly. Most insect larvae are defenseless and have developed special ways of hiding from predators. But many insect larvae are fierce predators themselves, consuming other creatures for nourishment as they grow.

Grub in pupal cell

Caterpillar rears up when threatened.

WELL HIDDEN
The larvae of chafer beetles live underground, safely hidden from most predators. The larvae, or grubs, may take many weeks to develop. They then produce a cell of hardened soil in which they will change into an adult.

Fearsome "face"

Sharp spines

True legs

Proleg

SPINY LARVA
Mexican bean beetle larvae eat leaves and develop rapidly. They are covered with long, branched spines which may deter birds and other predators from attacking them.

SCARY DISPLAY
Caterpillars are a favorite food of birds. Some caterpillars try to hide to stay safe. But if the puss moth caterpillar is threatened, it puts on a startling display which can frighten off birds.

WATER LARVA
Stone-fly larvae live in cold water and grow slowly, spending about three years as a larva. They are slow-moving and hide from predators under rocks and among plants.

NIGHT FEEDER
The mormon butterfly caterpillar feeds in the dark of night to avoid being seen by predators. In less than eight hours it will chew away a leaf which is more than twice its own length. During the day it rests as inconspicuously as possible.

For a more frightening display, the caterpillar waves these "tails" as if they were stings.

SOFT BODIES
Young mantids are fierce predators. The body of some species resembles a flower. This disguise helps them to go unnoticed by prey, and also by predators such as birds.

Eye

Leg

Pink flowerlike body

Legs are striped pink and green.

67

Nests and societies

Most insects lead solitary lives, but some, particularly wasps, ants, bees, and termites, live in societies which are sometimes very ordered. There are queens, kings, workers, and soldiers. Each of these has particular jobs to do. Social insects live in nests which are often elaborate, where they protect each other and rear their young.

TROPICAL WASP NEST MADE OF CHEWED-UP PLANT FIBERS

The nest is cemented together with wasp saliva.

Wasps, ants, and bees

These insects produce a wide range of nests. Some are small with only a few dozen members, while larger nests may contain thousands of insects. Most have a single queen, and all the nest members are her offspring.

Ants
A species of African tree ant builds its nest from fragments of plants and soil to produce a substance like dark cement. The ants live on a diet of honeydew that they get from aphids. The aphids feed on the sap of leaves in the tree tops and discharge the honeydew from their rear ends.

Bees
A bumblebee queen starts her nest alone in spring in a hole in the ground. She makes cells for her eggs out of wax. She also makes a wax pot which she fills with honey for food.

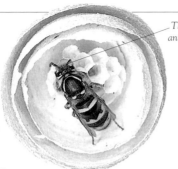

The queen uses her antennae to measure the cells as she builds them.

1 A NEW START

European wasp colonies die out each winter. In spring a queen begins a new nest of "paper" made with chewed-up wood. She makes a few cells for her eggs, building walls around the cells to shield them.

Entrance hole

2 PROTECTIVE LAYERS

The queen builds more and more paper layers around the cells. The layers will protect the larvae from cold winds as well as from predators. The queen leaves an entrance hole at the bottom.

Finished nest

3 HARD-WORKING FAMILY

The first brood the queen rears become workers, gathering food for more larvae and expanding the nest. By summer, a nest may have 500 wasps, all collecting caterpillars for the larvae. A large nest may be as much as 18 in (45 cm) in diameter.

INSIDE THE NEST

The queen lays a single egg in each cell. When the larvae hatch they stay in their cell and the queen feeds them with pieces of caterpillar.

Termite nests

Termites have the most complex insect societies. Their elaborate nests, which may be in wood or underground, last for several years. Each nest has a single large queen and king, which are served by specialized small workers and large soldiers. Termites feed and protect each other, and one generation will help raise the next generation of offspring.

QUEEN TERMITE
In a termite society, the queen lays all the eggs. She is too fat to move, so the workers bring food to her. The queen lays 30,000 eggs each day and, as she lays them, the workers carry them off to special chambers for rearing.

Layers of "umbrellas"

NEST DEFENDERS
Termite soldiers fight enemies that attack the nest. Most termite species have soldiers with enlarged heads and powerful jaws. In some species, each soldier's head has a snout that squirts poison at invaders.

STRANGE NEST
The function of the "umbrellas" on this African nest is a mystery to scientists. The termite species that build this type of nest live underground. If an "umbrella" is damaged, it does not get repaired, but a new one may be built.

Hot air rises up main chimney.

The fungus grows on pieces of grass the termites chew up and put in the nest.

COOLING SYSTEM
The biggest mounds are built by African termites and may be 42 ft (12.8 m) high. They have a series of chimneys which ventilate the nest below ground. Heat from the nest rises up a main chimney, and cooler air is drawn in through tunnels underground.

Animals that eat termites often try to break into the nests. Worker termites mend any holes made by intruders.

Fungus garden

Food store

Termites' ving chambers

King and queen live in central chamber.

The nest is molded from earth cemented together with termite saliva.

INSIDE THE NEST
The termites live in a complex series of chambers. Some termite species feed on a special fungus which they grow in an underground garden. Five million termites may live in a large nest, cultivating the fungus garden and feeding the young. They adjust the sizes of the chimneys to control the airflow in the nest, which regulates the nest's temperature.

HUNTING AND HIDING

SOME INSECT SPECIES are deadly hunters, killing prey with poisonous stings and sharp jaws. Insects are also hunted by a huge number of animals. To hide from predators, many insects have developed special disguises and patterns of behavior.

Hunting insects

About one-third of insect species are carnivorous (they eat meat). Some species eat decaying meat and dung, but most carnivorous insects hunt for their food.

KILLER BEETLE
Some insects are easily recognized as predators. The large jaws of this African ground beetle indicate that it is a hunter and its long legs show that it can run fast after its insect prey.

KILLER WASPS
There are many types of hunting wasp. Most adult hunting wasps are vegetarians – they hunt prey only as food for their larvae. Each hunting wasp species hunt a particular type of prey. The weevil-hunting wasp hunts only a type of beetle called a weevil.

ESSENTIAL INSECTS
Ants are the most important
carnivores on Earth. They eat
huge numbers of other insects, which
helps keep the insect population from
becoming too plentiful. Ants in turn are eaten
by other animals, such as birds and lizards.

Wasp cocoons

PARASITES
The larvae of many species of wasp are
parasites, which means they feed and
grow inside another insect's body. This
caterpillar has had about 50 wasp larvae
feeding inside it. The larvae are pupating
on the caterpillar's back. Soon they will
hatch as adult wasps.

*Wasp uses its
antennae and
sight to find
cockroaches.*

SPECIALIST HUNTER
Many predatory insects specialize
on one particular type of prey.
This jewel wasp hunts only
cockroaches, which it uses as
food for its larvae. The adult
wasp is not carnivorous – it
feeds on the nectar
in flowers.

ROVE BEETLE
Some rove beetles
specialize in feeding on
springtails. To catch
such elusive prey the
beetle can flick out a
long, sticky "tongue"
to pull an unwary
springtail into
its mouth.

*Beetle raises
tail before
attacking prey.*

73

Camouflage

Insects whose body coloring matches their background are almost impossible to see. This method of hiding is known as camouflage. One of the first rules of successful camouflage is to keep still, since movement can betray an insect to a sharp-eyed predator. Some insects use another type of camouflage called disruptive coloration. They disguise their body by breaking up its shape with stripes and blocks of color.

GRASSY DISGUISE
The stripe-winged grasshopper can be heard singing in meadow grasses, but its camouflaged body is very hard to spot.

Grasshopper kicks any attackers with its back legs.

DISRUPTIVE COLORATION
This tropical moth has disruptive coloration. The patterns on the wings break up their shape. A predator might notice the patterns, but not the whole moth.

LOOKING DISTASTEFUL
This treehopper has twiglike extensions on its thorax and abdomen. It looks like an inedible piece of wood, so hunters are likely to overlook it.

Wing

Extension on thorax

Eye

STILL HUNTER

Insect predators use camouflage so their prey cannot see them. The brown coloring of this mantid perfectly matches the brown leaf on which it sits. It completely surprises any prey which comes within striking distance.

Because of its brown coloring, the Indian leaf butterfly can rest only beside decaying, dried-out leaves.

Midvein on real leaf

Mantis is hard to spot.

Butterfly's head

Wing of butterfly

LEAF MIMIC

It is almost impossible to distinguish the Indian leaf butterfly from the other leaves where it rests. It looks just like a decaying leaf, complete with leaflike veins and mock fungus spots.

Bottom of wings are narrow to look like stalk of real leaf.

Marking like midvein of real leaf

75

Warning coloration

Birds, mammals, and other intelligent predators learn through experience that some insects are poisonous or harmful. Such insects do not camouflage themselves. Instead they have brightly colored bodies which warn predators that they have an unpleasant taste or a nasty sting. The most common warning colors are red, yellow, and black. Any insect with those colors is probably poisonous.

BASKER MOTH
Moths that fly by day are often brightly colored, particularly when they taste unpleasant. The red, yellow, and black coloring of this basker moth tells birds that it is not a tasty meal.

PAINFUL REMINDER
The saddle-back caterpillar is eye-catching with its vivid coloring and grotesque appearance. No young bird would ever forget the caterpillar if it tried a mouthful of the poisonous, stinging spines.

Poisonous spines

Vivid green coloring across back

Bright spot

WARNING SPOTS
This assassin bug is easily seen because of the two bright spots on its back. These bold markings warn predators that there is a reason for them to stay away. The bug's weapon is a needle-sharp beak which can give a very painful bite.

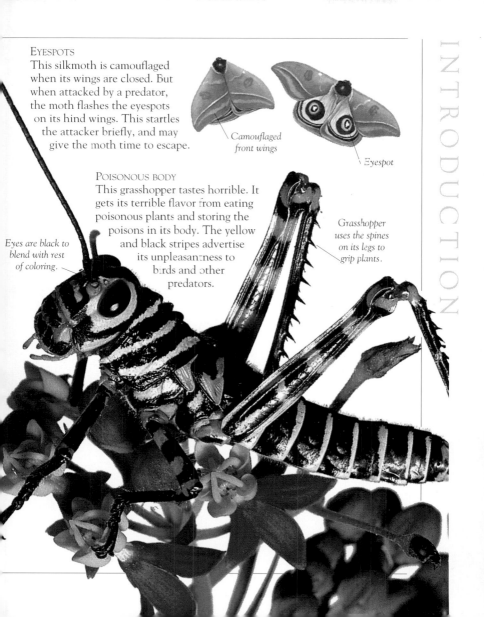

EYESPOTS
This silkmoth is camouflaged when its wings are closed. But when attacked by a predator, the moth flashes the eyespots on its hind wings. This startles the attacker briefly, and may give the moth time to escape.

Camouflaged front wings

Eyespot

POISONOUS BODY
This grasshopper tastes horrible. It gets its terrible flavor from eating poisonous plants and storing the poisons in its body. The yellow and black stripes advertise its unpleasantness to birds and other predators.

Grasshopper uses the spines on its legs to grip plants.

Eyes are black to blend with rest of coloring.

Mimicry

Predators usually avoid preying on dangerous animals. Many harmless insects take advantage of this by mimicking harmful creatures. Mimicking insects copy a dangerous animal's body shape and coloring. They also behave like the animal they're copying to make the disguise more convincing. Inedible objects, such as twigs and thorns, are also mimicked by insects.

The treehoppers move only when they need a fresh source of food.

Markings make head resemble alligator's head.

Real eye of bug

ALLIGATOR MIMIC
Scientists can often only guess at the reasons for the strange look and behavior of some animals. It is not known why this tree-living bug looks like a tiny alligator. Perhaps its appearance briefly startles monkey predators, giving the bug time to fly off to safety.

HORNET MIMIC
The hornet moth looks very like the large wasp called a hornet. When flying, it even behaves like a hornet. Many insects find protection by mimicking wasps – birds avoid them because they might sting.

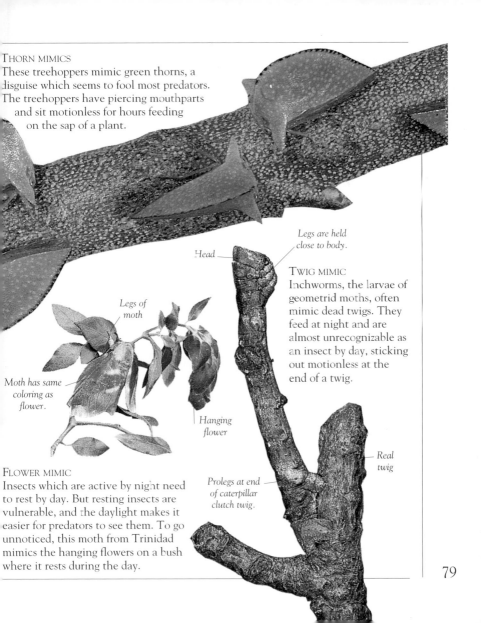

THORN MIMICS

These treehoppers mimic green thorns, a disguise which seems to fool most predators. The treehoppers have piercing mouthparts and sit motionless for hours feeding on the sap of a plant.

Legs are held close to body.

Head

TWIG MIMIC

Inchworms, the larvae of geometrid moths, often mimic dead twigs. They feed at night and are almost unrecognizable as an insect by day, sticking out motionless at the end of a twig.

Legs of moth

Moth has same coloring as flower.

Hanging flower

Real twig

FLOWER MIMIC

Insects which are active by night need to rest by day. But resting insects are vulnerable, and the daylight makes it easier for predators to see them. To go unnoticed, this moth from Trinidad mimics the hanging flowers on a bush where it rests during the day.

Prolegs at end of caterpillar clutch twig.

79

WHERE INSECTS LIVE

INSECTS LIVE everywhere there is warmth and moisture. Many of the one million or more species have specialized habitat requirements. They can live only in particular places, and easily become extinct when humans change or destroy their surroundings. Other species are able to adapt to changing conditions; these adaptable insects often become pests.

NORTH
AMERICA

SOUTH
AMERICA

TEMPERATE WOODLAND
The varied plant life and complex structure of temperate woodland provides insects with many different habitats. Trees, shrubs, and herbs all have flowers, fruits, and buds for insects to feed on, as well as stems and roots for insects to bore into.

GRASSLAND AND HEATHLAND
These habitats offer little shelter from bad weather. But they warm up quickly in the sun, and have a rich variety of flowering plants.

TOWNS AND GARDENS
Hundreds of insect species take advantage of human habitats. Insects find food and shelter in our roofs, cellars, food stores, kitchens, garbage cans, farms, and in our flower-filled gardens.

ARCTIC

EUROPE

ASIA

AFRICA

AUSTRALASIA

ANTARCTIC

DESERTS, CAVES, AND SOILS
These are inhospitable habitats. Food and water are scarce in deserts. Caves are dark and cold. It is hard for insects to move and communicate in dense soil.

TROPICAL FOREST
This is the richest habitat for insect species. Thousands of species of plants provide countless niches for insects to live in, from treetop fruits to dead leaves and twigs on the ground.

LAKES AND RIVERS
Freshwater insects are highly specialized. Their bodies have modified to allow them to swim and breathe underwater.

TEMPERATE WOODLAND

FIELD SCABIOUS
FLOWER

TEMPERATE WOODLANDS are often dominated by one tree species, such as oak, which is deciduous (the trees lose their leaves in winter). The types of insect found, and their numbers, will vary with the seasons, as well as with the types of tree species in the woodlands.

DRAINING
Forests in wetlands have many different plant species. But people often drain this habitat because it is good for farming. Draining kills plants such as milk-parsley, the only plant the English swallowtail butterfly will breed on. This beautiful insect is now rarely seen.

+1.75

Although the English swallowtail will lay eggs only on milk-parsley, adults eat a variety of flowers.

- The woodland edge supports the greatest number of insect species.

- Each pair of blue tits needs about 5,000 caterpillars to feed to their chicks.

- In Britain, over 280 species of insect live on native oak trees.

- Temperate rainforests in the northwestern United States are disappearing faster than tropical rainforests.

Bumblebees are very common in woodlands.

Q +2.5

FLOWERS
Woodlands contain many types of flower. These attract various species of insect, such as bumblebees, which nest in the ground in animal burrows and pollinate many woodland flowers.

Vaporer moth caterpillar is covered with tufts of hair.

VAPORER MOTH CATERPILLAR
This attractive caterpillar eats the leaves of many different trees in Europe and North America. It will also attack rosebushes and heather plants.

Processionary caterpillars are covered in poisonous hairs.

PROCESSIONS
Conifer forests have fewer types of plant and animal than deciduous forests, although some, such as processionary moth caterpillars, can be common. These are named for their habit of following each other head to tail.

83

OAK TREE

IN NORTH AMERICA and Europe, oak trees support a rich variety of insects. There are insects living on every part of the oak tree – the leaves, buds, flowers, fruits, wood, bark, and on decaying leaves and branches. All these insects provide food for the many birds and other animals found in oak woodland.

OAK TREE

GREEN OAK TORTRIX MOTH

CATERPILLAR

GREEN OAK TORTRIX
The green wings of the green oak tortrix moth camouflage the moth when it rests on a leaf. Green oak tortrix caterpillars are extremely common on oak trees. The caterpillars hide from hungry predators by rolling themselves up in a leaf.

Q +1.5

Q +2.5

Leaf rolled around green oak tortrix caterpillar

Mine

MAKING A TUNNEL
The caterpillars of some small moths tunnel between the upper and lower surfaces of a leaf. They eat the green tissues between these surfaces as they tunnel, and leave a see-through trail called a mine.

+15

Chalcid wasp larvae have eaten the gall wasp larvae

GALLS

Oak trees have many tiny growths called galls. Galls are grown by the tree around eggs laid by gall wasps. When the eggs hatch, the gall provides food and shelter for up to 30 wasp larvae. Parasitic wasps called chalcid wasps sometimes burrow inside galls and lay their eggs beside the gall wasp eggs. When the chalcid larvae hatch they eat the gall wasp larvae.

CHALCID WASP ON GALL

NUT WEEVILS

Acorns are used as food by nut weevils. They drill a hole in an acorn with their long, thin snout, and then lay their eggs inside. The larvae feed inside the acorn, and this turns the acorn black.

Black acorn

ACORNS

Long, thin snout

Antenna

+5

NUT WEEVIL

85

TREE CANOPY

THE UPPER BRANCHES and leaves of a tree are like a living green umbrella, forming a canopy over the lower plants. Countless insects find their food in the canopy and they are food for many different birds.

Inchworm on leaf

Silken thread suspends inchworm.

INCHWORMS

Some young birds like to feed on inchworms, the caterpillars of Geometrid moths. When in danger, inchworms can drop from a leaf and hang below by a silken thread.

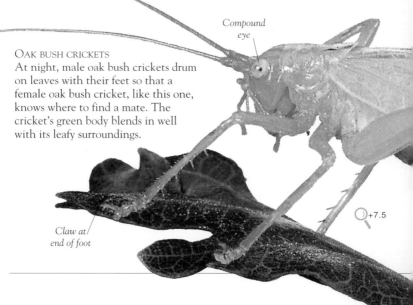

Very long antennae help the cricket find its way in the dark. They also alert the cricket to the approach of an enemy.

Compound eye

OAK BUSH CRICKETS

At night, male oak bush crickets drum on leaves with their feet so that a female oak bush cricket, like this one, knows where to find a mate. The cricket's green body blends in well with its leafy surroundings.

Claw at end of foot

+7.5

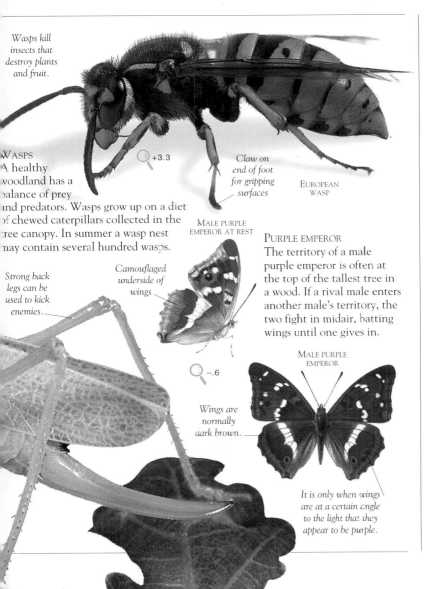

Wasps kill insects that destroy plants and fruit.

+3.3

Claw on end of foot for gripping surfaces

EUROPEAN WASP

WASPS

A healthy woodland has a balance of prey and predators. Wasps grow up on a diet of chewed caterpillars collected in the tree canopy. In summer a wasp nest may contain several hundred wasps.

MALE PURPLE EMPEROR AT REST

Camouflaged underside of wings

Strong back legs can be used to kick enemies.

PURPLE EMPEROR

The territory of a male purple emperor is often at the top of the tallest tree in a wood. If a rival male enters another male's territory, the two fight in midair, batting wings until one gives in.

−.6

MALE PURPLE EMPEROR

Wings are normally dark brown.

It is only when wings are at a certain angle to the light that they appear to be purple.

WOODLAND BUTTERFLIES

THE RICH VARIETY of habitats in woodland supports many butterfly species. Some live in the canopy; others feed on low shrubs. But most butterflies need sunshine and can be found on flowers in sunny clearings.

Q –.6

SILVER-WASHED FRITILLARY
This butterfly lays its eggs in cracks in the bark of mossy tree trunks, close to where violets are growing. The caterpillars feed on the leaves of these plants.

Brown upperside

Green underside

Q –.8

GREEN HAIRSTREAK
Whether it is sitting on a branch or resting on a leaf, the green hairstreak butterfly is well camouflaged. Its upperside is a woody brown while its underside is a leafy green.

PURPLE HAIRSTREAK BUTTERFLY

Female

Male

PURPLE HAIRSTREAK
High in the canopy of oak trees the caterpillars of the purple hairstreak butterfly feed on flowers and young leaves. Adult purple hairstreaks spend most of their lives in the treetops feeding and sunbathing with their wings open.

Eyespots on underwings

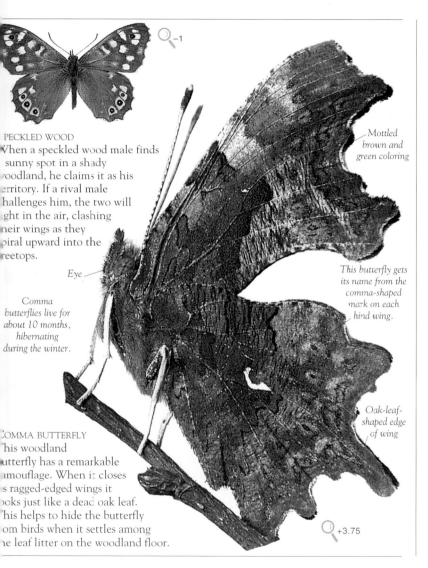

Q -1

SPECKLED WOOD

When a speckled wood male finds a sunny spot in a shady woodland, he claims it as his territory. If a rival male challenges him, the two will fight in the air, clashing their wings as they spiral upward into the treetops.

Eye

Comma butterflies live for about 10 months, hibernating during the winter.

COMMA BUTTERFLY

This woodland butterfly has a remarkable camouflage. When it closes its ragged-edged wings it looks just like a dead oak leaf. This helps to hide the butterfly from birds when it settles among the leaf litter on the woodland floor.

Mottled brown and green coloring

This butterfly gets its name from the comma-shaped mark on each hind wing.

Oak-leaf-shaped edge of wing

Q +3.75

TREE TRUNKS AND BRANCHES

CRACKS IN THE bark of trees provide a hiding place fo
many species of insect. Some burrow into the wood
and live completely concealed from predators. Many
insects also live and feed among the different plant lif
that grows on tree trunks and branches.

BARK INSECTS
Insects which live on bark
are usually camouflaged,
such as barklice, which
feed on tiny fungi and
algae. Another bark insect,
the snakefly, is a predator.
When it hunts, it looks
like a tiny snake about to
strike, holding its head
high looking for prey.

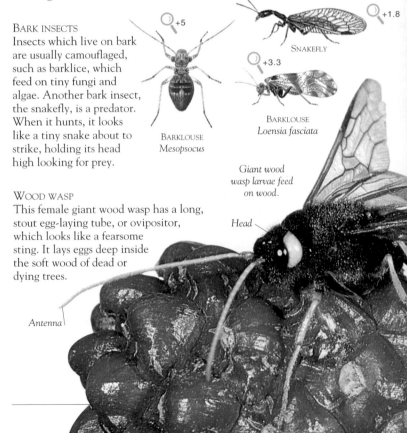

+5

+1.8

SNAKEFLY

+3.3

BARKLOUSE
Mesopsocus

BARKLOUSE
Loensia fasciata

WOOD WASP
This female giant wood wasp has a long,
stout egg-laying tube, or ovipositor,
which looks like a fearsome
sting. It lays eggs deep inside
the soft wood of dead or
dying trees.

*Giant wood
wasp larvae feed
on wood.*

Head

Antenna

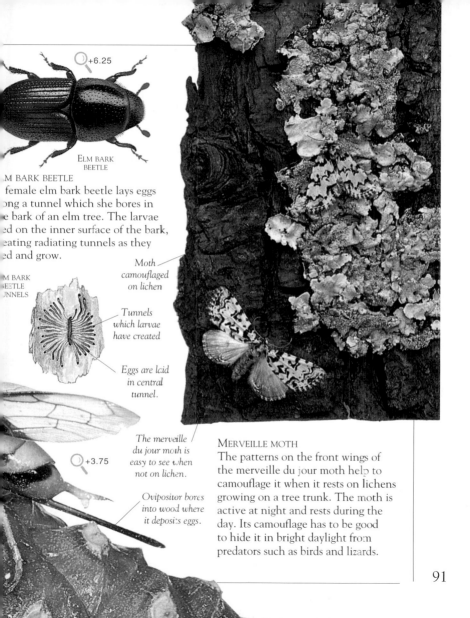

+6.25

ELM BARK
BEETLE

M BARK BEETLE

female elm bark beetle lays eggs
ong a tunnel which she bores in
e bark of an elm tree. The larvae
ed on the inner surface of the bark,
eating radiating tunnels as they
ed and grow.

M BARK
EETLE
UNNELS

*Moth
camouflaged
on lichen*

*Tunnels
which larvae
have created*

*Eggs are laid
in central
tunnel.*

*The merveille
du jour moth is
easy to see when
not on lichen.*

+3.75

*Ovipositor bores
into wood where
it deposits eggs.*

MERVEILLE MOTH
The patterns on the front wings of
the merveille du jour moth help to
camouflage it when it rests on lichens
growing on a tree trunk. The moth is
active at night and rests during the
day. Its camouflage has to be good
to hide it in bright daylight from
predators such as birds and lizards.

91

GROUND LEVEL

THE WOODLAND floor does not get much sunlight, so few plants grow there. Most insects at ground level feed on plant and animal debris falling from the canopy, or, if they are carnivorous, eat other insects.

ANT NEST
The wood ant is a voracious predator. Colonies build huge nests of plant debris, with a network of tunnels below ground providing a home for thousands of ants.

WOOD CRICKET
Most crickets are nocturnal (active at night). But the wood cricket is active on sunny days when it can be heard chirping loudly. It is unable to fly because of its short wings.

Strong jaws bite into prey.

WOOD ANT
Wood ants forage out from their nest for hundreds of yards, making distinct paths on the woodland floor. They catch huge numbers of insects and bring them to the nest in pieces as food for their young.

Ant can squirt poison from abdomen.

+10

–1.25

⬤IOLET GROUND BEETLE
⬤his beetle can run fast
⬤ its long legs, catching
⬤her insects among the
⬤af litter. It hunts mainly
⬤ night and grips its prey
⬤ith powerful jaws.

⬤TAG BEETLE
⬤he larvae of stag beetles spend about
⬤ree years feeding on rotting wood
⬤side a dead tree. These handsome
⬤etles are now becoming rare
⬤cause dead wood is often
⬤eared away and burned.

WHITE ADMIRALS
On sunny days, white
admiral butterflies can
be spotted near the
ground feeding on the
nectar of bramble
flowers. They can often
be seen in the morning
sipping water from
puddles. They spend
much of their time in
the tree canopy, basking
in the sunshine.

+3

UPPERSIDE OF
WHITE ADMIRAL

UNDERSIDE OF
WHITE ADMIRAL

Antenna

*Only male
stag beetles
have enlarged
jaws.*

+3.75

This grass is called cocks-foot.

FIELD CHAFER

GRASSLAND AND HEATHLAND

HERE, THE LACK OF PROTECTIVE tree canopy results in quick changes in the weather. Grassland and heathland habitats provide fewer dwelling places for insects than forest or woodland, since there is little wood to burrow into and hardly any leaf litter to dwell in.

+1.5

FOOD SOURCE
Plant roots are an important food for insects in these habitats. Field chafer larvae eat roots, while the adults fly from plant to plant seeking a mate.

SPRINGTAILS
Cultivated grass fields, such as sport fields, support few insect species. But they do contain vast numbers of tiny insects called springtails. An area the size of a tennis court might be home to up to three hundred million springtails.

94

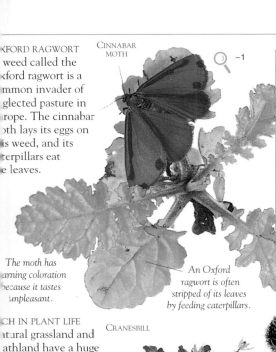

CINNABAR MOTH

Q −1

GRASSLAND AND HEATHLAND FACTS

- The grassland of Argentina are called Pampas, or "plains" in the language of the native people.

- Prairies of the US have tall grasses.

- Steppes (prairielike land) of Siberia have short grasses.

[X]FORD RAGWORT
weed called the [O]xford ragwort is a [co]mmon invader of [ne]glected pasture in [Eu]rope. The cinnabar [m]oth lays its eggs on [th]is weed, and its [ca]terpillars eat [th]e leaves.

The moth has [w]arning coloration [b]ecause it tastes [u]npleasant.

An Oxford ragwort is often stripped of its leaves by feeding caterpillars.

[RI]CH IN PLANT LIFE
[Na]tural grassland and [he]athland have a huge [va]riety of grasses [an]d flowering [pl]ants. These rich [ha]bitats buzz with [in]sect life [in] the [su]mmer [m]onths.

CRANESBILL

EXTINCT BUTTERFLY
The English large copper butterfly was once common in fenland but is now extinct. This is a result of intensive land development for agriculture, which destroyed the butterfly's special food plant.

GRASSLAND INSECTS

MOST INSECT species cannot survive in cultivated grass lands, such as garden lawns, since they usually contain only one type of grass. Also, weedkillers and other chemicals harm many insects. But natural grasslands, with their variety of plants, support thousands of insect species that have adapted to this open, windy habitat.

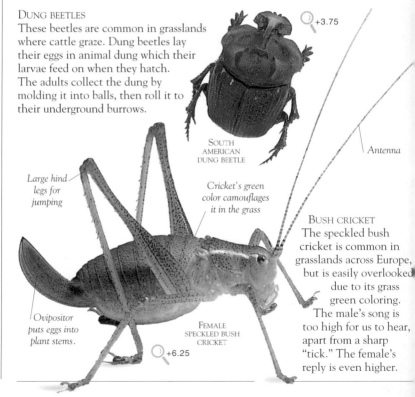

DUNG BEETLES
These beetles are common in grasslands where cattle graze. Dung beetles lay their eggs in animal dung which their larvae feed on when they hatch. The adults collect the dung by molding it into balls, then roll it to their underground burrows.

Q +3.75

SOUTH AMERICAN DUNG BEETLE

Antenna

Large hind legs for jumping

Cricket's green color camouflages it in the grass

BUSH CRICKET
The speckled bush cricket is common in grasslands across Europe, but is easily overlooked due to its grass green coloring. The male's song is too high for us to hear, apart from a sharp "tick." The female's reply is even higher.

Ovipositor puts eggs into plant stems.

FEMALE SPECKLED BUSH CRICKET

Q +6.25

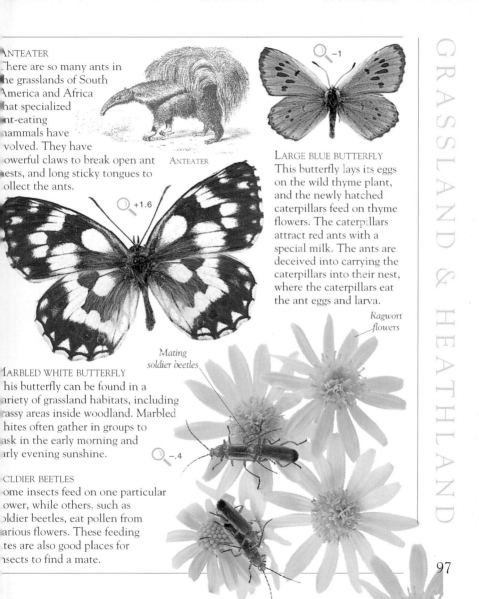

ANTEATER
There are so many ants in
the grasslands of South
America and Africa
that specialized
ant-eating
mammals have
evolved. They have
powerful claws to break open ant
nests, and long sticky tongues to
collect the ants.

ANTEATER

○ −1

LARGE BLUE BUTTERFLY
This butterfly lays its eggs
on the wild thyme plant,
and the newly hatched
caterpillars feed on thyme
flowers. The caterpillars
attract red ants with a
special milk. The ants are
deceived into carrying the
caterpillars into their nest,
where the caterpillars eat
the ant eggs and larva.

*Ragwort
flowers*

○ +1.6

*Mating
soldier beetles*

MARBLED WHITE BUTTERFLY
This butterfly can be found in a
variety of grassland habitats, including
grassy areas inside woodland. Marbled
whites often gather in groups to
bask in the early morning and
early evening sunshine.

○ −.4

SOLDIER BEETLES
Some insects feed on one particular
flower, while others, such as
soldier beetles, eat pollen from
various flowers. These feeding
sites are also good places for
insects to find a mate.

97

HEATHLAND INSECTS

MANY BURROWING insects live in heathland since the soil is loose and easy to dig into. Heathland occurs in parts of the world with a climate of rainy winters and warm, dry summers. It has a rich mixture of plants, and the soil, which is often sandy, warms up quickly in the sunshine.

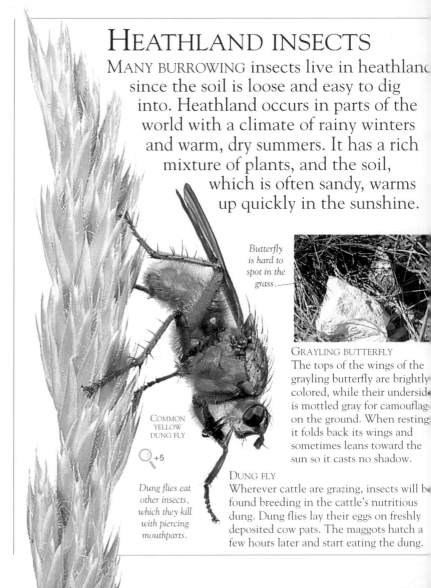

Butterfly is hard to spot in the grass.

GRAYLING BUTTERFLY
The tops of the wings of the grayling butterfly are brightly colored, while their underside is mottled gray for camouflage on the ground. When resting it folds back its wings and sometimes leans toward the sun so it casts no shadow.

COMMON YELLOW DUNG FLY

+5

Dung flies eat other insects, which they kill with piercing mouthparts.

DUNG FLY
Wherever cattle are grazing, insects will be found breeding in the cattle's nutritious dung. Dung flies lay their eggs on freshly deposited cow pats. The maggots hatch a few hours later and start eating the dung.

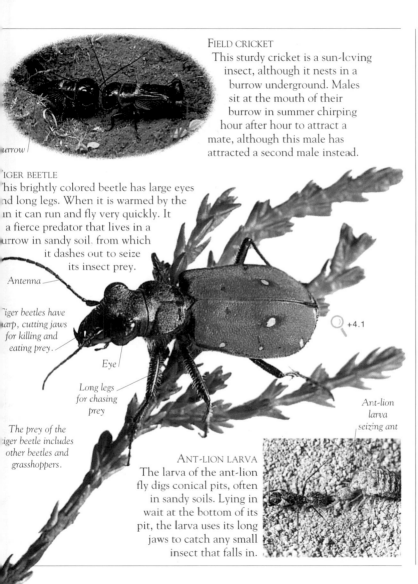

FIELD CRICKET

This sturdy cricket is a sun-loving insect, although it nests in a burrow underground. Males sit at the mouth of their burrow in summer chirping hour after hour to attract a mate, although this male has attracted a second male instead.

urrow

IGER BEETLE

his brightly colored beetle has large eyes
nd long legs. When it is warmed by the
un it can run and fly very quickly. It
a fierce predator that lives in a
urrow in sandy soil, from which
it dashes out to seize
its insect prey.

Antenna

iger beetles have
harp, cutting jaws
for killing and
eating prey.

Eye

Long legs
for chasing
prey

+4.1

The prey of the
iger beetle includes
other beetles and
grasshoppers.

Ant-lion
larva
seizing ant

ANT-LION LARVA

The larva of the ant-lion
fly digs conical pits, often
in sandy soils. Lying in
wait at the bottom of its
pit, the larva uses its long
jaws to catch any small
insect that falls in.

99

LAKES AND RIVERS

INSECTS CAN be found in all sorts of freshwater habitats: lakes, fast-flowing streams, ponds, puddles, damp moss, and wet leaf litter. These insects have many adaptations for surviving in their watery homes.

This case is made of a mixture of leaves and stones.

+3.75

The stony case is held together by silk woven by the larva.

Head

Legs hold onto plant.

Flowers attract nectar-eating insects.

CADDIS FLY LARVAE
Insects are in danger of being swept away in fast-flowing water. Caddis fly larvae build a case around their body for protection, and often the cases are made of heavy stone to weigh the larvae down.

The flat leaves have a water-repellent waxy covering so they don't get waterlogged.

FRINGED WATERLILY
The tangled stems of the fringed waterlily are a good hiding place for pond insects. Dragonflies also find the leaves and stems a safe place on which to lay their eggs.

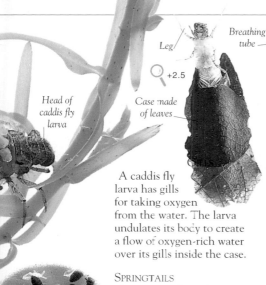

Leg

Breathing tube

+2.5

Head of caddis fly larva

Case made of leaves

GILLS

A caddis fly larva has gills for taking oxygen from the water. The larva undulates its body to create a flow of oxygen-rich water over its gills inside the case.

SPRINGTAILS
In corners of ponds sheltered from the wind, swarms of springtails sometimes gather on the surface of the water. They feed on organic debris that has blown into the pond.

FAST STREAMS
Insects that live in fast-flowing streams have streamlined bodies and strong claws to help them cling to stones. The water that passes over their gills is always rich in oxygen, but cool temperatures mean that larvae develop more slowly than they would in a shallow, sun-warmed pond.

WATER SCORPION
The water scorpion has a breathing tube on its rear end so it can breathe the outside air while it is underwater. Insects with breathing tubes can survive in warm ponds or polluted waters that are low in oxygen.

LAKES AND RIVERS FACTS

• Fish populations depend on plenty of insects as food.

• Dragonfly larvae are considered a delicacy in New Guinea.

• Swarms of nonbiting midges are sometimes so dense over African lakes that fishermen have been suffocated.

WATER SURFACE INSECTS

A WATER SURFACE behaves like a skin due to a force called surface tension. This force enables certain insects to walk on the "skin," and others to hang just beneath it. Many of these insects are predators, and much of their food comes from the constant supply of flying insects which have fallen into the water.

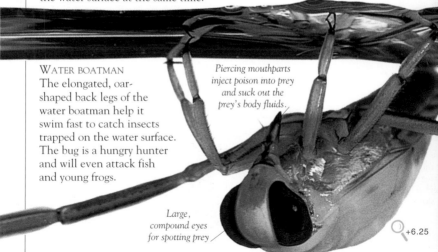

Q +7.5

WHIRLIGIG
The whirligig beetle swims around and around very fast on the water surface. It hunts insects trapped on the surface tension. The whirligig's eyes are divided into two halves, allowing it to see both above and below the water surface at the same time.

WATER BOATMAN
The elongated, oar-shaped back legs of the water boatman help it swim fast to catch insects trapped on the water surface. The bug is a hungry hunter and will even attack fish and young frogs.

Piercing mouthparts inject poison into prey and suck out the prey's body fluids.

Large, compound eyes for spotting prey

Q +6.25

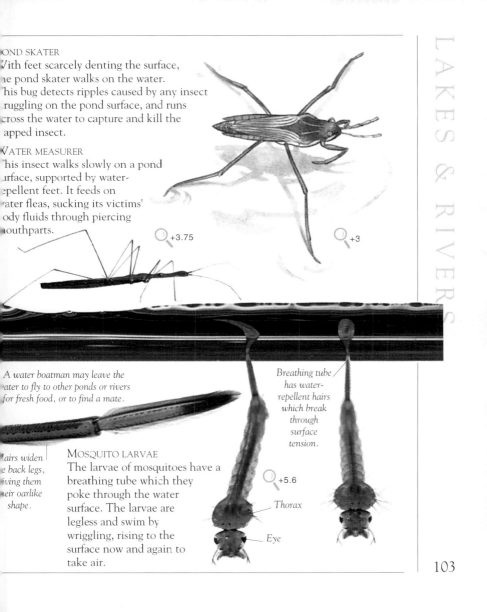

POND SKATER
With feet scarcely denting the surface,
the pond skater walks on the water.
This bug detects ripples caused by any insect
struggling on the pond surface, and runs
across the water to capture and kill the
trapped insect.

WATER MEASURER
This insect walks slowly on a pond
surface, supported by water-
repellent feet. It feeds on
water fleas, sucking its victims'
body fluids through piercing
mouthparts.

+3.75

+3

*A water boatman may leave the
water to fly to other ponds or rivers
for fresh food, or to find a mate.*

*Breathing tube
has water-
repellent hairs
which break
through
surface
tension.*

*Hairs widen
the back legs,
giving them
their oarlike
shape.*

MOSQUITO LARVAE
The larvae of mosquitoes have a
breathing tube which they
poke through the water
surface. The larvae are
legless and swim by
wriggling, rising to the
surface now and again to
take air.

+5.6

Thorax

Eye

103

UNDERWATER INSECTS

MANY OF THE insects that live underwater are carnivorous, either hunting their prey or scavenging. Some of these insects are fierce, sometimes killing prey larger than themselves.

DIVING BEETLE
The great diving beetle collects air from the water surface and stores it under its wings to breathe as it swims underwater.

+1.8

This mighty beetle can catch insects, small fish and tadpoles.

Nymph waits for prey to swim past.

+1.8

The great diving beetle sometimes flies from one pond to another.

Antenna

Water plants provide food and shelter for water insects.

DAMSELFLY NYMPH

LARVAL CASES
Caddis fly larvae sometimes use pieces of plant to make their protective cases. This body armor also acts as camouflage.

Pieces of plant

MAYFLY NYMPH
A mayfly spends one year as a nymph living underwater before it leaves the water to become an adult. The nymph breathes through gills along the side of its abdomen.

+0

ADULT DRAGONFLY
Male darter dragonflies perch
on plants that emerge from the
water. They fiercely attack and
drive away any rival males of
the same species, but attempt
to mate with any female darter
dragonfly that flies past.

−.8

DRAGONFLY EGGS
Darter dragonflies scatter their
eggs in water. The eggs are
surrounded by a jelly-like
substance, and hatch
after a few days.

*Jelly holds
eggs in place.*

−.8

BEETLE LARVA
The larva of the great diving beetle
injects juices into prey with its jaws.
The juices turn the prey's insides
into liquid for the larva to suck out.

DRAGONFLY NYMPH
Dragonfly nymphs breathe by
pumping water in and out of their
rear end, where they have
complex gills.

+1.8

ORCHID

TROPICAL FOREST

INSECTS THRIVE in the humid heat and flourishing plant life of tropical forests. These forests have a complex structure that provides many habitats for insects. Trees vary in shape and size; vines and dead branches are everywhere, and thick leaf litter covers the ground.

ORCHIDS

Tropical forests contain a spectacular variety of plants – there are about 25,000 species of orchid alone. It is quite dark beneath the forest canopy and orchids are strongly scented to help insects find them.

EPIPHYTES

Many plants grow on the trunks and branches of trees where birds have wiped seeds from their beaks. These tree-dwelling plants, called epiphytes, provide extra habitats for insects.

INSECT PREDATORS

A tropical forest is a rich habitat for birds as well as insects. Tropical birds feed on countless insects each day. This high rate of predation is a major reason for the evolution of camouflage and mimicry in tropical insects.

FRUITY NOURISHMENT

Some tropical butterflies live for several months. An important source of fuel for their continued activity is rotting fruit and dung on the forest floor. This gives them not only sugars for energy, but also amino acids and vitamins needed for survival.

Until recently, this insect was known only from dull brown museum specimens.

Blue face

Red eye

TROPICAL FORESTS

Bright colors are typical of tropical forests, and they can be seen in both the plant and animal life. This Central American grasshopper looks as if it would be easy to spot with its multicolored body, but it is camouflaged among the shining leaves of the forest trees.

The bright colors of this grasshopper surprised even entomologists.

Bright green abdomen

Q +2.5

The grasshopper's colors fade when it dies.

TROPICAL FOREST FACTS

• Tropical forests cover about five percent of the Earth's land surface.

• They contain over half of all living species.

• Around 1,200 species of butterfly have been recorded in one forest in southern Peru.

• Over half the world's rainforest has been cut since 1945.

107

IN THE CANOPY

THERE IS WARMTH, light, and plenty of food to eat in the canopy of tropical trees. The canopy provides living space for thousands of insec[t] species. In one day 3,000 different species were collected from a single tree in a forest in Borneo.

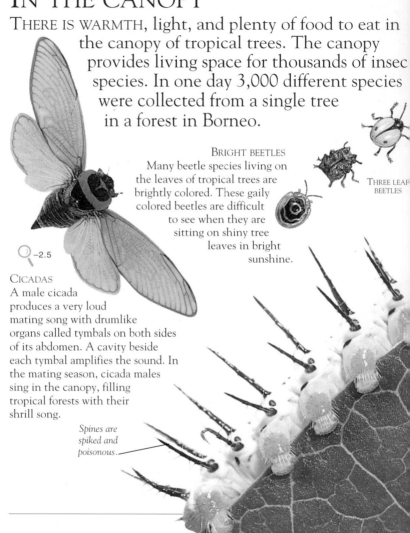

BRIGHT BEETLES
Many beetle species living on the leaves of tropical trees are brightly colored. These gaily colored beetles are difficult to see when they are sitting on shiny tree leaves in bright sunshine.

THREE LEAF BEETLES

–2.5

CICADAS
A male cicada produces a very loud mating song with drumlike organs called tymbals on both sides of its abdomen. A cavity beside each tymbal amplifies the sound. In the mating season, cicada males sing in the canopy, filling tropical forests with their shrill song.

Spines are spiked and poisonous.

FROG BEETLE

This vividly colored jeweled frog beetle is probably less noticeable in the bright sunshine of its leafy habitat. Despite its name, the froglike hind legs are not used for jumping, but for holding onto a female while mating.

Froglike hind leg

+0

−3.1

VIOLIN BEETLE

Little is know about the curious violin beetle, which got its name because of its violin-like shape. It is very flat, and has been found living between layers of shelf fungi on tree trunks in Indonesian forests.

Six simple eyes on either side of the head can sense whether it is light or dark.

+5

POISON SPINES

The body of the postman butterfly caterpillar contains poisons. It gets the poisons from chemicals in the leaves of the passionflower vines that it eats. The prickly spines remind birds to avoid it.

PASSIONFLOWER

NESTS IN THE CANOPY

WITH SO MANY insects feeding in the forest canopy, it is not surprising that the insect-eating ants and wasps build their nests there. But these ants and wasps are in turn hunted by mammals and lizards, so their nests must give protection.

Nest is made of paperlike material.

GREEN WEAVER ANTS
Each green weaver ant colony has several nests made of leaves. To make a nest, the ants join forces to pull leaves together and sew the edges. They sew using silk which the larvae produce when they are squeezed by the adult ants. These carnivorous ants hunt through the tree canopy, catching other insects and carrying the prey in pieces back to the ants' nests.

Ants' pulling leaves together.

WASP NESTS
Each wasp species makes a different type of nest. This nest from South America has been cut in half to reveal the "floors" which house the larvae. There is one small opening at the bottom where the wasps defend the nest from invading ants.

This nest hangs from a branch of a tree.

There may be half a million ants in one weaver ant colony.

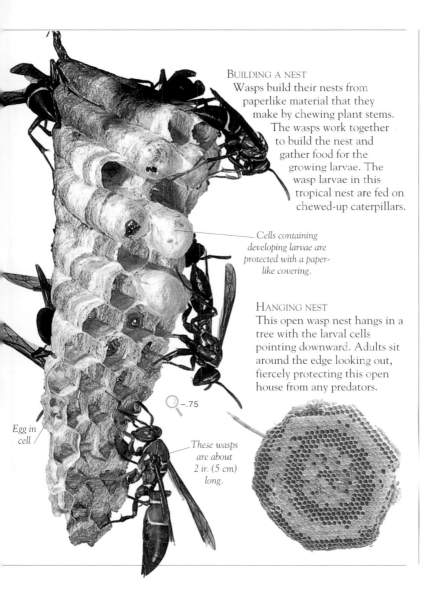

BUILDING A NEST

Wasps build their nests from paperlike material that they make by chewing plant stems. The wasps work together to build the nest and gather food for the growing larvae. The wasp larvae in this tropical nest are fed on chewed-up caterpillars.

Cells containing developing larvae are protected with a paper-like covering.

HANGING NEST

This open wasp nest hangs in a tree with the larval cells pointing downward. Adults sit around the edge looking out, fiercely protecting this open house from any predators.

Egg in cell

–.75

These wasps are about 2 in (5 cm) long.

111

BRILLIANT BUTTERFLIES

MANY TROPICAL butterflies are large and brilliantly colored, which ought to make it easy for predators to catch them. But they fly rapidly and erratically, flash their bright colors in the sun, and then seem to disappear, darting into the deep shade of the forest.

BLUE MORPHO
The iridescent blue of South American morpho butterflies is so vivid it can be seen from a great distance. But its underwings are a muddy brown for camouflage when feeding on the ground.

○ .4
SOUTHEAST ASIAN MOTH
The vivid colors of this southeast Asian moth shows that some day-flying moths can be as colorful as butterflies. The bright colors warn predators that this moth is poisonous.

○ .6

○ +2.5

NERO BUTTERFLY
The bright yellow Nero butterfly drinks from streams and puddles near mammal dung. This habit is common in butterflies of tropical forests, and supplies them with nutrients that are not available in flowers.

+2.5

Tops of wings are bright and colorful

POSTMAN
BUTTERFLY
Brightly colored
and slow-flying, the
postman butterfly is
poisonous to predators, who
quickly learn to avoid them.
Groups of postman butterflies
often sleep together on branches.

FEMALE BIRDWING
BUTTERFLY

−4

BIRDWING
BUTTERFLIES
The males of
southeast Asian
birdwing butterflies
differ in size, color, and behavior from the
females. The brightly colored males sometimes
fly near the ground, but the larger brownish
females remain in the treetops.

−3.5

MALE BIRDWING BUTTERFLY

TROPICAL BUTTERFLIES

THOUSANDS OF butterfly species live in tropical forests. Each butterfly has to recognize members of its own species among all the others in order to mate They find each other by sight – butterflies have a good sense of color– and by smell.

Q-.75

Tail brush

USING SCENTS
Striped blue crow butterfly males have a yellow brush at the end of their abdomen. When a male has found a female, he uses his brush to dust scented scales on her. The arousing scent encourages the female to mate with him.

DETECTING SCENTS
Butterfly and moth antennae are covered in sense organs that detect scents. This is a silkmoth antenna viewed at high magnification. It is divided into segments, and each segment has two branches. The branches increase the antenna's surface area, making it more sensitive.

Branches on each segment

Scent chemicals stimulate nerves in the antennae.

Q-3.1

SITTING TOGETHER
At sunny spots in the forest, butterflies gather at muddy puddles to drink water and salts. Butterflies of the same species usually sit together, so that white-colored species form one group, blue another, and so on.

Postman butterflies and small postman butterflies are two different species. But they share the same wing patterns in different parts of South America.

SMALL POSTMAN BUTTERFLY
FROM SOUTHERN ECUADOR

POSTMAN BUTTERFLY
FROM SOUTHERN ECUADOR

SMALL POSTMAN BUTTERFLY
FROM SOUTHERN BRAZIL

POSTMAN BUTTERFLY
FROM SOUTHERN BRAZIL

SMALL POSTMAN BUTTERFLY
FROM WESTERN BRAZIL

POSTMAN BUTTERFLY
FROM WESTERN BRAZIL

.8

COPYING PATTERNS

Sometimes two or more different species of poisonous butterfly share the same wing pattern. This kind of mimicry means that the different species protect each other. Birds only need to learn that one species is poisonous to avoid the other.

HORNED BEETLES

WITH SO MANY millions of insects in tropical forests, individuals must sometimes compete for the best living space in which to mate and lay eggs. Horned beetles have horns which they use as weapons in battle. A male may lock horns with other males to claim a good territory, and then attract females to him.

Jaws have spines running along them.

Darwin's beetle is from Brazil.

Antenna

Spiny front leg

Q—.6

DARWIN'S BEETLE
This beetle probably uses its long jaws to drive away rival males. Darwin's beetle is supposed to have bitten Charles Darwin, the famous naturalist, when he was in Brazil.

Q—.6

The rhinoceros beetle can lift 850 times its own weight.

The beetle may use its horns to lift a rival out of the way.

RHINOCEROS BEETLE
Within the same species, rhinoceros beetle males and their horns can vary greatly in size. Sometimes, when the biggest males are fighting, one of the smallest will sneakily mate with the female of one of the fighting males.

This male rhinoceros beetle is 3½ in (9 cm) long.

Clawed feet

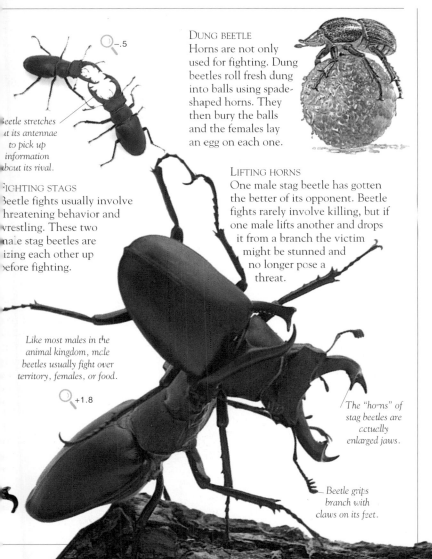

_-.5_

Beetle stretches
out its antennae
to pick up
information
about its rival.

DUNG BEETLE
Horns are not only
used for fighting. Dung
beetles roll fresh dung
into balls using spade-
shaped horns. They
then bury the balls
and the females lay
an egg on each one.

FIGHTING STAGS
Beetle fights usually involve
threatening behavior and
wrestling. These two
male stag beetles are
sizing each other up
before fighting.

LIFTING HORNS
One male stag beetle has gotten
the better of its opponent. Beetle
fights rarely involve killing, but if
one male lifts another and drops
it from a branch the victim
might be stunned and
no longer pose a
threat.

_Like most males in the
animal kingdom, male
beetles usually fight over
territory, females, or food._

_+1.8_

_The "horns" of
stag beetles are
actually
enlarged jaws._

_Beetle grips
branch with
claws on its feet._

117

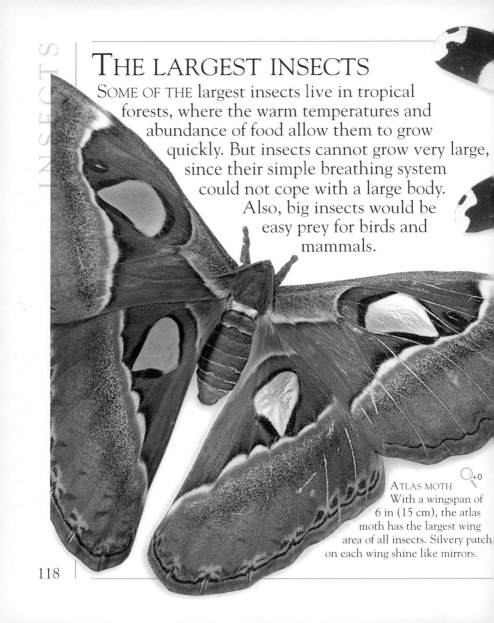

THE LARGEST INSECTS

SOME OF THE largest insects live in tropical
forests, where the warm temperatures and
abundance of food allow them to grow
quickly. But insects cannot grow very large,
since their simple breathing system
could not cope with a large body.
Also, big insects would be
easy prey for birds and
mammals.

ATLAS MOTH
With a wingspan of
6 in (15 cm), the atlas
moth has the largest wing
area of all insects. Silvery patch
on each wing shine like mirrors.

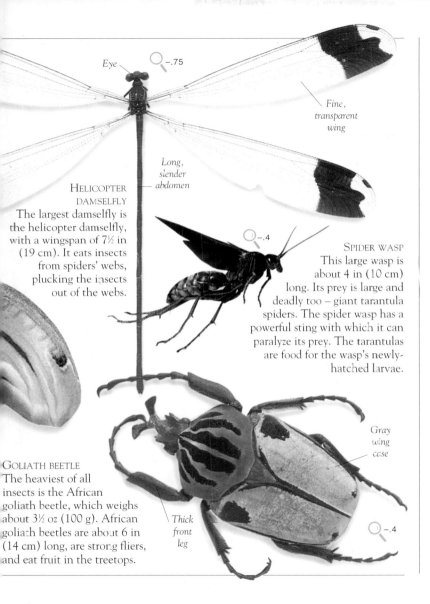

Eye ⊙ –.75

Fine,
transparent
wing

Long,
slender
abdomen

HELICOPTER DAMSELFLY
The largest damselfly is
the helicopter damselfly,
with a wingspan of 7½ in
(19 cm). It eats insects
from spiders' webs,
plucking the insects
out of the webs.

⊙ –.4

SPIDER WASP
This large wasp is
about 4 in (10 cm)
long. Its prey is large and
deadly too – giant tarantula
spiders. The spider wasp has a
powerful sting with which it can
paralyze its prey. The tarantulas
are food for the wasp's newly-
hatched larvae.

Gray
wing
case

GOLIATH BEETLE
The heaviest of all
insects is the African
goliath beetle, which weighs
about 3½ oz (100 g). African
goliath beetles are about 6 in
(14 cm) long, are strong fliers,
and eat fruit in the treetops.

Thick
front
leg

⊙ –.4

119

STICK AND LEAF INSECTS

A TROPICAL FOREST is alive with animals, most of which eat insects. To survive, insects adopt many strategies. Stick and leaf insects hide from predators by keeping still to resemble their background of leaves and sticks.

STICK INSECTS
Some stick insects are slender, brown, or green, just like the twigs and leaf stalks they sit on. Other species are shorter and fatter, with spines and other projections. These often look like curled dead leaves.

Winged male of Macleay's spectre

Wingless female of Macleay's spectre

Indian stick insect

Spiny green nymph

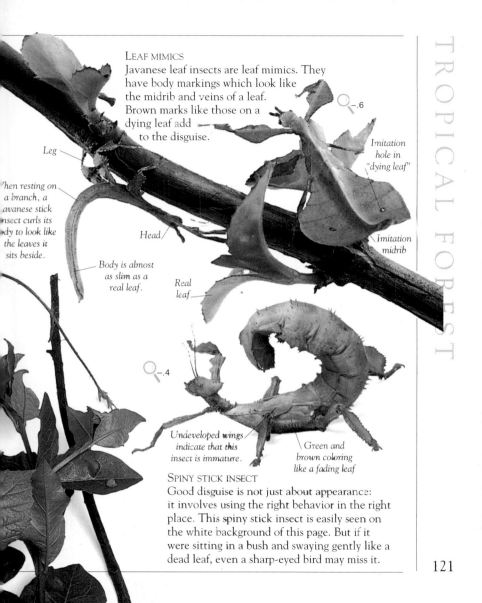

Javanese leaf insects are leaf mimics. They
have body markings which look like
the midrib and veins of a leaf.
Brown marks like those on a
dying leaf add
to the disguise.

○-.6

Imitation
hole in
"dying leaf"

Leg

When resting on
a branch, a
Javanese stick
insect curls its
body to look like
the leaves it
sits beside.

Head

Imitation
midrib

Body is almost
as slim as a
real leaf.

Real
leaf

○-.4

Undeveloped wings
indicate that this
insect is immature.

Green and
brown coloring
like a fading leaf

SPINY STICK INSECT
Good disguise is not just about appearance:
it involves using the right behavior in the right
place. This spiny stick insect is easily seen on
the white background of this page. But if it
were sitting in a bush and swaying gently like a
dead leaf, even a sharp-eyed bird may miss it.

121

ARMIES ON THE GROUND

ANTS ARE THE dominant creatures of tropical forests. They live in colonies made up of any number from 20 individuals to many thousands. Ants are mostly carnivorous. Some species make slaves of other ant species by invading their nest and killing their queen

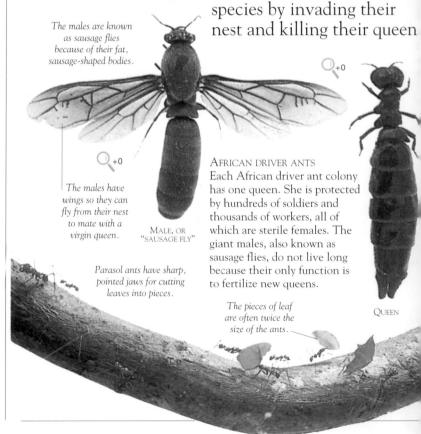

The males are known as sausage flies because of their fat, sausage-shaped bodies.

Q +0

Q +0

The males have wings so they can fly from their nest to mate with a virgin queen.

MALE, OR "SAUSAGE FLY"

Parasol ants have sharp, pointed jaws for cutting leaves into pieces.

AFRICAN DRIVER ANTS

Each African driver ant colony has one queen. She is protected by hundreds of soldiers and thousands of workers, all of which are sterile females. The giant males, also known as sausage flies, do not live long because their only function is to fertilize new queens.

The pieces of leaf are often twice the size of the ants.

QUEEN

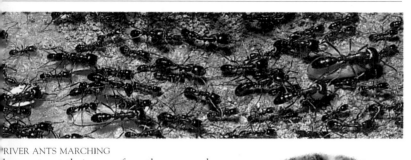

DRIVER ANTS MARCHING

These ants get their name from the way a colony sweeps through an area catching all the insects it can find. They move their nests from place to place regularly, unlike most ants which have a permanent nest and territory.

+4

Beetle pupae are among the prey of driver ants.

CARRYING PREY

Ants in a column collaborate to cut large insects they have caught into smaller pieces. This is so they can carry their food back to the nest. Smaller prey can be carried whole.

ATTENTIVE SOLDIER

Driver ant soldiers have very large jaws. Often they can be seen standing beside a marching column of ants with their jaws wide open, waiting to attack intruders such as parasitic flies.

Ant returning for more leaves

PARASOL ANTS

These South American ants are not carnivorous. They feed on fungus which they cultivate in huge underground nests. The fungus is grown on pieces of leaf which the ants bring to the nest.

123

DESERTS, CAVES, AND SOILS

SOME INSECTS flourish in habitats where it is difficult for living things to survive. Desert habitats, for example, lack water and have very high temperatures. Caves are dark and lack plant life for food. Life in soil makes communication, by both scent and sight, difficult for insects.

Q +5

Tiger beetle larva has hooks on body to help it climb upward.

HIDING IN SOIL
Life in the soil is only a passing phase for some insect species. This tiger beetle larva hides underground by day. At night it waits in its vertical tunnel with its jaws projecting at the ground surface, and snatches passing insects to devour in its burrow.

CAVE DWELLER
This cockroach lives all its life in the dark. Like other cave creatures, it feeds on debris from the outside world. Bat dung, dead animals, and pieces of plants washed into the cave provide the cockroach with its nourishment.

DESERT BEETLE
The lack of water in deserts forces insects to find ingenious ways of obtaining moisture. This darkling beetle lives in the Namib Desert, where sea winds bring mists each night. The beetle holds its abdomen high to catch the moisture, which then runs down into its mouth.

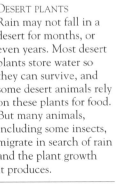

DESERT HEAT
The hot and dry days in deserts can lead to rapid water loss and death for animals. Most living creatures hide under stones or in the sand to avoid drying out. These animals are active at night when it is much cooler.

DESERT FACTS

• The Sahara Desert is spreading at a rate of 3 miles (5 km) per year.

• In deserts the temperature may range from 90°F (30°C) in the day to below 32°F (0°C) at night.

• Caves are a nearly constant temperature throughout the year.

• 20% of the Earth's land surface is desert.

CACTUS
FLOWER

DESERT PLANTS
Rain may not fall in a desert for months, or even years. Most desert plants store water so they can survive, and some desert animals rely on these plants for food. But many animals, including some insects, migrate in search of rain and the plant growth it produces.

DESERT INSECTS

HOT, DRY DESERTS are dangerous places in which to live. Animals often die from sunstroke and dehydratic (drying out). To prevent this, insects avoid the sun by staying in the shade or burrowing in the sand. Some insects have special methods of collecting water. Mar feed only at night, because the surface of the sand is too hot for them to walk on during the day.

−.8

NAMIB DESERT BEETLE
Long legs keep the body of the Namib desert beetle off the hot sand. The larvae live in the sand, scavenging on detritus (organic debris), and complete development in about six months. The adults live for several years.

Antenna

DESERT LOCUSTS
Adult desert locusts fly in swarms to find fresh food. When there is enough food they breed rapidly, and huge groups of wingless nymphs hop across the desert sand.

Grasses and other plants form the diet of desert locusts.

Desert locusts get water from plant food.

TWO DESER LOCUST NYM

+2.5

DESERT CRICKET
The large feet of
this desert cricket
allow it to dig speedily
in the sand. It can
bury itself in a few
seconds, either to hide
from predators or to
escape from the
intense heat
of the midday sun. Its
wingtips are coiled to
protect them when
underground.

–.6

End of
wings
coiled up

Large feet

Strong back
legs for long
leaps

Wing
buds

This hard
collar protects
the thorax.

Long
antenna

HONEYPOT ANTS
Honeypot ants are living water
stores. During the rainy season,
certain worker ants in a colony
are fed with water and nectar
until their abdomens are full
and swollen. In the dry season
the other ants feed from them
until the rainy season returns.

JEWEL WASP
These shiny green wasps
catch other insects, such as
cockroaches, for their young
to eat. Adult jewel wasps are
vegetarians, drinking nectar
from desert flowers. +1.5

Long antenna

-4.3

AFRICAN CRICKET
Some insects have developed very long antennae to make up for lack of vision in dark caves. This African cricket has the longest antennae for its body size of any insect.

CAVE INSECTS

ALL LIFE DEPENDS on the sun's energy. Plants change sunlight into food by a process called photosynthesis. In dark, sunless caves, nothing grows, and cave-dwelling insects must find food from outside. This food is sometimes washed in on floods, or dropped by bats and birds.

Long back legs for jumping out of danger

FEMALE AFRICAN CAVE CRICKET

Two sensitive spines, called cerci, can detect enemies approaching from behind.

Cricket uses its ovipositor (egg-laying tube) to lay eggs in soil.

+3.1

PEACOCK BUTTERFLY

For some insects, caves provide shelter from the uncomfortable weather conditions. During cold northern winters a cave is an ideal place for peacock butterflies to hibernate.

Dark underside of wings camouflages the peacock butterfly as it hibernates.

Top of wings are brightly colored.

−1

PEACOCK BUTTERFLY

CAVE CRICKET

Crickets living in caves have smaller eyes and paler bodies than crickets living in sunlight. Cave crickets breed all year because the temperature and the amount of food in the cave stay constant.

Very long, sensitive antennae

COCKROACH

Cave-dwelling cockroaches eat bat droppings and bat carcasses, as well as mites and fungi. Cockroaches often eat each other, too. Caves make an ideal home for cockroaches since they love dark, damp places.

+3.75

SURINAM COCKROACH

SOIL INSECTS

WHEN PLANTS and animals die, their remains usually get absorbed into the soil. Insects that live in soil are among the most important creatures on Earth because they help to recycle these remains, releasing their nutrients and so helping new crops and forests to grow. Soil insects are also an important food for many mammals and birds.

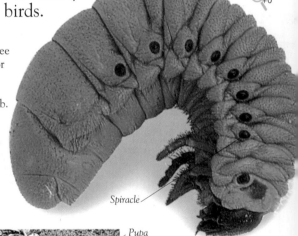

Q_{+0}

BEETLE LARVA
Roots and decaying tree trunks provide food for many types of insect larva, such as this lamellicorn beetle grub. The grub breathes through holes called spiracles, which occur along the side of its body. Although there is not very much air underground, there is enough for insects.

Spiracle

Pupa

GOOD HABITAT
Living in soil has advantages. Insects are unlikely to dehydrate, and there is plenty of food in plant roots and decaying plants. This spurge hawk-moth pupa has sharp plates on its abdomen which help it climb to the surface just before the adult emerges.

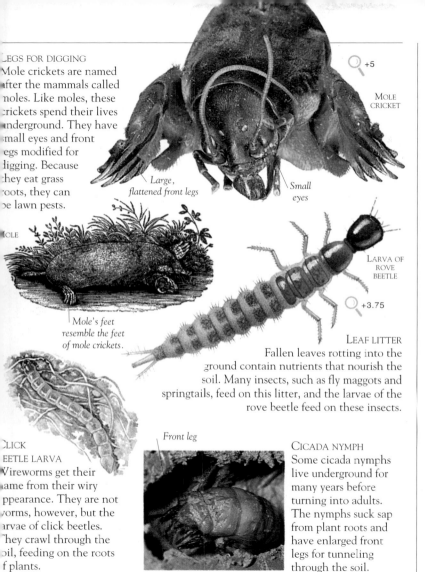

LEGS FOR DIGGING
Mole crickets are named after the mammals called moles. Like moles, these crickets spend their lives underground. They have small eyes and front legs modified for digging. Because they eat grass roots, they can be lawn pests.

+5

MOLE
CRICKET

Large, flattened front legs

Small eyes

MOLE

LARVA OF ROVE BEETLE

Mole's feet resemble the feet of mole crickets.

+3.75

LEAF LITTER
Fallen leaves rotting into the ground contain nutrients that nourish the soil. Many insects, such as fly maggots and springtails, feed on this litter, and the larvae of the rove beetle feed on these insects.

CLICK
BEETLE LARVA
Wireworms get their name from their wiry appearance. They are not worms, however, but the larvae of click beetles. They crawl through the soil, feeding on the roots of plants.

Front leg

CICADA NYMPH
Some cicada nymphs live underground for many years before turning into adults. The nymphs suck sap from plant roots and have enlarged front legs for tunneling through the soil.

131

TOWNS AND GARDENS

SINCE INSECTS HAVE managed to make homes for themselves in practically every natural habitat, it is no surprising that they have turned human habitats into their homes, too. Insects live in our houses, feeding on our furniture, clothes, foodstores, and garbage dumps. Our gardens and farms are also teeming with insect life, nourished by the abundance of flowers, fruits and vegetables.

Colorado beetle

-1.75

POTATO PESTS
When potatoes were brought to Europe from South America, the Colorado beetle came with them. This insect eats potato plant leaves, and can cause great damage to crops.

Leaves of potato plant

Potato

CABBAGE EATERS
Cabbage white butterflies lay eggs on cabbage plants so the larvae can eat the leaves. Farms provide acres of cabbages, and the butterflies become pests since they breed at an unnaturally high rate because of the abundance of food.

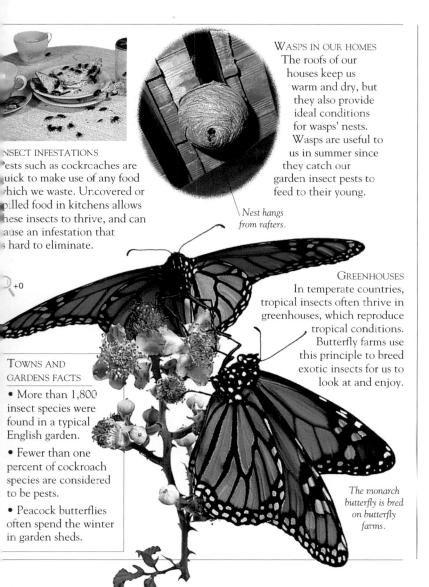

WASPS IN OUR HOMES
The roofs of our houses keep us warm and dry, but they also provide ideal conditions for wasps' nests. Wasps are useful to us in summer since they catch our garden insect pests to feed to their young.

Nest hangs from rafters.

INSECT INFESTATIONS
Pests such as cockroaches are quick to make use of any food which we waste. Uncovered or spilled food in kitchens allows these insects to thrive, and can cause an infestation that is hard to eliminate.

+0

GREENHOUSES
In temperate countries, tropical insects often thrive in greenhouses, which reproduce tropical conditions. Butterfly farms use this principle to breed exotic insects for us to look at and enjoy.

TOWNS AND GARDENS FACTS

• More than 1,800 insect species were found in a typical English garden.

• Fewer than one percent of cockroach species are considered to be pests.

• Peacock butterflies often spend the winter in garden sheds.

The monarch butterfly is bred on butterfly farms.

133

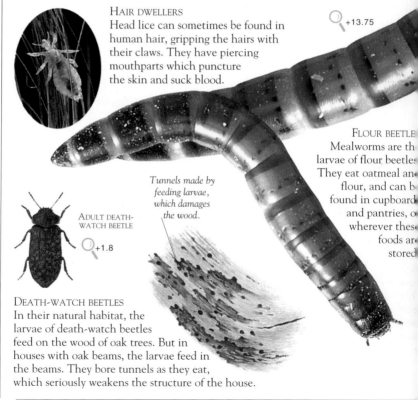

HOUSEHOLD INSECTS

SINCE PREHISTORIC times, insects have lived in human
homes, attracted by warmth, shelter, and food. These
insects eat our food, our furniture, and some even eat
our carpets. Parasitic insects also live in our homes,
feeding on the human inhabitants.

HAIR DWELLERS
Head lice can sometimes be found in
human hair, gripping the hairs with
their claws. They have piercing
mouthparts which puncture
the skin and suck blood.

+13.75

FLOUR BEETLE
Mealworms are the
larvae of flour beetles.
They eat oatmeal and
flour, and can be
found in cupboards
and pantries, or
wherever these
foods are
stored

*Tunnels made by
feeding larvae,
which damages
the wood.*

ADULT DEATH-
WATCH BEETLE

+1.8

DEATH-WATCH BEETLES
In their natural habitat, the
larvae of death-watch beetles
feed on the wood of oak trees. But in
houses with oak beams, the larvae feed in
the beams. They bore tunnels as they eat,
which seriously weakens the structure of the house.

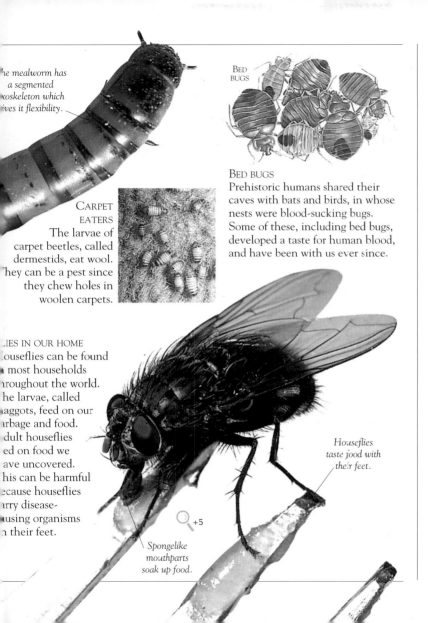

The mealworm has a segmented exoskeleton which gives it flexibility.

BED BUGS

BED BUGS
Prehistoric humans shared their caves with bats and birds, in whose nests were blood-sucking bugs. Some of these, including bed bugs, developed a taste for human blood, and have been with us ever since.

CARPET EATERS
The larvae of carpet beetles, called dermestids, eat wool. They can be a pest since they chew holes in woolen carpets.

FLIES IN OUR HOME
Houseflies can be found in most households throughout the world. The larvae, called maggots, feed on our garbage and food. Adult houseflies feed on food we have uncovered. This can be harmful because houseflies carry disease-causing organisms on their feet.

Houseflies taste food with their feet.

Q_{+5}

Spongelike mouthparts soak up food.

135

GARDEN INSECTS

A GARDEN IS a good place to watch and study insects. Many different insects are attracted into gardens to feed on the flowers, vegetables, and other plants. Som predatory insects come to eat the plant-eating insects. But most garden insects are just tourists, feeding on flower nectar a they pass through.

ROVE BEETLES
Rove beetles hunt at night, scouring the garden for insects to eat. These large beetles are common in compost piles, scurrying away from the daylight when the compost is turned.

+3.1

GARDENER'S FRIENDS
Hoverflies hover in front of flower on hot, sunny days as they feed on nectar. They are particularly attracted to thistle flowers. Hoverfly larvae are the gardener's friends, feeding voraciously on plant-damaging aphids.

+3.75

Eye

Antenna

SPHINX-MOTH

The caterpillars of sphinx-moths can be recognized by their short, erect "tail." Most adult sphinx-moths fly at night, hovering in front of flowers to gather nectar with their long tongues.

SILVER-STRIPED SPHINX-MOTH CATERPILLAR

"Tail"

+0

Caterpillar has eyespots to frighten off predators.

Eyespot

Fuchsia flower

GARDEN GRASSHOPPER

The common field grasshopper is widespread in Europe on short grass in sunny places, and often finds a home in gardens. Like tropical locusts, common field grasshoppers sometimes migrate in swarms, but on a much smaller scale.

RED ADMIRAL

−.4

Butterflies often stop to sunbathe for a while.

FOOD FOR BUTTERFLIES

The flower border of a garden is like a filling station for passing butterflies. They feed on nectar to give them energy as they search for suitable mates or plants on which to lay eggs.

PEACOCK

SILVER-SPOTTED SKIPPER

−.75

−.4

FRIENDS AND FOES

THE RELATIONSHIP between insects and humans is not always good. Many insec are useful to us, although others are pests. We destroy their habitats, and deny other wild animals of food.
Ecology, involving the study of the balance between our needs and the needs of other animals and plants, helps us to understand this conflict

APHIDS

Aphids are major pests on our food plants and flower Some aphid species are common on roses, while others spread diseases which ruin potatoes and strawberries, as well as many other food crops.

Aphids drink the rose's sap. This may kill the rose, because the sap is like the plant's blood.

Intricate pattern of veins in wings

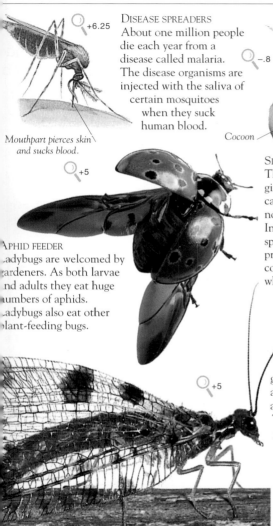

DISEASE SPREADERS
About one million people die each year from a disease called malaria. The disease organisms are injected with the saliva of certain mosquitoes when they suck human blood.

Mouthpart pierces skin and sucks blood.

Q +6.25

Q −.8

Moth

Cocoon

Q +5

SILK PROVIDERS
The silk we use in clothes is given to us by silkworm moth caterpillars. Silkworm moths no longer occur in the wild. Instead, they are bred in special farms. The caterpillars produce the silk to form cocoons that protect them when they pupate.

APHID FEEDER
Ladybugs are welcomed by gardeners. As both larvae and adults they eat huge numbers of aphids. Ladybugs also eat other plant-feeding bugs.

Q +5

PEST EATERS
Lacewings are delicate insects, often with shining golden eyes. Their larvae are voracious predators of aphids and other plant lice. They have long, tubular jaws through which they suck the body contents of their prey. Lacewing larvae hide themselves from predators by sticking the remains of their prey onto small hairs on their backs.

BEES AND POLLINATION

BEES AND PLANTS depend on each other. Plants need bees to carry pollen between flowers to produce seeds. Bees collect pollen and nectar from flowers to feed their larva. Nectar in a hive is made into honey for winter food.

BEE-KEEPING

For thousands of years people have kept bees for their honey. Modern hives have racks of frames, each with a ready-made comb of cells. Individual frames can be removed and the honey drained.

POLLINATION

Other insects, such as butterflies, also pollinate flowers. Many flowers are a special color or shape to attract particular insects. These insects receive pollen and nectar in the process of carrying pollen to another flower.

+2.5

+7.5

POLLEN BASKETS
Bees carry pollen back to their nest in
special pollen baskets on their back legs.
The baskets are made from curved
bristles. A bee uses its front legs to
comb pollen from its furry body and
put it in the baskets.

*Shape of dance
shows bees
direction
of flowers.*

BEE COMMUNICATION
When a honeybee finds
flowers with nectar it tells
other bees in the hive by
dancing. The bee conveys
the distance of the flowers
by how fast it shakes its
abdomen, and the
direction by the angle
of its dance.

*Pollen
basket*

FISH

FISH

WHAT IS A FISH?

THE FIRST FISH appeared in the oceans 470 million years ago. Today, more than 20,000 species have been discovered. Fish live in water, breathe through gills, have a scaly body, and maneuver themselves using fins. All fish are vertebrates, which means that they have a backbone or similar structure, and an internal skeleton. The three main fish groups are bony fish, cartilaginous fish, and jawless fish.

Caudal fin or tail for stabilizing fish

Lateral line helps fish feel vibrations

BONY FISH FINS
Most bony fish have a dorsal fin, paired pectoral and pelvic fins, and a tail for movement. In some fish, fins have become specialized as lifting foils, walking legs, suckers for holding on, or poisoned spines for protection.

Anal fin

Pelvic fin for maneuvering

WHALE SHARK

CARTILAGINOUS FISH
Sharks are cartilaginous fish, which means that they have skeletons made of extremely hard cartilage, not bone. The world's biggest fish is the whale shark, which grows to 49 ft (15 m) in length.

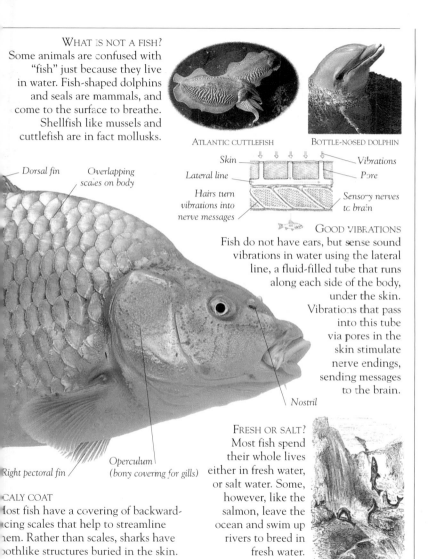

WHAT IS NOT A FISH?
Some animals are confused with "fish" just because they live in water. Fish-shaped dolphins and seals are mammals, and come to the surface to breathe. Shellfish like mussels and cuttlefish are in fact mollusks.

ATLANTIC CUTTLEFISH

BOTTLE-NOSED DOLPHIN

Skin — Vibrations
Lateral line — Pore
Hairs turn vibrations into nerve messages — Sensory nerves to brain

GOOD VIBRATIONS
Fish do not have ears, but sense sound vibrations in water using the lateral line, a fluid-filled tube that runs along each side of the body, under the skin. Vibrations that pass into this tube via pores in the skin stimulate nerve endings, sending messages to the brain.

Dorsal fin

Overlapping scales on body

Nostril

Right pectoral fin

Operculum (bony covering for gills)

SCALY COAT
Most fish have a covering of backward-facing scales that help to streamline them. Rather than scales, sharks have toothlike structures buried in the skin.

FRESH OR SALT?
Most fish spend their whole lives either in fresh water, or salt water. Some, however, like the salmon, leave the ocean and swim up rivers to breed in fresh water.

145

FISH ANATOMY

FISH HAVE MANY of the same internal organs found in reptiles, birds, and mammals, such as a heart, brain, lungs, and liver. However, in order to live and "breathe" under water, a fish also needs some unique body parts.

Fish "breathe" in water using their gills. Oxygen passes from the water through the thin gill membranes into the fish's blood, and is then distributed around the body, to power the muscles.

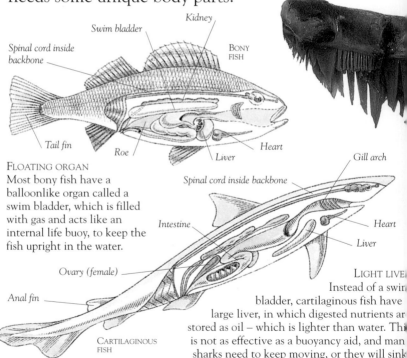

Swim bladder

Kidney

Spinal cord inside backbone

BONY FISH

Tail fin

Roe

Liver

Heart

FLOATING ORGAN
Most bony fish have a balloonlike organ called a swim bladder, which is filled with gas and acts like an internal life buoy, to keep the fish upright in the water.

Spinal cord inside backbone

Gill arch

Intestine

Heart

Liver

Ovary (female)

Anal fin

LIGHT LIVE
Instead of a swin bladder, cartilaginous fish have large liver, in which digested nutrients ar stored as oil – which is lighter than water. Thi is not as effective as a buoyancy aid, and man sharks need to keep moving, or they will sink

CARTILAGINOUS FISH

146

Stiff gill rakers sieve in clean water passing over gills

Bony support of gill arch

Gill filaments, through which oxygen in the water passes into the fish's blood

TUNA FISH GILL

WATER FLOW
To obtain oxygen, the fish takes in a mouthful of water, while the gill cover shuts flat to stop water escaping. The fish then closes its mouth, forcing the water inside to flow past the gills. On its way out, the water pushes open the flaplike gill cover.

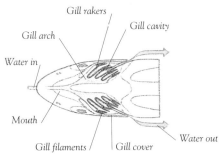

Gill rakers

Gill cavity

Gill arch

Water in

Mouth

Gill filaments

Gill cover

Water out

147

FISH BONES

ALL FISH HAVE internal skeletons.
Sharks and rays have skeletons
made of cartilage, but most
fish have skeletons
made of bone (bony
fish or teleosts.)

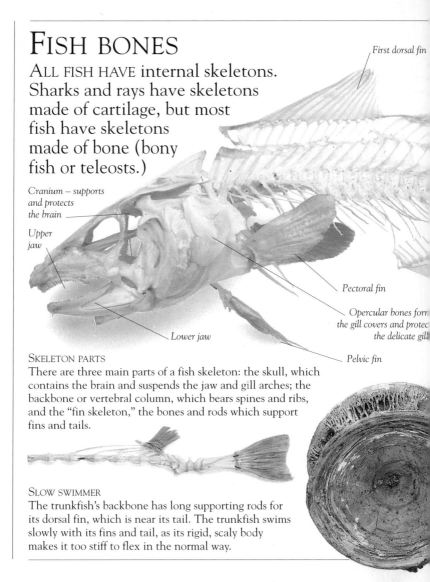

First dorsal fin

*Cranium – supports
and protects
the brain*

*Upper
jaw*

Lower jaw

Pectoral fin

*Opercular bones form
the gill covers and protect
the delicate gills*

Pelvic fin

SKELETON PARTS

There are three main parts of a fish skeleton: the skull, which
contains the brain and suspends the jaw and gill arches; the
backbone or vertebral column, which bears spines and ribs,
and the "fin skeleton," the bones and rods which support
fins and tails.

SLOW SWIMMER

The trunkfish's backbone has long supporting rods for
its dorsal fin, which is near its tail. The trunkfish swims
slowly with its fins and tail, as its rigid, scaly body
makes it too stiff to flex in the normal way.

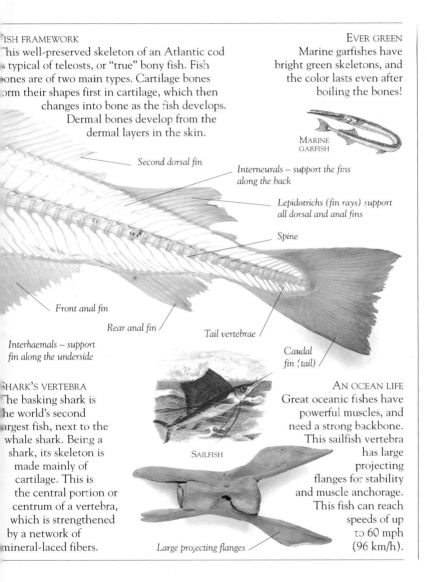

FISH FRAMEWORK
This well-preserved skeleton of an Atlantic cod is typical of teleosts, or "true" bony fish. Fish bones are of two main types. Cartilage bones form their shapes first in cartilage, which then changes into bone as the fish develops. Dermal bones develop from the dermal layers in the skin.

EVER GREEN
Marine garfishes have bright green skeletons, and the color lasts even after boiling the bones!

MARINE GARFISH

Second dorsal fin

Interneurals – support the fins along the back

Lepidotrichs (fin rays) support all dorsal and anal fins

Spine

Front anal fin

Rear anal fin

Tail vertebrae

Caudal fin (tail)

Interhaemals – support fin along the underside

SHARK'S VERTEBRA
The basking shark is the world's second largest fish, next to the whale shark. Being a shark, its skeleton is made mainly of cartilage. This is the central portion or centrum of a vertebra, which is strengthened by a network of mineral-laced fibers.

SAILFISH

AN OCEAN LIFE
Great oceanic fishes have powerful muscles, and need a strong backbone. This sailfish vertebra has large projecting flanges for stability and muscle anchorage. This fish can reach speeds of up to 60 mph (96 km/h).

Large projecting flanges

149

COLOR FOR SURVIVAL

MANY FISH USE color for survival tactics, and have
evolved almost every imaginable hue and pattern,
for various reasons. Color is an excellent means of
camouflage or defense, or of advertising a territory,
whether it be in the open
ocean, in rivers or lakes,
or on a coral reef.

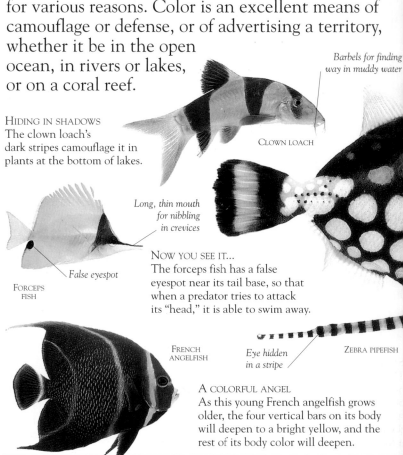

*Barbels for finding
way in muddy water*

HIDING IN SHADOWS
The clown loach's
dark stripes camouflage it in
plants at the bottom of lakes.

CLOWN LOACH

*Long, thin mouth
for nibbling
in crevices*

False eyespot

FORCEPS
FISH

NOW YOU SEE IT...
The forceps fish has a false
eyespot near its tail base, so that
when a predator tries to attack
its "head," it is able to swim away.

FRENCH
ANGELFISH

*Eye hidden
in a stripe*

ZEBRA PIPEFISH

A COLORFUL ANGEL
As this young French angelfish grows
older, the four vertical bars on its body
will deepen to a bright yellow, and the
rest of its body color will deepen.

Eye hidden by head stripe

Eyespot

LOTS TO LOOK AT
The threadfin butterfly fish, which lives in warm Australian seas, is a highly patterned and colored fish. It has a white mustard-lined forehead, zig-zags on the front half of the body, and a false eyespot on the rear of the dorsal fin.

THREADFIN
BUTTERFLY FISH

CUBAN
HOCK

DIRTY DEALER
Scattered darker scales on the Cuban hock's body and fins give it a slightly "dirty" appearance, aiding camouflage.

CLOWN
TRIGGERFISH

REGAL
TANG

CONFUSING CLOWN
The contrasting patterns of the clown triggerfish confuse predators, making it less likely to be attacked.

INTO THE BLUE
The regal tang starts life mostly yellow, but turns blue gradually.

BLUE-RINGED
ANGELFISH

STRIPY CAMOUFLAGE
The zebra pipefish hides horizontally in the stems of waterweed. Its stripes blend in with the weed, disguising it from predators.

LOOK AT ME!
The electric-blue bands of this blue-ringed angelfish give a strong visual signal to members of the same species.

151

SKATES AND RAYS

IT IS HARD TO BELIEVE that flat, slow-moving skates and rays, which live on the bed of the ocean, are related to fast, streamlined sharks. However, rays' and sharks' anatomy is very similar: for example, both have cartilaginous skeletons, and up to seven gill slits.

Underside is pale in colour, while upper surface is camouflaged

SEABED FEEDER
Rays feed mainly on sand-living creatures, so their mouths are on the underside of their bodies. There is a hole called a spiracle on the upper side through which clean water for breathing is taken in and passed over the gills.

MOLLUSKS
Rays feed on hard-shelled animals, such as sea snails, that live in the sand.

Grinding teeth crush the armor of prey

POISON GLAND
Some rays have sharp sawlike stings on their tails. These are good protection against their enemies.

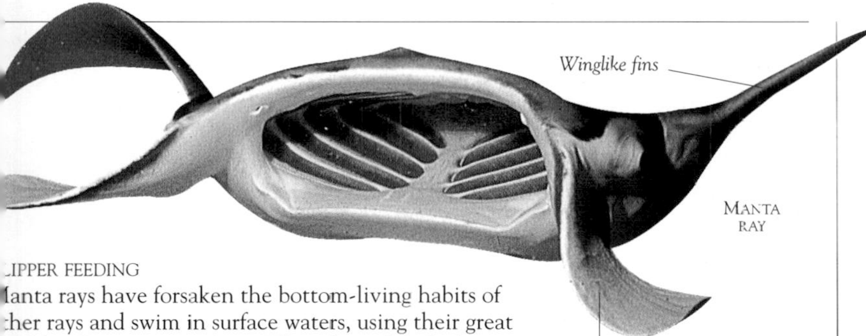

Winglike fins

MANTA
RAY

Flippers for
guiding food

FLIPPER FEEDING
Manta rays have forsaken the bottom-living habits of
other rays and swim in surface waters, using their great
fins like slow-moving wings. These huge fish feed on
plankton, which they guide into their mouths with
flipperlike organs on either side of their heads.

SUN BATHER
The pygmy devil ray is smaller than
the great manta. In warm oceans, it can
sometimes be seen lying on the surface,
before leaping out of the water
and speeding away.

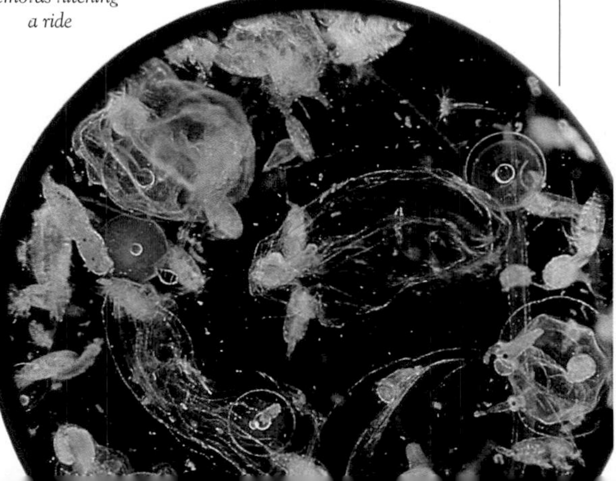

MOBULA
WITH
REMORAS

Remoras hitching
a ride

FLOATING FOOD
Plankton is largely made up
of tiny marine plants and
animals that float at the
mercy of the currents.
This nutritious "soup"
drifts on or near the
surface of the ocean.

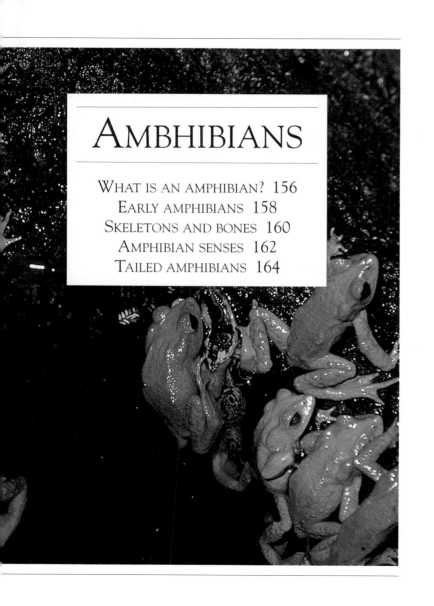

AMBHIBIANS

WHAT IS AN AMPHIBIAN?

AMPHIBIANS ARE DIVIDED into frogs and toads, salamanders, sirens, and the wormlike caecilians. They are vertebrates, and are cold-blooded, which means that their body temperature varies with their surroundings. Amphibians have no hair, feathers, or surface scales on their skin, and can breathe through their skin, as well as their lungs.

Smooth, slimy skin of frog is typical

EUROPEAN
COMMON FROG

FROG FEATURES
Frogs and toads have a distinctive body shape – a large head and wide mouth, prominent eyes, no tail, and back legs longer than the front ones.

FIRE SALAMANDER

156

NOT AMPHIBIANS
Lizards and snakes are
reptiles, although
they look similar to
some amphibians.
Reptiles can be easily
distinguished by their dry, scaly skin.
Some tadpoles may look like small fish,
but the lack of scales and body fins
shows that they are quite different.

TEGU LIZARD

Typical dry, scaly
skin of a reptile

AMPHIBIAN ODDITY
The body rings on a caecilian
make it look like a worm, but
the sharklike head and
needle-sharp teeth
show it is not!

The smooth,
damp skin of a
salamander is
typical of many
amphibians

A SPECIFIC SHAPE
Newts and salamanders have
narrower heads with smaller eyes and
mouths than frogs and toads. The body is
also longer and more lizard-shaped,
and there is always a well-developed tail.

157

EARLY AMPHIBIANS

THE FIRST AMPHIBIANS appeared some 360 million years ago. They evolved from fishes with fleshy fins that looked like legs, and had fishlike features. These amphibians may have been attracted onto land by a good food supply, and relatively few enemies to prey on them. Most amphibians had become extinct by the Triassic period, leaving only a few to evolve into modern amphibians.

SKELETON OF ICHTHYOST[EGA]

FISH-LIKE AMPHIBIAN
Ichthyostega was an early amphibian from the Devonian period in Greenland. It had some fishlike features, but also had legs suitable for walking.

RECONSTRUCTION OF ICHTHYOSTEGA

SWAMP DWELLER
This skeleton is of *Eryops*, a crocodile-like amphibian that lived in swamps in Texas about 270 million years ago. These terrestrial creatures used their strong limbs to move around.

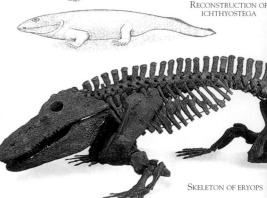

SKELETON OF ERYOPS

Wide, flat skull, like modern frogs

FOSSIL SANDWICH

This fossil is the only known specimen of *Triadobatrachus*, which was found in France, dating from the Triassic period about 210 million years ago. It has a wide, flat, froglike skull, but contains more vertebrae than modern frogs do, and also has a bony tail and short hind legs.

Short tail

KEEPING WELL

Well-preserved fossil frog skeletons like *Rana pueyoi* show how little some groups have changed in the last 25 million years.

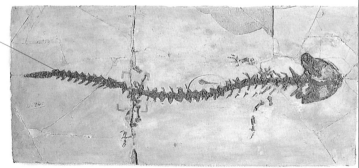

Body shape of fossil salamander is like that of modern hellbender

Short, stout legs supporting heavy body

LONG LOST RELATIVE

This fossil salamander was found in Switzerland and is about eight million years old. It is a close relative of the hellbender salamander, the only living member now found in the southeastern US.

SKELETONS AND BONES

AMPHIBIANS HAVE SIMPLE SKELETONS with fewer bone
than other modern vertebrates and many fewer than
their fishy ancestors. This shows an
evolutionary trend in amphibians –
towards reducing the
number of bones
in the skull and
vertebra (spine.)

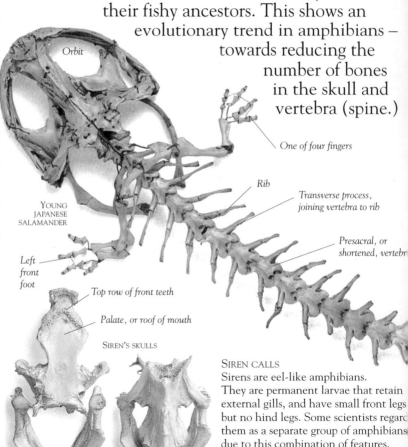

Orbit

One of four fingers

Rib

*Transverse process,
joining vertebra to rib*

YOUNG
JAPANESE
SALAMANDER

*Presacral, or
shortened, vertebr*

*Left
front
foot*

Top row of front teeth

Palate, or roof of mouth

SIREN'S SKULLS

SIREN CALLS

Sirens are eel-like amphibians.
They are permanent larvae that retain
external gills, and have small front legs
but no hind legs. Some scientists regard
them as a separate group of amphibians
due to this combination of features.

160

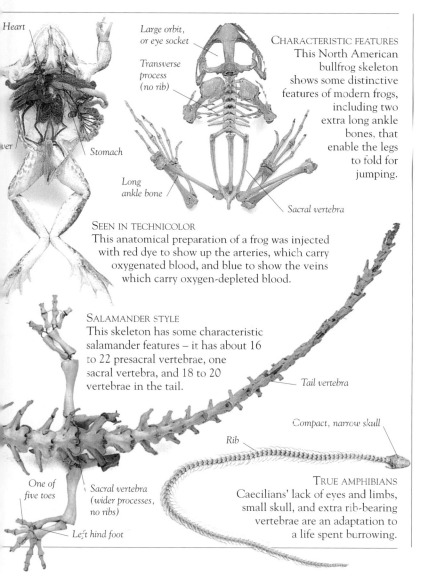

Heart

Large orbit, or eye socket

Transverse process (no rib)

ver

Stomach

CHARACTERISTIC FEATURES
This North American bullfrog skeleton shows some distinctive features of modern frogs, including two extra long ankle bones, that enable the legs to fold for jumping.

Long ankle bone

Sacral vertebra

SEEN IN TECHNICOLOR
This anatomical preparation of a frog was injected with red dye to show up the arteries, which carry oxygenated blood, and blue to show the veins which carry oxygen-depleted blood.

SALAMANDER STYLE
This skeleton has some characteristic salamander features – it has about 16 to 22 presacral vertebrae, one sacral vertebra, and 18 to 20 vertebrae in the tail.

Tail vertebra

Compact, narrow skull

Rib

One of five toes

Sacral vertebra (wider processes, no ribs)

Left hind foot

TRUE AMPHIBIANS
Caecilians' lack of eyes and limbs, small skull, and extra rib-bearing vertebrae are an adaptation to a life spent burrowing.

AMPHIBIAN SENSES

AMPHIBIANS HAVE THE FIVE basic senses of touch, taste, sight, hearing, and smell. But they can also detect ultraviolet and infrared light, and the Earth's magnetic field. Through touch, amphibians can feel temperature and pain, and respond to irritants, such as acids in the environment. As cold-blooded animal with porous skin, amphibians need to respond quickly to external changes.

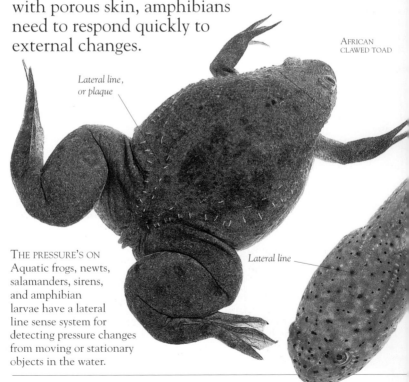

AFRICAN CLAWED TOAD

Lateral line, or plaque

Lateral line

THE PRESSURE'S ON
Aquatic frogs, newts, salamanders, sirens, and amphibian larvae have a lateral line sense system for detecting pressure changes from moving or stationary objects in the water.

PAINTED REED FROG

RED-EYED TREEFROG

ORIENTAL FIRE-BELLIED TOAD

EELING HOT?
In hot or drying conditions, amphibians lose body water by evaporation. They control their body temperature by basking in the sun if too cold, or going into the shade if too hot. By tucking in its legs, the painted reed frog reduces the amount of body area exposed to the sun.

EYE SEE
Eye color and pupil shape are variable in frogs. The red-eyed treefrog has vertical, catlike pupils for night vision or quick response to rapidly changing light conditions. The fire-bellied toad has heart-shaped pupils.

Ear of American bullfrog

AMERICAN BULLFROG TADPOLE

LISTEN UP
Hearing is one of the most important senses in frogs. The size of, and distance between, a frog's ears are related to the wavelength and frequency of the sound of the male's call.

TAILED AMPHIBIANS

SALAMANDERS, NEWTS, AND SIRENS
make up a group of about 360
species of tailed amphibians,
which, like frogs and toads, have
adopted a wide range of lifestyles.
Some live on land in damp areas,
although they may go into the
water to breed. Some lungless
salamanders even live in trees.
Others spend their whole lives
in water. Caecilians are found
only in the tropics, and
burrow in soft earth or
mud, often near water,
or else swim in rivers
and streams.

*Short hind legs – toe
more equal in siz
than in frog*

*Long
body tha
frogs an
toa*

*Tip of cre
on male's t
only grow
during mati
seaso*

Well-developed tail

TIGER SALAMANDER

SHY AWAY
"Salamander"
is a term generally
used to refer to land-based
amphibians with tails, although newts
and sirens are also members of this family. Land-dwelling
salamanders are shy and live mostly in damp, hidden areas.

...nger body than ...gs and toads

One of four toes on hind foot

A LIFE IN THE WATER
Sirens are distinct from
salamanders – they have
lungs as well as gills and are
permanent aquatic larvae
(they never leave the water.)

LESSER SIREN

Gills

*One of five
toes on
hind foot*

*...ewts are
...mi-aquatic
...lamanders,
...at return to
...e water to breed*

MALE GREAT
CRESTED NEWT

165

REPTILES

MEDUSA
Throughout history, reptiles have been feared. Medusa, a monster from Greek mythology, had snakes for hair.

WHAT IS A REPTILE?

LIKE FISH, amphibians, birds, and mammals, reptiles are vertebrates (have backbones). But what makes them different from fish and amphibians is that they are basically land animals – they do not have to live in or keep returning to water. And unlike birds and mammals, they are cold-blooded. That is, their bodies remain at the same temperature as their surroundings.

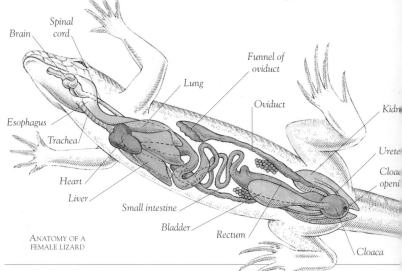

Brain

Spinal cord

Funnel of oviduct

Lung

Oviduct

Kidn

Esophagus

Trachea

Ovidct

Urete

Heart

Cloac openi

Liver

Small intestine

Bladder

Rectum

Cloaca

ANATOMY OF A FEMALE LIZARD

SEEN FROM THE OUTSIDE

Lizards are typical reptiles. The crested water dragon, shown below, is found in Asia. It has scaly skin that is waterproof – thus retaining moisture inside the reptile's body.

Long tail for balance

Long toes for support

Scaly skin

CRESTED WATER DRAGON

Eye

GLASSY STARE

Snakes and some lizards do not have movable eyelids. Instead the eye is covered with a transparent membrane, called the spectacle, that protects the eye from damage.

EGG LAYERS

Some reptiles produce active young, but most species lay eggs. Here a young rat-snake is hatching.

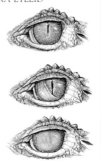

RATSNAKE

INSIDE A REPTILE

A reptile has a small brain and a heart with three chambers (a human heart has four). The cloaca, a chamber at the rear of the gut, is used by the bladder when excreting and by the reproductive system during sexual reproduction.

AN EXTRA EYELID

Crocodiles have three eyelids. There are two above and below the eye. An extra see-through lid covers the eye from the inner corner to protect the surface of the eye under water.

169

REPTILES

REPTILE GROUPS

REPTILES FIRST APPEARED about 340 million years ago, during the Carboniferous period (see diagram). Their ancestors were amphibians, but the first reptiles could breed without having to return to water. Today, four main groups remain: turtles and tortoises (chelonians) snakes and lizards, crocodilians, and the tuatara.

GIANT SEA SNAKE

PALAEOPHIS
Snakes first appeared in the late Jurassic period. *Palaeophis* was an ancient sea snake.

MODERN PYTHON
These vertebrae are from a python that is four times smaller than *Palaeophis*.

Scaly skin

Mouth

FIRST REPTILE
Westlothiana, the earliest known reptile, existed 338 million years ago. Its waterproof, scaly skin enabled it to live all its life on land.

MODEL OF WESTLOTHIANA

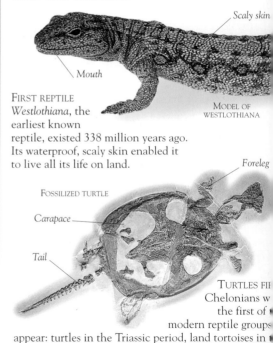

FOSSILIZED TURTLE

Carapace

Foreleg

Tail

TURTLES FIR
Chelonians w
the first of
modern reptile groups
appear: turtles in the Triassic period, land tortoises in
Cenozoic period. This fossil is about 200 million years o

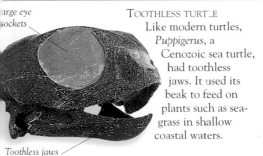

large eye sockets

TOOTHLESS TURTLE
Like modern turtles, *Puppigerus*, a Cenozoic sea turtle, had toothless jaws. It used its beak to feed on plants such as sea-grass in shallow coastal waters.

Toothless jaws

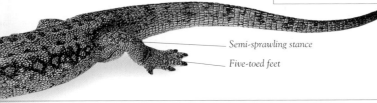

Semi-sprawling stance

Five-toed feet

REPTILE GROUP FACTS

• Rhynchocephalians were common in the Triassic period. The only one left is the tuatara.

• Mammal-like reptiles appeared in the Permian period giving rise to the first mammals in the Triassic period.

REPTILE EVOLUTION
This diagram shows the evolution of reptiles. The column on the left shows when they existed and how many millions of years ago that was.

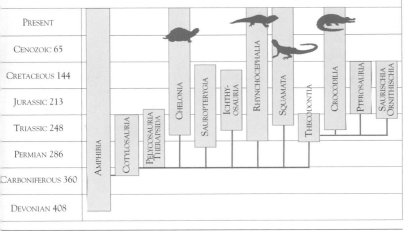

	AMPHIBIA	COTYLOSAURIA	PELYCOSAURIA THERAPSIDA	CHELONIA	SAUROPTERYGIA	ICHTHY-OSAURIA	RHYNCHOCEPHALIA	SQUAMATA	THECODONTIA	CROCODILIA	PTEROSAURIA	SAURISCHIA ORNITHISCHIA
PRESENT												
CENOZOIC 65												
CRETACEOUS 144												
JURASSIC 213												
TRIASSIC 248												
PERMIAN 286												
CARBONIFEROUS 360												
DEVONIAN 408												

PREHISTORIC REPTILES

THE FIRST REPTILES encountered no competition for the wide range of land habitats available. Over millions of years they adapted to every possible type of lifestyle and diet. Some of them even learned to fly. Others returned to living in the sea.

The "sail" was probably used to help control body temperature

DIMETRODON

SAIL BACK
Dimetrodon was mammal-like reptile of the Permian period. Its relatives were the ancestors of modern mammals.

Fangs and sharp cheek-teeth for eating flesh

CYNOGNATHUS

Sharp claws

REPTILE DOG
Cynognathus lived in the early Triassic period. It was about 7 ft (2 m) long and looked like a large dog. Scientists have discovered that it probably had hair

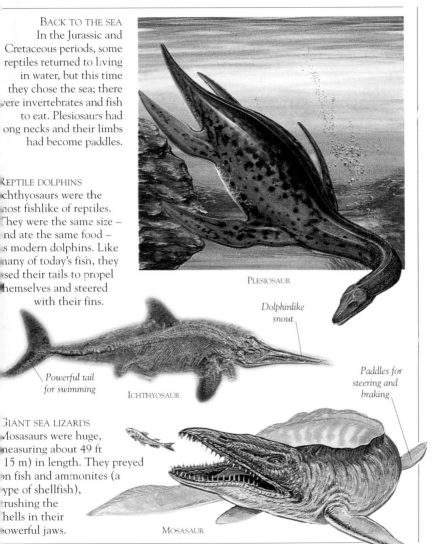

BACK TO THE SEA
In the Jurassic and Cretaceous periods, some reptiles returned to living in water, but this time they chose the sea; there were invertebrates and fish to eat. Plesiosaurs had long necks and their limbs had become paddles.

REPTILE DOLPHINS
Ichthyosaurs were the most fishlike of reptiles. They were the same size – and ate the same food – as modern dolphins. Like many of today's fish, they used their tails to propel themselves and steered with their fins.

PLESIOSAUR

Dolphinlike snout

Powerful tail for swimming

ICHTHYOSAUR

Paddles for steering and braking

GIANT SEA LIZARDS
Mosasaurs were huge, measuring about 49 ft (15 m) in length. They preyed on fish and ammonites (a type of shellfish), crushing the shells in their powerful jaws.

MOSASAUR

173

More prehistoric reptiles

During the Jurassic and Cretaceous periods, reptiles ruled the land. Among these reptiles were the dinosaurs ("terrible lizards"). Some dinosaurs were gentle herbivores; others were ferocious carnivores. At the same time, a number of reptiles adapted to life in the air, 100 million years before flying birds appeared.

RHAMPHORHYNCIDS
The first flying reptiles, or pterosaurs, appeared during the Triassic period. *Rhamphorhynchus* and its relatives were Jurassic pterosaurs. They had long tails, curved snouts, and jaws with teeth. *Rhamphorynchus* may have used its teeth for spearing fish.

Claws on wings

Vane on tail for steering

Hairy body

RHAMPHORHYNCHUS

Throat pouch – possibly for holding fish

Tail may have aided balance while eating

GLIDERS ANCIENT AND MODERN
Pterosaurs probably could not fly like birds. Instead, they launched themselves from cliffs and glided through the air, using updrafts – just like modern hang-gliders. The largest pterosaurs, such as *Pteranodon*, had wingspans of 26 ft (8 m) or more.

PTERANODON AND HANG-GLIDER

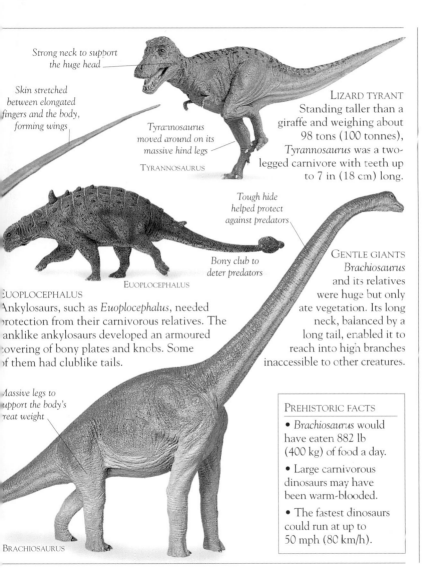

Strong neck to support the huge head

Skin stretched between elongated fingers and the body, forming wings

Tyrannosaurus moved around on its massive hind legs

TYRANNOSAURUS

LIZARD TYRANT
Standing taller than a giraffe and weighing about 98 tons (100 tonnes), *Tyrannosaurus* was a two-legged carnivore with teeth up to 7 in (18 cm) long.

Tough hide helped protect against predators

Bony club to deter predators

EUOPLOCEPHALUS

EUOPLOCEPHALUS
Ankylosaurs, such as *Euoplocephalus*, needed protection from their carnivorous relatives. The tanklike ankylosaurs developed an armoured covering of bony plates and knobs. Some of them had clublike tails.

Massive legs to support the body's great weight

GENTLE GIANTS
Brachiosaurus and its relatives were huge but only ate vegetation. Its long neck, balanced by a long tail, enabled it to reach into high branches inaccessible to other creatures.

PREHISTORIC FACTS

• *Brachiosaurus* would have eaten 882 lb (400 kg) of food a day.

• Large carnivorous dinosaurs may have been warm-blooded.

• The fastest dinosaurs could run at up to 50 mph (80 km/h).

BRACHIOSAURUS

175

SCALY SKIN

REPTILES TYPICALLY have skins covered in overlapping, horny scales. They act as a waterproof covering and help retain precious body moisture. In some reptiles, the scales form an armored protection. As a reptile grows, its old skin becomes too small and starts to wear out. A new skin replaces it.

ARMORED ALLIGATOR
Like all crocodilians, this Chinese alligator is covered in large, tough, partly ossified (turned into bone) scales. As it grows, the scales flake off and are replaced by new ones.

SECTION THROUGH SKIN

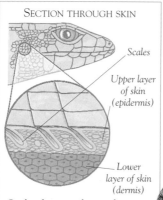

Scales

Upper layer of skin (epidermis)

Lower layer of skin (dermis)

Scales form in the epidermis. They are made mostly of keratin – the same substance found in hair and nails.

Each time a new piece is added, the oldest one falls off the end

WARNING RATTLE
A rattlesnake's rattle is made up of hollow pieces of keratin formed at the end of the tail. A new segment is added when the snake sheds its skin.

The rattle warns off attackers

Old skin
peeling off

SHEDDING
SNAKESKIN
A snake sheds its skin in one
piece, beginning at the head. A new
skin, complete with scales, has already
formed underneath, and when the
process is finished an entire
transparent skin is left.

New skin

A SHED SNAKESKIN

A LEOPARD CHANGING ITS SPOTS
Lizards, like this leopard
gecko, change their skins
regularly – about once a
month. The old skin
comes off in large flakes
(some lizards scrape it
off). A new layer of
skin is revealed,
complete with the gecko's
black spots, underneath.

Old skin

LEOPARD GECKO

SLOW WORM

New skin

SLOW WORM SHEDDING
A slow worm looks like a snake
but is, in fact, a legless lizard found
in Europe. Like other lizards, it
loses its skin in large flakes.

177

COLD-BLOODED CREATURES

REPTILES ARE DESCRIBED as cold-blooded. This does not mean that their blood is always cold. But, unlike birds and mammals, they do not make their own heat by using the chemical reactions in their bodies. Instead, a reptile relies on heat from the outside, and its body temperature goes up or down with the surrounding temperature.

CHILLING OUT
To cool, a reptile finds shade, or angles its body to expose the smallest possible area to the sun.

Reptiles warm up by basking in the sun

AGAMA LIZARD

COLD-BLOODED FACTS

• Scientists call "cold-blooded" animals poikilotherms or ectotherms.

• For digestion to take place, a high body temperature is needed. A snake that has just eaten may die if it is not warm enough.

WARMING UP
When a reptile starts to get too cold, it warms itself by basking in the sun, presenting as much of its body as possible to the sun's rays. By moving regularly between sun and shade, a reptile is able to maintain an almost constant body temperature.

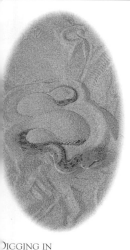

REPTILE CIRCULATION

LIZARD HEART
Most reptiles have three-chambered hearts. When blood-pressure increases, as when turtles dive, this arrangement allows oxygen-poor blood to mix with oxygen-rich blood from the lungs.

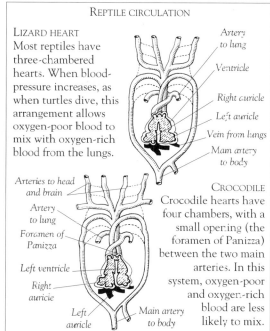

Artery to lung
Ventricle
Right auricle
Left auricle
Vein from lungs
Main artery to body

Arteries to head and brain
Artery to lung
Foramen of Panizza
Left ventricle
Right auricle
Left auricle
Main artery to body

CROCODILE
Crocodile hearts have four chambers, with a small opening (the foramen of Panizza) between the two main arteries. In this system, oxygen-poor and oxygen-rich blood are less likely to mix.

DIGGING IN
Shade is difficult to find in the desert. A sand viper solves this problem by wriggling its body down into the sand. If it did not do this it would literally fry in the heat.

Water evaporates from mouth

Like all reptiles, the crocodile cannot sweat to lose heat

OPEN-MOUTHED COOLING
One way of cooling is to let water evaporate from the body. A crocodile lies with its mouth open to let water evaporate from its mouth. American crocodiles lie in burrows when they get too hot. Other species cool down in water.

SENSES

MOST REPTILES have eyes
and ears. Snakes and
lizards also "taste"
their surroundings
using their tongues.
The tuatara, and
many lizards, also have a
light-sensitive organ on
their heads, which may be
important to temperature
regulation and to reproduction.

*Scaly skin contain:
sensors that detec
touch, pain, heat
and cold*

*Notched iris
with vertical slit*

*Heat-sensitive
pit*

HEAT SENSITIV
A pit viper has
heat-sensitive pit o
either side of its head
Using these it ca
follow the he
trail of a warm
blooded animal b
day or night. A p
viper can detec
temperature changes
0.002°C (0.002°F

SLIT EYES
A gecko is active mostly
at night and its eyes
are very sensitive. In
daylight, the iris of
each eye closes to a slit,
stopping too much light
from reaching the retina.
Notches in the iris allow
the animal to see.

TEGU SENSES

A tegu lizard's well-developed eyes are designed for use in daylight and are protected by movable eyelids. Its eardrums are visible as small patches on the sides of its head behind the jaws. Its flicking, forked tongue is used, in conjunction with its Jacobson's organ, to "taste" the air.

Eye with movable eyelid

Eardrum picks up sounds

Jacobson's organ

Forked tongue collects chemicals from the air

SWIVELING EYES

To see without being seen, a chameleon remains perfectly still, while swiveling its eyes to see in almost any direction. The eyes swivel independently of each other.

TASTING THE AIR

Jacobson's organ is a pit in the roof of the mouth of snakes and lizards. The tongue is flicked out to pick up chemicals in the air and is then inserted into the pit, where sense cells detect the nature of the chemicals.

SENSES FACTS

• A chameleon can use one eye to hunt and the other to watch out for predators.

• Most snakes "hear" by feeling vibrations through the ground; however, most lizards hear airborne sounds.

181

MOVEMENT

THE LEGS OF A typical reptile, such as a lizard, protrude sideways from its body. Heavier reptiles may require considerable physical effort to lift their bodies off the ground. Larger, land-based reptiles tend to move slowly, but smaller, lighter ones can be fast-moving and agile. Some reptiles, notably snakes, have dispensed with legs altogether.

GECKO

STICKY FEET
Geckos are small and light, and able to move rapidly. Pads on their feet have millions of tiny hooks that enable them to cling to smooth surfaces, even glass.

Fringelike scales on feet

SANDFISH

SWIMMING IN SAN[D]
A sandfish (a type of skink[) has fringelike scales on its fee[t to help it move on sand. I[t can also dive into the sand[, wriggling like a snak[e.

SIDEWINDING
Some desert snakes move over the sand by looping their bodies sideways and moving in a series of sidewa[ys steps, known as sidewindin[g.

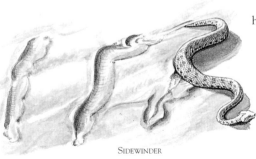

SIDEWINDER

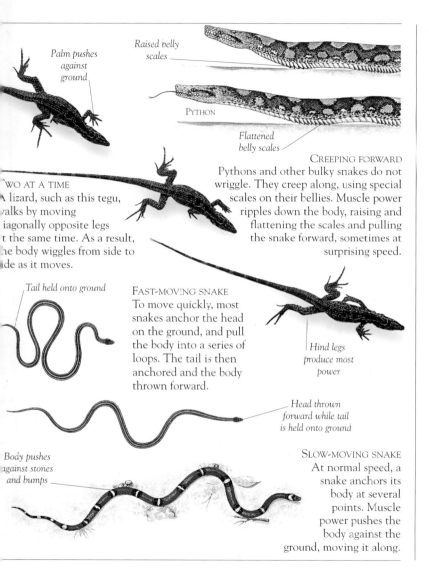

Palm pushes
against
ground

Raised belly
scales

PYTHON

Flattened
belly scales

CREEPING FORWARD
Pythons and other bulky snakes do not
wriggle. They creep along, using special
scales on their bellies. Muscle power
ripples down the body, raising and
flattening the scales and pulling
the snake forward, sometimes at
surprising speed.

TWO AT A TIME
A lizard, such as this tegu,
walks by moving
diagonally opposite legs
at the same time. As a result,
the body wiggles from side to
side as it moves.

Tail held onto ground

FAST-MOVING SNAKE
To move quickly, most
snakes anchor the head
on the ground, and pull
the body into a series of
loops. The tail is then
anchored and the body
thrown forward.

Hind legs
produce most
power

Head thrown
forward while tail
is held onto ground

Body pushes
against stones
and bumps

SLOW-MOVING SNAKE
At normal speed, a
snake anchors its
body at several
points. Muscle
power pushes the
body against the
ground, moving it along.

183

Flying reptiles

Reptiles have never learned to fly like bats or birds. The first "flying" reptiles, the pterosaurs of the Triassic period, were gliding animals rather than fliers, and the same is true of the modern species that have taken to the air. Nevertheless, the ability to glide can be very useful in escaping quickly from predator or simply moving swiftly from one tree branch to the next in the search for food.

CROSS SECTION
OF FLYING SNAKE

*Normal shape
of body*

*Body flattened
for gliding*

A flying snake turns itself into a wing by pushing out its ribs and holding in its belly, so that the body becomes flattened.

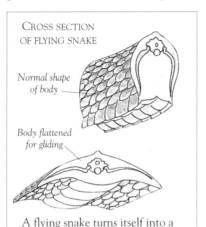

FLYING DRAGON
The "wings" of the flying dragon of Southeast Asia are flaps of skin supported by elongated ribs. They normally lie folded against the body, but can be spread out wide for gliding flights.

*Six or seven pairs of
ribs support skin flaps*

*Limbs spread
out to help
steering*

Rough scales on
the snake's belly
help it climb trees

Flying snakes fly to
escape predators,
such as hawks

FLYING SNAKE
A flying snake uses its whole body
as a "wing." It takes off from high in
the treetops by uncoiling quickly
and glides in a series of long curves.
It steers by twisting its body from
side to side. Flying snakes are found
in Southeast Asia.

Webbed feet
help in
flying

GECKO AND FOOT
Flying geckos
live in Asian
rain forests. They glide by unfurling
flaps of skin along the sides of the
body, using the flattened tail to help
steer. When at rest on tree
bark, a flying gecko is
very hard to see.

FLYING FACTS

• There are five species
of Asian snake that are
able to glide.

• There are
unsubstantiated claims
that large flying reptiles
resembling pterosaurs
still exist in the Jiundu
swamp of Zambia.

185

COURTSHIP

LIKE ALL ANIMALS, reptiles need to attract members of the opposite sex in order to reproduce. They do this in various ways: by signals, colorful displays, or eye-catching ornaments, such as frills or crests.

Male's head

SNAKES MATING

Tails intertwined

Mating may take several hours

SNAKE CHARMERS
Once a male snake has attracted a female he stimulates her into mating by rubbing his chin along her back. She then allows him to intertwine her body with his. Their cloacal openings meet, allowing sperm to pass from male to female.

A CLASH OF SHELLS
Tortoise mating, especially in large species such as these Galápagos tortoises, is a laborious affair. The males roar during mating.

All anoles have very long tails

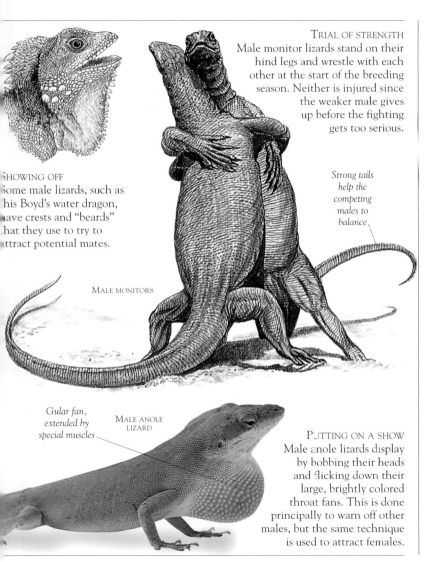

TRIAL OF STRENGTH
Male monitor lizards stand on their hind legs and wrestle with each other at the start of the breeding season. Neither is injured since the weaker male gives up before the fighting gets too serious.

Strong tails help the competing males to balance

SHOWING OFF
Some male lizards, such as this Boyd's water dragon, have crests and "beards" that they use to try to attract potential mates.

MALE MONITORS

Gular fan, extended by special muscles

MALE ANOLE LIZARD

PUTTING ON A SHOW
Male anole lizards display by bobbing their heads and flicking down their large, brightly colored throat fans. This is done principally to warn off other males, but the same technique is used to attract females.

187

NESTS AND EGGS

ANIMALS THAT TAKE CARE of their young usually have fewer offspring than those that leave their young to fend for themselves. Some reptiles, such as the marine turtles, lay thousands of eggs, but because they abandon them, only a few hatchlings reach maturity. A crocodile, on the other hand, guards not only her eggs but also her young for some time after they hatch. So a higher percentage of eggs and young survive.

ALLIGATOR NEST

ROTTEN NEST
A female American alligator builds a mound of mud and decaying vegetation, in which she lays 15 to 80 eggs. The heat produced by the rotting material incubates the eggs for two to three months.

The mother uncovers the eggs when they hatch

ON GUARD
The estuarine, or saltwater, crocodile of Southeast Asia and northern Australia builds a mound of leaves for her eggs. She builds her nest near water and shade so she can keep cool as she guards her offspring against predators, including lizards, herons, mongooses, turtles, and other crocodiles.

The female covers the nest with her body

SAFE IN MOTHER'S MOUTH
After baby Nile
crocodiles have
hatched, their mother
gathers as many as she
can in her mouth and
carries them to the
safety of a pool,
making several trips
to complete the task.
She remains to
defend her offspring.

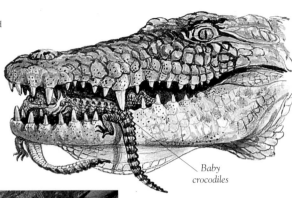

Baby
crocodiles

GREEN TURTLE LAYING EGGS

NO SAFETY IN NUMBERS
A marine turtle lays up to 200
eggs, burying them in a nest in
the sand. If the nest remains
undiscovered, the eggs hatch
6 to 10 weeks later, but the
hatchlings fall prey to crabs,
seabirds, and other predators
on the way to the sea.

LIVE BIRTH
A rattlesnake keeps her
eggs inside her body
until they hatch, which
greatly improves their
chances of survival.
Approximately 10 to 20
young are born, measuring
about 13½ in (35 cm) in
length. The mother abandons
them soon after birth.

RATTLESNAKE AND YOUNG

189

More nests and eggs

Reptile eggs have shells that retain moisture so they can be laid on land. Most reptile eggs have soft, leathery shells, but some, such as a crocodile's, have hard shells. In most cases the eggs hatch outside the mother's body, although a few reptiles produce live young. In some cases the eggs hatch just before laying; in others, the embryos obtain nourishment from their mother through a placenta.

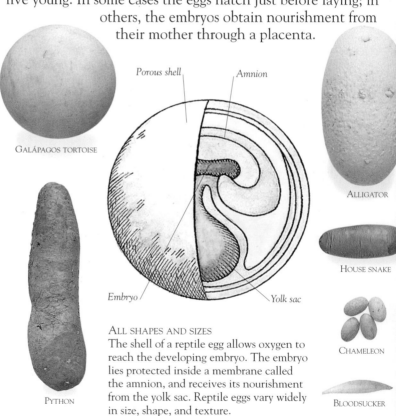

GALÁPAGOS TORTOISE

Porous shell

Amnion

Embryo

Yolk sac

PYTHON

ALLIGATOR

HOUSE SNAKE

CHAMELEON

BLOODSUCKER

ALL SHAPES AND SIZES

The shell of a reptile egg allows oxygen to reach the developing embryo. The embryo lies protected inside a membrane called the amnion, and receives its nourishment from the yolk sac. Reptile eggs vary widely in size, shape, and texture.

ᴳG TOOTH

s it grows inside the egg, a young lizard
‹ snake develops a sharp "egg tooth" on
ᴇ tip of its upper jaw. When the time
r hatching arrives, the animal escapes
ᴏm the shell by using the egg tooth to
ᴜt its way out.

Egg tooth

HOW A SNAKE HATCHES

Just before a snake hatches, the yolk sac is drawn into the snake's body and the
remaining yolk is absorbed into its intestine. Then, using its egg tooth, the snake
cuts a slit large enough to push its head through. It may remain like this for up to
two days before finally emerging from the egg. When it is fully hatched, the
snake may be up to seven times longer
than the egg from which it came.

*The young snake checks
its surroundings.*

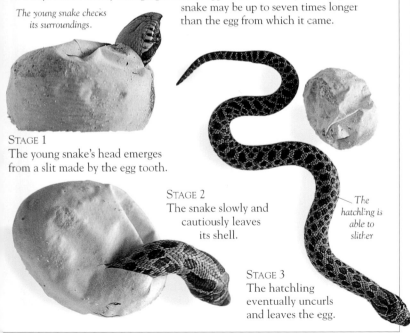

STAGE 1
The young snake's head emerges
from a slit made by the egg tooth.

STAGE 2
The snake slowly and
cautiously leaves
its shell.

*The
hatchling is
able to
slither*

STAGE 3
The hatchling
eventually uncurls
and leaves the egg.

191

DEADLY ENEMIES

MOST REPTILES are predators, but they are also preyed upon by other animals. Sometimes reptiles eat other reptiles. Eggs and young are especially vulnerable and in many cases adults, too, have their enemies. Even the largest and most dangerous reptiles may fall victim to human hunters.

A secretary bird either bites or tramples its reptile prey

SECRETARY BIRD
This African bird hunts tortoises, snakes, and lizards, flushing them from grass by stamping its feet. It uses its wings as a shield against venomous snakes.

The mongoose has lightning reactions

ENEMY FACTS

• When they are away from water, Nile crocodiles are vulnerable to attack by lions.

• The giant tortoises of Mauritius and Reunion Island were wiped out by hunters in the late 1700s.

Faced with a mongoose, a cobra looks fierce but its chances are slim

LEGENDARY ENEMIES
The mongoose is the only mammal that includes poisonous snakes in its diet. Although smaller than some of its prey, it is very courageous and is immune to snake venom. When tackling a snake, such as a spitting cobra, it bites the head of its prey with lightning speed.

SNAKE EATS SNAKE

Kingsnakes, some of which are also known as milk snakes, feed on small mammals, lizards, frogs, and other snakes. Kingsnakes, which squeeze their prey, are not afraid to tackle venomous snakes, such as copperheads.

Kingsnake

A kingsnake swallows a copperhead

Copperhead

A gull has easy pickings when a turtle nest hatches

HATCHLINGS AND GULL

GULL GAUNTLET

Young turtles hatch out from eggs buried high on the beach. They immediately head for the sea but, in doing so, run the gauntlet of numerous predators. Seabirds, such as gulls, gather in large numbers to feast on the hatchlings, and many of them never reach the safety of the water.

HUMAN HUNTERS

Humans hunt reptiles for various reasons – for food, for their skins, or simply because they are poisonous. Humans have also reduced the natural habitat of many species. A combination of these factors has brought some species to extinction and made others very rare.

The cobra was pulled out of a hole

SOUTH INDIAN VILLAGERS DISPLAY A LIVE COBRA

193

BATTLE FOR SURVIVAL

SURVIVAL IN THE ANIMAL WORLD means not only being able to find something to eat but also avoiding being eaten by other animals. Large reptiles deter predators by their sheer size, but smaller species have to use a range of strategies, including camouflage, warning colours, mimicry, and bluff.

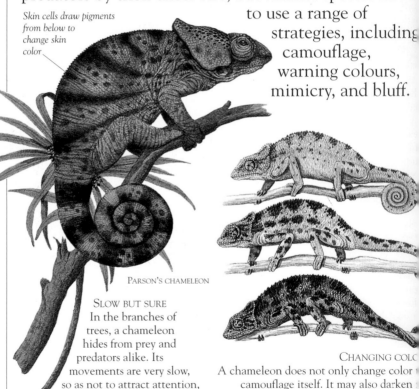

Skin cells draw pigments from below to change skin color

PARSON'S CHAMELEON

SLOW BUT SURE
In the branches of trees, a chameleon hides from prey and predators alike. Its movements are very slow, so as not to attract attention, and it adjusts its coloring to blend in with its surroundings.

CHANGING COLO
A chameleon does not only change color
camouflage itself. It may also darken
heat or sunlight, or to indicate a change
mood – an angry chameleon turns blac

194

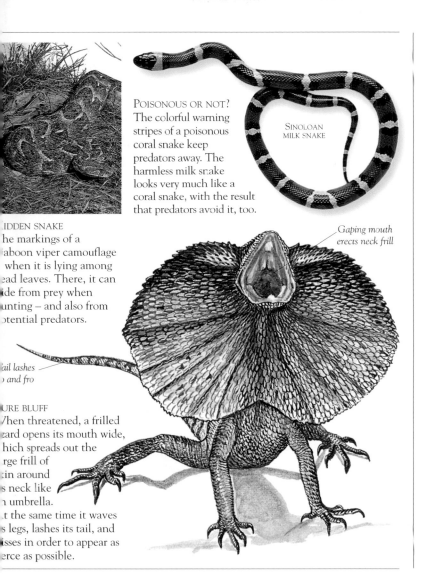

POISONOUS OR NOT?
The colorful warning
stripes of a poisonous
coral snake keep
predators away. The
harmless milk snake
looks very much like a
coral snake, with the result
that predators avoid it, too.

SINOLOAN
MILK SNAKE

HIDDEN SNAKE
The markings of a
gaboon viper camouflage
it when it is lying among
dead leaves. There, it can
hide from prey when
hunting – and also from
potential predators.

Gaping mouth
erects neck frill

Tail lashes
to and fro

PURE BLUFF
When threatened, a frilled
lizard opens its mouth wide,
which spreads out the
large frill of
skin around
its neck like
an umbrella.
At the same time it waves
its legs, lashes its tail, and
hisses in order to appear as
fierce as possible.

Defense strategies

Reptiles have evolved many ways to avoid being eaten. Small lizards often use speed to escape, and many species retreat into underground burrows or rock crevices. Some use water as a means of escape. When cornered, many lizards, particularly large ones like monitors, will turn to face their attackers. Two lizards, the Gila monster and the beaded lizard, are venomous.

The snake lies absolutely stil[l]

The stinkpot is very aggressive

PLAYING DEA[D]

When it cannot escape, a grass snake tur[ns] over, curls up, then lies still. It is playin[g] dead, hoping its attacker will go awa[y]

STINKING STINKPOT
The stinkpot turtle is the reptile equivalent of the skunk. It produces such an unpleasant smell that predators avoid it.

As it loses speed, [the] basilisk drops into [the] water and must s[wim]

SURVIVAL FACTS

• Horned lizards squirt blood at their attackers from their eyes.

• Some skinks have a bright blue tail that attracts predators away from vital body parts.

BASILISK

LOSING A TAIL TO SAVE A LIFE
In many cases a lizard can shed
its tail if it is grabbed by an
attacker. The tail is equipped with
special breaking points in the vertebrae,
and the shed tail usually twitches for a
while after it breaks off, distracting the
attacker long enough for the lizard to
make good its escape. A new tail grows.

Tail recently shed

New tail after eight months

Growing the new tail uses up energy

TREE SKINK

Tail can only break in the old part, where there are still breakable vertebrae

Tail helps lizard balance as it runs

RUNNING ON WATER
Basilisks have long hind legs for running,
and their feet have broad soles with a
fringe of scales around the toes.
This enables them to run
across water in
order to escape
from potential predators.

197

LIVING IN WATER

ALTHOUGH REPTILES EVOLVED as land animals, many species have become adapted to living in water, where food is often plentiful. For these species, swimming is more important than walking and many are equipped with paddles instead of feet. But they are still air-breathing animals and so have special adaptations enabling them to cope with a watery environment.

GOGGLE EYES
Crocodilians, like this caiman, lie submerged in the water, waiting for prey. The eyes and nostrils are placed high on the head so that only these parts show above the water.

The spectacled caiman has a bony ridge between its eyes, resembling the frame of a pair of glasses

SNORKELING TURTLE

The matamata turtle of Brazil waits for its prey on the river bed. It pokes its nostrils out of the water to breathe, without moving – thus it avoids disturbing the fish.

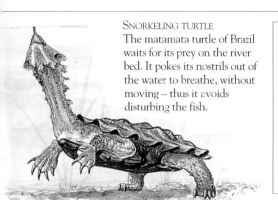

WATER FACTS

- Sea turtles excrete salt absorbed in sea water from their eyes, which is why they seem to cry.

- To prevent water from getting into its lung, a sea snake closes off its nostrils with a spongelike tissue.

Sea snakes are very poisonous

Powerful tail moves the snake forward

PADDLE TAIL

A sea snake is virtually helpless on land but is an excellent swimmer. Its tail is flattened vertically to form a powerful, oarlike paddle.

The four paddles propel the turtle

WEB-FOOTED SLIDER

Freshwater chelonians, such as terrapins, have webbed feet for swimming. The red-eared slider has a habit of sliding back into the water if disturbed.

PADDLE FEET
A marine turtle can tolerate high levels of carbon dioxide in its blood and so can swim under water for long periods.

REPTILES

CHELONIAN ANATOMY

CHELONIANS are reptiles whose bodies are protected by shells. The shells are made up of the plastron which protects the belly, and the carapace, which covers the back. There are between 250 and 300 species of chelonian. Some live in salt water, others in fresh water, and yet others on land. Water dwellers are usually called turtles or terrapins, while land dwellers are known as tortoises.

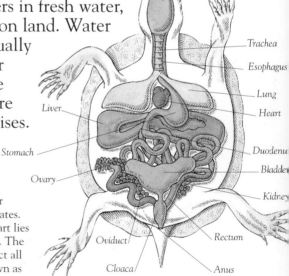

Carapace

FROM THE OUTSIDE
The red-eared terrapin is a typical chelonian. It has a carapace made up of several layers. The outer layer consists of horny shields, known as scutes.

INTERNAL ANATOMY OF A FEMALE TORTOIS

Mouth cavity

Trachea

Esophagus

Lung

Heart

Liver

Stomach

Duodenu

Ovary

Bladder

Kidney

Oviduct

Rectum

Cloaca

Anus

INSIDE A CHELONIAN
The internal anatomy of a chelonian is similar to that of other vertebrates. A three-chambered heart lies between a pair of lungs. The gut, bladder, and oviduct all lead to a chamber known as the cloaca (meaning "sewer").

FUSED VERTEBRAE

The carapace is made up of about 50 bony plates formed in the skin. The shell has an outer layer of horny shields and an inner one of bone. The vertebrae, with the ribs and the two limb girdles, are fused to the carapace. This has resulted in the limb girdles being inside the ribs.

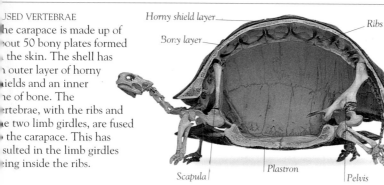

Horny shield layer

Bony layer

Ribs

Scapula

Plastron

Pelvis

SKELETON OF A TURTLE

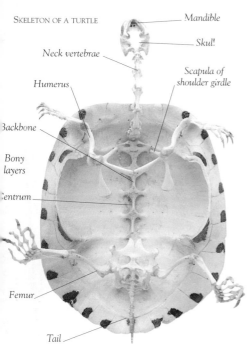

Mandible

Skull

Neck vertebrae

Scapula of shoulder girdle

Humerus

Backbone

Bony layers

Centrum

Femur

Tail

FLEXIBLE NECK

Inside the horny outer layer, the carapace is made of several layers of bone. The eight neck vertebrae are very flexible. The upper limb bones are short, with enlarged ends to take the weight of the animal's body and shell.

CHELONIAN FACTS

- Some female turtles produce eggs four years after mating.

- All chelonians lay eggs on land, even the marine turtles.

- Some turtles can live for more than a year without food.

MARINE TURTLES

TURTLES INVADED the world's seas and oceans during the Triassic period, some 200 million years ago. Today there are seven species, six of which are grouped together in the one family, the Chelonidae. The leatherback turtle is classified by itself in another family, called the Dermochelidae.

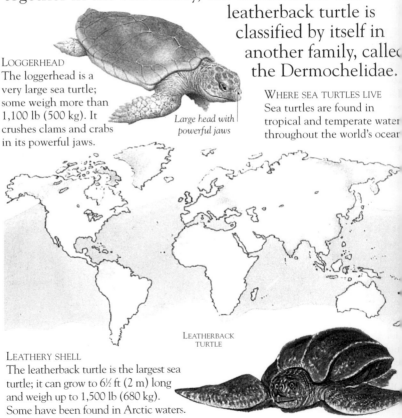

LOGGERHEAD
The loggerhead is a very large sea turtle; some weigh more than 1,100 lb (500 kg). It crushes clams and crabs in its powerful jaws.

Large head with powerful jaws

WHERE SEA TURTLES LIVE
Sea turtles are found in tropical and temperate waters throughout the world's ocean

LEATHERBACK
TURTLE

LEATHERY SHELL
The leatherback turtle is the largest sea turtle; it can grow to 6½ ft (2 m) long and weigh up to 1,500 lb (680 kg). Some have been found in Arctic waters.

IMMUNE TO POISON
Hawksbill turtles are found near coral reefs. They feed on invertebrates, such as sponges, many of which contain poisons. These do not affect the turtles but may kill animals that eat them.

NESTING TOGETHER
Ridley turtles come ashore in large numbers to nest together on certain beaches. Each female digs a hole in which she lays about 100 eggs. Olive ridleys live in the Atlantic, Indian, and parts of the Pacific Oceans.

CHELONIAN FEET

The limbs of marine turtles are very different from those of land and freshwater chelonians. Land tortoises have large, clawed feet. Freshwater turtles have webbing between the toes. Marine turtles have no claws; instead, their limbs have evolved into flippers.

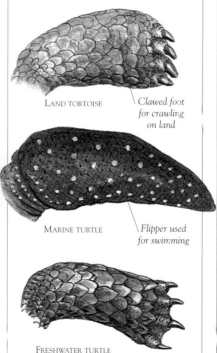

LAND TORTOISE
Clawed foot for crawling on land

MARINE TURTLE
Flipper used for swimming

FRESHWATER TURTLE

203

Turtles in danger

Sea turtles are among the world's most vulnerable animals. They are relatively slow moving and easy to catch, and their nest sites are mostly well known – for example, Kemp's ridley turtles only nest on one beach in Mexico. Turtle products are much in demand, and large numbers of turtles are killed. In addition, their overall rate of reproduction is slow; although a green turtle may lay 1,000 eggs in one season, only a few survive into adulthood.

TURTLE EXPLOITATION

Turtles are large, meaty animals and in many places are hunted for food; green turtles are especially prized, particularly for turtle soup. When polished, the shell of a green turtle is a popular tourist souvenir. Pieces of turtle shell are also used in furniture-making.

GREEN TURTLE EGGS

END OF THE LINE
Green turtle eggs are a popular food. The nests are easy to find since the females leave an obvious trail to the nest.

TURTLES FOR SALE
Rows of stuffed turtles provide an income for a local trader. Trade in wild turtles is banned under the provisions of international agreements on trade in endangered animal products. Some trade in specially bred animals is allowed.

STUFFED TURTLES

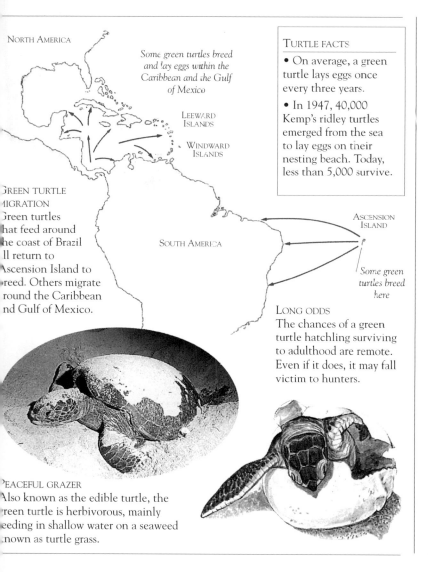

NORTH AMERICA

Some green turtles breed and lay eggs within the Caribbean and the Gulf of Mexico

LEEWARD ISLANDS

WINDWARD ISLANDS

TURTLE FACTS

• On average, a green turtle lays eggs once every three years.

• In 1947, 40,000 Kemp's ridley turtles emerged from the sea to lay eggs on their nesting beach. Today, less than 5,000 survive.

GREEN TURTLE MIGRATION
Green turtles that feed around the coast of Brazil will return to Ascension Island to breed. Others migrate round the Caribbean and Gulf of Mexico.

SOUTH AMERICA

ASCENSION ISLAND

Some green turtles breed here

LONG ODDS
The chances of a green turtle hatchling surviving to adulthood are remote. Even if it does, it may fall victim to hunters.

PEACEFUL GRAZER
Also known as the edible turtle, the green turtle is herbivorous, mainly feeding in shallow water on a seaweed known as turtle grass.

TURTLES AND TORTOISES

THE ORIGINS of the first chelonians are obscure because there is very little fossil evidence. However, it seems likely that their ancestors belonged to an early group of reptiles known as diadectomorphs that lived in swamplands. As some of them moved farther onto the land, they acquired protective shells. Some ancestors of modern chelonians remained on land; others returned to the water.

Soft shell

Snorkel-like nose for breathing when underwater

SOFT KILLER
The shell of a soft-shelled turtle is covered in leathery skin instead of horny plates. Soft-shelled turtles are found in southern Asia, Africa, and North America. They live in rivers where they feed on water creatures, striking with lightning speed.

Fish being sucked in

FISH SUCKER
Disguised as a rock, the matamata turtle of South America lurks on the river bed patiently waiting for a fish to swim close by. When its prey approaches, it expands its throat and sucks the fish into its gaping mouth.

TERRAPIN HEAPS
The red-eared slider lives in ponds
and rivers in the US and Central
America. These terrapins like to bask
on logs in the sun and may pile up
several terrapins deep. The name
slider comes from its habit of sliding
back into the water when disturbed.

Distinctive red
markings on
side of head

Sharp beak for
grabbing fish

Mouth contains
a wormlike
appendage to
attract fish

TURTLE SNAPPER
The alligator snapping turtle from the US is
the largest freshwater turtle; some males have
carapaces measuring more than 2½ ft (75 cm)
long and weigh more than 198 lb (90 kg).

BONE HEAD
The head of the big-headed
turtle is too large to be
retracted into the shell, and
so it has a bony roof with a
tough outer scute. A skillful
climber, this turtle may feed
away from water.

BIG-HEADED TURTLE

207

More chelonians

Tortoises are among the most popular reptiles, being slow-moving, peaceful herbivores. Species of tortoise that have evolved in isolated places, where predators are few and competition for food is slight, may live to great ages and grow to vast sizes. Freshwater turtles are carnivorous and tend to be much more active.

RED-LEGGED TORTOISE

RED FEET
The red-legged tortoise is common in South America where it lives in rainforests. Large specimens can reach 19½ in (50 cm) in length.

PANCAKE TORTOISES
An African pancake tortoise's shell is light and flattened in shape, enabling it to move quickly and climb over rocks. It can also squeeze into small spaces when danger threatens.

PANCAKE TORTOISE

HINGE-BACK
The hinge-back tortoises of southern Africa have a hinge of cartilaginous tissue that allows the back of the shell to drop and protect the animal's rear. Hinge-backs sometimes share their burrow with lizards.

STARRED CAMOUFLAGE
The starred tortoise is found in
India and Sri Lanka. It is well
camouflaged; its shell blends in
with dry grassland. Less than
½ in (25 cm) long, it crawls
slowly, at little over ⅛ mph
(0.2 km/h).

STARRED
TORTOISE

Sturdy legs

*Shell may be up to
foot (30 cm) long*

SNAKE-NECK
The snake-necked turtles of Australia live in rivers,
where they hunt freshwater animals. However, like all
chelonians, they leave the water to lay eggs in a nest on
dry land. When threatened, they fold the head back
into the shell.

*Neck is nearly as
long as the shell*

SNAKE-NECKED TURTLE

GALÁPAGOS
TORTOISE

GALÁPAGOS GIANT
The lumbering giant tortoises of
the Galápagos Islands weigh up to
98 lb (90 kg). They were
originally present in large
numbers, but predation by
humans, dogs, and pigs, plus
competition for food with
goats, have brought about a
severe decline in numbers.

209

CROCODILE-
BONE
FIGURINE

CROCODILE ANATOMY

CROCODILES AND ALLIGATORS are the only remaining group of archosaurs, or "ruling reptiles" – the group to which the dinosaurs belonged. They are large animals with an armored skin that covers the whole body. Apart from the estuarine crocodile, they are found near the shores of freshwater rivers and lakes in warm regions of the world.

CROCODILE BONE
Animal bones have often been used to make ornaments. This Egyptian figurine was carved from a crocodile bone.

NILE CROCODILE
The Nile crocodile is found in many parts of Africa, although its range has been much reduced due to hunting. It often swims out to sea, and so is also found in Madagascar.

Powerful tail

ANATOMY FACTS

• A crocodile's skin is composed of partly ossified (converted into bone) horny plates.

• Crocodilians propel themselves through the water with their powerful tails.

SKELETON
Like all crocodilians, a caiman has a long skull, with nostrils and eyes set high. The body is long with two pairs of short legs held out sideways from the body.

Hind feet with four toes

Tail vertebrae

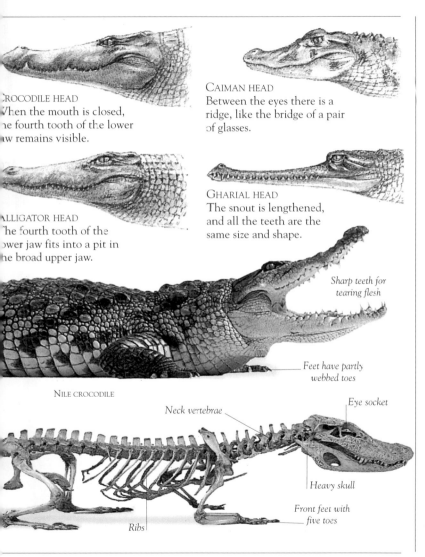

CROCODILE HEAD
When the mouth is closed, the fourth tooth of the lower jaw remains visible.

CAIMAN HEAD
Between the eyes there is a ridge, like the bridge of a pair of glasses.

ALLIGATOR HEAD
The fourth tooth of the lower jaw fits into a pit in the broad upper jaw.

GHARIAL HEAD
The snout is lengthened, and all the teeth are the same size and shape.

Sharp teeth for tearing flesh

Feet have partly webbed toes

NILE CROCODILE

Neck vertebrae

Eye socket

Heavy skull

Front feet with five toes

Ribs

REPTILES

CROCODILES

CROCODILES ARE FOUND in many tropical parts of the world. Large species include the American crocodile, the Orinoco crocodile, the Nile crocodile, and the saltwater crocodile, all of which can grow to more than 23 ft (7 m) in length. Smaller species include the mugger of India and Sri Lanka, and the Australian crocodile.

Prominent tooth

SKULL
A crocodile's skull is almost solid bone. The jaws are long, for holding prey, but the teeth cannot slice or chew, only tear.

SALTWATER TRAVELER
Unlike other crocodiles, the estuarine, or saltwater, crocodile is never found in freshwater. It lives near coasts in the sea or in the brackish waters of estuaries. It can travel long distances.

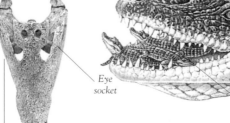

Eye socket

CROCODILE SKULL
(TOP VIEW)

Female guards young in mouth

212

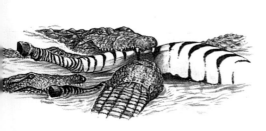

Sharing a Meal

In Africa, crocodiles feed mostly on antelopes, which are seized as they come near the water to drink. However, other animals are also taken, and crocodiles will feed on animals that have died, such as this zebra.

Lying in Wait

Even large animals, such as wildebeest, may fall victim to a crocodile attack. With a sudden rush, the crocodile grabs the prey in its jaws and drags it into the water to drown.

Unlikely Partners

As a crocodile lies with its mouth open, to keep cool, a spur-winged plover picks food from between its teeth. This looks dangerous for the bird, but the crocodile may benefit from having its teeth cleaned and the plover's cry warns the crocodile of danger.

ESTUARINE CROCODILE

213

Crocodiles

An adult crocodile swallows stones, which accumulate in its stomach. The stones do not break up food, but scientists believe that they may act as ballast, allowing the animal to remain submerged under the water.

CROCODILE SKIN

NILE CROCODILE

CRACKING EGGS
When her eggs are about to hatch, the female uncovers them. She may gently crack them to help the young emerge.

SHOES AND HANDBAGS
Formerly many wild crocodiles and alligators were hunted for their skins used for making shoes, handbags, and suitcases. Wild crocodiles are now protected, but are still illegally killed

CROCODILE FACTS

• A saltwater crocodile arrived at the Cocos Islands in the Indian Ocean, having swum 684 miles (1,100 km).

• The ancient Egyptians worshiped a crocodile-headed god named Sebek.

ESTUARINE CROCODILE

CROCODILE TEARS
The estuarine crocodile gets rid of the excess salt it swallows with its food by excreting it via the tear glands in its eyes.

THE GHARIAL

The family Gavialidae contains just one species, the gharial, or Indian gavial. The Gavialidae is thought to have arisen during the Cretaceous period, some 100 million years ago. The modern gharial has rather weak limbs and spends nearly all its life in water, using its oar-like tail for swimming. It lives in the deep waters of the Ganges, Mahanadi, and Brahmaputra Rivers of India, as well as the Koladan and Maingtha Rivers in Southeast Asia.

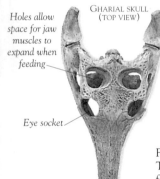

Holes allow space for jaw muscles to expand when feeding

GHARIAL SKULL
(TOP VIEW)

Eye socket

NO PROTECTION
For a long time, the gharial was protected from hunters because it was sacred to the Hindu god Vishnu. Today, however, it is illegally hunted for its skin.

FISH FEEDER
The gharial feeds entirely on fish. It lies in wait, moving its head from side to side to cover a large area, and catches its prey with a sudden jerk of its head.

LONG SNOUT
The main characteristic of the gharial is its long snout. At the tip it widens into an oval area that bears the nostrils; in males this region is bulbous. Each jaw contains more than 50 sharp teeth.

Nasal opening

ALLIGATORS AND CAIMANS

ALLIGATORS AND CAIMANS have shorter snouts than crocodiles, and they live solely in freshwater. There are two species of alligator, the American alligator and the rare Chinese alligator. The various species of caiman are all found in the Americas, ranging from Mexico to South America and the Caribbean.

SLOW DOWN, LIVE LONGER
Alligators are more sluggish than crocodiles. This may be why they live longer – there are records of alligators living for up to 50 years. Widespread hunting, however, severely threatens the animal's survival in the wild.

AMERICAN ALLIGATOR

Males roar during breeding season

SKULL
An alligator's skull is shorter and broader than a crocodile's. The fearsome jaws can carry young with surprising delicacy.

HUNTED DOWN
American alligators can grow to 20 ft (6 m) in length, but because of hunting it is rare nowadays to find individuals longer than 10 ft (3 m).

CAIMAN

The skin on a caiman's belly is reinforced with bony plates, making it difficult for use as leather. Caimans are still hunted – to protect livestock.

Caimans can move surprisingly quickly on land

Hind foot is used to scratch body, rub eyes, and tear food

Caimans hiss when threatened

ALLIGATOR YOUNG

Alligators are 8 in (20 cm) long at hatching. They grow 1 ft (30 cm) each year, reaching maturity at six. The young are vulnerable to predators, including mammals, birds, and fish, and, at any age, may be eaten by other alligators.

YOUNG ALLIGATORS

Adults feed on fish and small mammals

ALLIGATOR FACTS

• The English word "alligator" comes from the Spanish for lizard, *largato*.

• The Chinese alligator is nearly extinct. It is killed for food and to make charms and medicines.

LIZARD ANATOMY

THE FIRST LIZARDS appeared 220 million years ago, in the Triassic period. They fed on insects and looked similar to modern lizards. Typically, a lizard has a broad head, a long, slender body with limbs held out sideways, and a long tail. However, there are more specialized forms, such as chameleons and legless lizards.

ANATOMY OF A
FEMALE LIZARD

Heart

Ovary

Lungs

Intestine

Opening
of cloaca

INTERNAL ANATOMY
A lizard's body is symmetrically arranged both externally and internally. As in nearly all reptiles, the heart has three chambers and the gut, oviduct, and ureter empty into a common chamber, the cloaca.

UNUSUAL LIZARD
A chameleon does not have the flexible spine of most lizards. In addition, its legs are proportionately longer, and it can raise its body higher than other lizards.

Spine is less
flexible than
other lizards'

Prehensile tail
for gripping
onto branches

CHAMELEON SKELETON

Broad body
with many ribs

Toes designed
for grasping

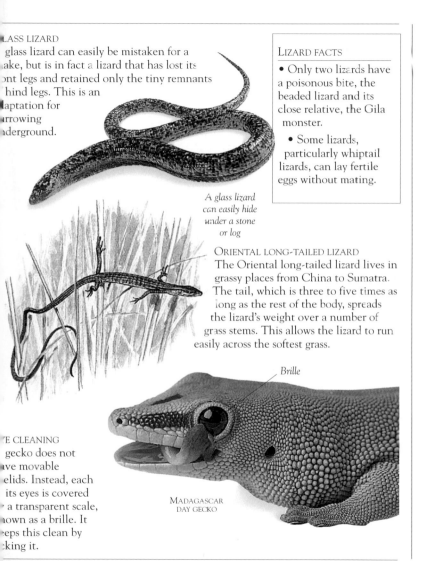

GLASS LIZARD

A glass lizard can easily be mistaken for a snake, but is in fact a lizard that has lost its front legs and retained only the tiny remnants of hind legs. This is an adaptation for burrowing underground.

A glass lizard can easily hide under a stone or log

LIZARD FACTS

• Only two lizards have a poisonous bite, the beaded lizard and its close relative, the Gila monster.

• Some lizards, particularly whiptail lizards, can lay fertile eggs without mating.

ORIENTAL LONG-TAILED LIZARD

The Oriental long-tailed lizard lives in grassy places from China to Sumatra. The tail, which is three to five times as long as the rest of the body, spreads the lizard's weight over a number of grass stems. This allows the lizard to run easily across the softest grass.

Brille

EYE CLEANING

A gecko does not have movable eyelids. Instead, each of its eyes is covered by a transparent scale, known as a brille. It keeps this clean by licking it.

MADAGASCAR
DAY GECKO

219

HOW LIZARDS FEED

SOME LIZARDS eat almost anything; others, such as the plant-eating Galápagos iguanas, have a specialized diet. Many lizards prey on insects, and some of them also eat vegetable matter. Some species prey on other animals, such as birds, small mammals, and other lizards.

VEGETARIAN
The Galápagos land iguana feeds only on plants, particularly the fleshy leaves and fruits of the prickly pear cactus. It deals with the spines by working the food around in its mouth until they break off.

GALÁPAGOS LAND IGUANA

CHAMELEON

Insect trapped in sticky mucus

Muscular tongue is as long as the lizard's body

STICKY TONGUE
A chameleon moves very slowly and deliberately toward its potential prey. When within range, it shoots out its long, muscular tongue at incredible speed. The insect is trapped on the end of the lizard's sticky tongue and drawn into its mouth.

EYED LIZARD

CATCHING INSECTS

The eyed lizard feeds on insects, small birds, rodents, and some fruits. An insect, such as a cricket, is shaken rapidly to stun it and then passed to the back of the lizard's mouth. It is then crushed by the jaws in a series of rapid, powerful snaps.

The eyed or jeweled lizard is native to southern Europe and North Africa

ANT EATER

Despite its fierce appearance, the Australian thorny devil, or moloch, lives solely on ants, which it eats in large quantities. It obtains much of its water from dew, which condenses on its spines and runs into its mouth.

THORNY DEVIL

KOMODO DRAGON

PREDATORY DRAGON

The huge Komodo dragon is a large monitor lizard found only on a few Indonesian islands, including Komodo. It feeds mostly on carrion, but is capable of catching and killing a small deer.

FEEDING FACTS

• The caiman lizards of South America feed almost exclusively on marsh snails.

• In crowded conditions, chameleons have been known to eat the young of their own species.

THE WORLD'S LIZARDS

BECAUSE THEY ARE COLD-BLOODED and use their environment to maintain body temperature, lizards prefer warm climates. Thus most species are found in tropical and subtropical regions. There are 14 families, the largest of which are the skinks (about 1000 species), the geckos (830 species), the iguanids (650 species), and the agamids (300 species).

Large toes with hooked pads

GECKO

HOUSE GUE
Pads on th
gecko's feet help
cling to any surfac
Geckos can often be se
hunting for insects o
walls in the tropi

MARINE IGUANA

BY THE SEA
The Galápagos marine iguana can often be seen sunning itself on seashore rocks. It feeds solely on seaweed and is an excellent swimmer.

MADAGASCAR
DAY GECKO

FORE
DWELL
This geck
bright green coloratio
is perfect camouflage for
home – the forests
Madagascar. Unlike mo
geckos, it hunts during the da

LIZARD FACTS

• Some lizards, such as the common lizard and slow worm of Britain, do live in temperate climates.

• On West Indian islands, numbers of anoles (which belong to the iguanids) exceed 20,000 per acre.

THE JUNGLE

ome rain forest iguanas are
ender animals with long toes.
ales are often larger and
ore brightly colored than
males. In some species,
the colors become
more apparent
during the
breeding season.

Long hind legs

PLUMED BASILISK
The most spectacular
species of basilisk is the
entral and South American
umed basilisk, which has a
il-like crest along its head and
ack. The male displays its crest
uring the breeding season.

ON WATER
Basilisks are found in
Central and South
America, near streams and
lakes. Their splayed feet and long
tails enable them to run across the
surface of the water.

PLUMED BASILISK

COMMON IGUANA

ESERT ISLANDER
he common, or
een, iguana is
und in Central
d South
merica and on many
aribbean islands.
here are about
0 species of iguana.

The Agamid family

Agamids, of which there are about 300 species, are found in central, south, and Southeast Asia, Australia, and Africa. The only species found in Europe is the starred lizard, or hardun, which lives on some Greek islands, in North Africa, and in southwest Asia. Many species spend their lives in the branches of trees, but agamids have adapted to a wide range of habitats. Some species live at high altitudes; *Agama himalayama* is found on Himalayan slopes at 11,000 ft (3,300 m).

GARDEN LIZARD

BLOODSUCKER
Like a chameleon, the garden lizard, or blood-sucker, can change color rapidly. It is found in India, Afghanistan, and China.

Large scales protect underside of jaw

BEARDED DRAGON
Some seven species of Australian lizard are known as bearded dragons because of the long, pointed scales on their throats.

BEARDED DRAGON

THORNY DEVIL

Spines provide excellent defense

HOT AND SPINY
The thorny devil, or moloch, is an Australian desert dweller. It allows its body to heat up to an almost lethal temperature so that it can spend as much time as possible feeding in the open.

Spring-tailed lizards tolerate very high temperatures and are among the hardiest lizards of the African Sahara. They feed on plants and insects and survive on the moisture they obtain from their food and from dew.

Channels between scales guide water condensed from the air toward the mouth

"Eyebrows" protect eyes from twigs and leaves

Spiny tail is used for defense and acts as a fat store

SPRING-TAILED LIZARD

Dorsal crest of pointed scales

PRICKLY NECK

The pricklenape agama lives high in the trees in mountain forests from China to Indonesia. Its name comes from the long, sharp spines on its neck. Its long toes have fringed scales that help it cling to branches.

PRICKLENAPE AGAMA

WATER DRAGON

The crested water dragon is an Asian species. It lives mainly in trees that grow near water. If disturbed on the ground, it escapes by rearing up on its hind legs and running off in a burst of speed.

CRESTED WATER DRAGON

Tail acts as balance when running

225

REPTILES

More lizards of the world

Many lizards are specially adapted for particular environments. A chameleon's body, for example, is greatly modified for living in trees. The body is flattened from side to side, a shape that helps the reptile avoid the heat of the sun during the hottest part of the day, but absorb heat in the early morning and late evening. It also helps to camouflage the body and makes it easier to balance on the branches of trees.

CHAMELEON
Chameleons have pincerlike toes for gripping branches. The largest species, found in Madagascar, may be over 2 ft (60 cm) in length.

JEWEL OF THE TREES
The emerald tree skink of Indonesia is a typical member of the skink family. Its long slender body is designed for scuttling rapidly among tree branches.

Long tail helps balance

EMERALD TREE SKINK

Coloration makes skink hard to see among trees

THREE HORNS
Jackson's chameleon is found around Mt. Kenya in Africa. Males have horns or crests on their heads and use them for combat and defense.

WHIPTAIL

Most whiptails have long stripes

WHIPTAIL
Whiptails are slender, agile lizards that are found in a variety of habitats from southern North America southward to Argentina. This species lives in dry grasslands.

Long toes assist grip

LIZARD FACTS
• Estimates of the number of species of skink vary from 600 to over 1,200; there are probably about 1,000.

• Blue-tongued skinks scare predators away by sticking out their bright blue tongues.

SKINK IN DANGER
The giant skink of the Solomon Islands grows to more than 2 ft (70 cm) and is the largest of the family. It lives in trees, feeding on leaves. Like many reptiles, it is threatened by the destruction of its habitat. It is also hunted for food.

Large, overlapping scales

Head-shaped tail

STUMP-TAILED SKINK

TWO HEADS
Southern Australia's stump-tailed skink (also known as the shingleback or pinecone lizard) has a tail that looks almost exactly like a head. This often confuses predators long enough for it to escape.

GIANT SKINK

227

Lizard protection

For a small animal that lives in the open, a scaly skin affords only limited protection, and so some lizards have additional protective features. Girdle-tailed lizards and their relatives are well armored, and the armadillo lizard makes good defensive use of its spines. Beaded lizards, such as the Gila monster, defend themselves with poison, while monitor lizards are protected by their sheer size.

Hissing warns off an attacker

ON GUARD
Gould's monitor uses i tail as a third hind leg to threaten an attacke or simply raise itself up and survey its surroundings. Monitor include a number of large lizards, and 20 o̅ the 30 known species are Australian.

GOULD'S MONITOR

Thick scales protect body

Male is brigl colored duri the breedir season

Food consists mostly of insects, with some plant material

Female lays a few eggs in a communal nesting site

FLAT LIZARD

STUCK FAST
The flat lizards of southern Africa live in rock crevices When threatened, a flat lizard inflates its body, jamming it into a crevice and making it impossible fc a predator to prize out.

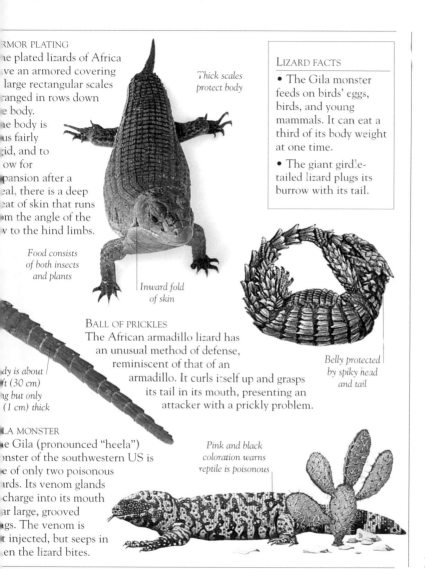

RMOR PLATING
1e plated lizards of Africa
ve an armored covering
large rectangular scales
ranged in rows down
e body.
1e body is
us fairly
gid, and to
ow for
pansion after a
eal, there is a deep
eat of skin that runs
om the angle of the
w to the hind limbs.

*Thick scales
protect body*

*Food consists
of both insects
and plants*

*Inward fold
of skin*

LIZARD FACTS

• The Gila monster
feeds on birds' eggs,
birds, and young
mammals. It can eat a
third of its body weight
at one time.

• The giant girdle-
tailed lizard plugs its
burrow with its tail.

BALL OF PRICKLES
The African armadillo lizard has
an unusual method of defense,
reminiscent of that of an
armadillo. It curls itself up and grasps
its tail in its mouth, presenting an
attacker with a prickly problem.

*Belly protected
by spiky head
and tail*

dy is about
t (30 cm)
1g but only
(1 cm) thick

LA MONSTER
1e Gila (pronounced "heela")
onster of the southwestern US is
e of only two poisonous
ards. Its venom glands
charge into its mouth
ar large, grooved
1gs. The venom is
t injected, but seeps in
en the lizard bites.

*Pink and black
coloration warns
reptile is poisonous*

THE TUATARA

THE TUATARA LOOKS LIKE A LIZARD, but it differs from true lizards in the structure of its skeleton and skull. In fact, it is the sole survivor of the rynchocephalians, a primitive reptile group that thrived between 15 and 240 million years ago, during the Jurassic and Triassic periods.

"Tuatara" is Maori for "peaks on the back"

LIVING FOSSIL
The tuatara is called a living fossil because it has changed little in 200 million years. All its closest relatives died out; no one knows why the tuatara alone survived.

LONG LIFE
Male tuataras grow to about 2 ft (61 cm) long; females are slightly shorter. Both sexes reach sexual maturity at the age of 20, and may live for another 100 years.

LIZARD ANCESTORS
Homoeosaurus, a relative of the tuatara, lived about 140 million years ago. Its ancestors probably evolved from lizards 200 million years ago.

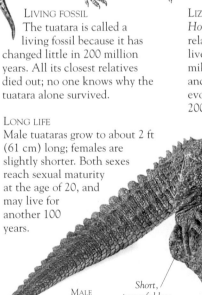

MALE
TUATARA

Short, powerful legs for burrowing

A third, or pineal, eye under the skim may act as a thermostat or help to regulate the tuatara's "biological clock"

Crest runs down the back and tail

FEMALE TUATARA

Teeth are fused with the jaws

Two bony arches

Tuatara has large, wedge-shaped teeth at the front

TUATARA SKULL

A LONG WAIT

After mating, a female tuatara stores the male's sperm for 10–12 months before fertilization occurs. She then lays 5–15 eggs in a shallow burrow.

SKULL STRUCTURE

The tuatara's skull is different from that of lizards. It resembles a crocodile's in having two bony arches at the back. Most lizards have just one arch, while in burrowing lizards and snakes the arches have disappeared.

AND HOME

Tuataras are found on a few small islands off the coast of New Zealand. They live in burrows (which they often share with seabirds) and are active at night, when they come out to search for insects and earthworms. They grow very slowly.

TUATARA FACTS

• Eggs hatch 15 months after laying – the longest incubation period of any reptile.

• A tuatara breathes very slowly, about once every seven seconds, and can hold its breath for nearly an hour.

SNAKE ANATOMY

SNAKES ARE PROBABLY descended from burrowing lizards that gradually lost their legs as they adapted to an underground life. Today's snakes do not generally live underground, but they have retained their ancestral form and found new ways of getting around.

RHINOCEROS VIPER

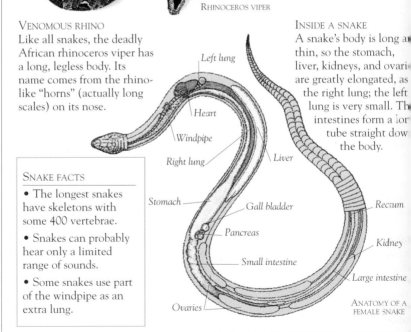

VENOMOUS RHINO
Like all snakes, the deadly African rhinoceros viper has a long, legless body. Its name comes from the rhino-like "horns" (actually long scales) on its nose.

INSIDE A SNAKE
A snake's body is long and thin, so the stomach, liver, kidneys, and ovaries are greatly elongated, as is the right lung; the left lung is very small. The intestines form a long tube straight down the body.

Left lung

Heart

Windpipe

Right lung

Liver

Stomach

Gall bladder

Pancreas

Small intestine

Ovaries

Rectum

Kidney

Large intestine

ANATOMY OF A
FEMALE SNAKE

SNAKE FACTS

• The longest snakes have skeletons with some 400 vertebrae.

• Snakes can probably hear only a limited range of sounds.

• Some snakes use part of the windpipe as an extra lung.

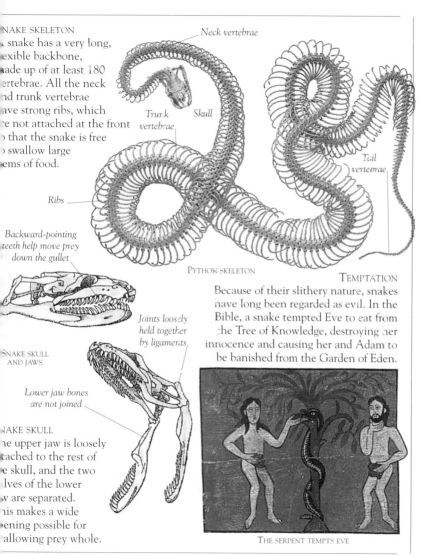

SNAKE SKELETON

A snake has a very long, flexible backbone, made up of at least 180 vertebrae. All the neck and trunk vertebrae have strong ribs, which are not attached at the front so that the snake is free to swallow large items of food.

Neck vertebrae

Trunk vertebrae

Skull

Tail vertebrae

Ribs

PYTHON SKELETON

Backward-pointing teeth help move prey down the gullet

SNAKE SKULL AND JAWS

Joints loosely held together by ligaments

Lower jaw bones are not joined

SNAKE SKULL

The upper jaw is loosely attached to the rest of the skull, and the two halves of the lower jaw are separated. This makes a wide opening possible for swallowing prey whole.

TEMPTATION

Because of their slithery nature, snakes have long been regarded as evil. In the Bible, a snake tempted Eve to eat from the Tree of Knowledge, destroying her innocence and causing her and Adam to be banished from the Garden of Eden.

THE SERPENT TEMPTS EVE

233

CONSTRICTORS

BOAS, PYTHONS, AND ANACONDAS are known as
constrictors – snakes that kill by wrapping prey in
their strong body coils until the animal suffocates.
Their victims are usually mammals, but
many constrictors kill birds
as well, and some are
known to prey
on other
reptiles.

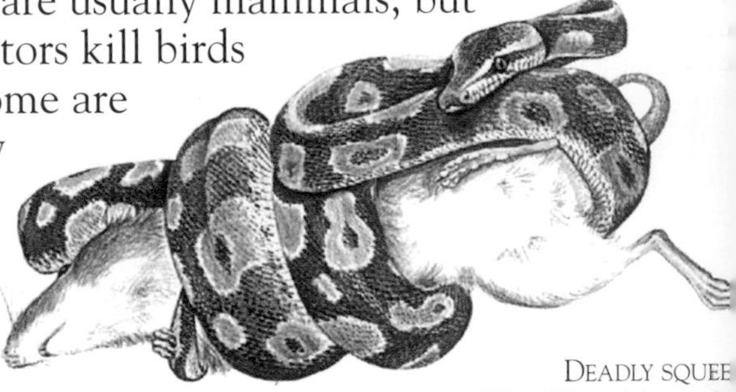

*Coils tighten
each time the
rat breathes out*

BALL PYTHON

DEADLY SQUEE[...]
This West African b[...]
python is killing its prey, a rat, by coili[...]
itself around the animal's chest a[...]
gradually tightening its grip. Soon, t[...]
rat will not be able to inhale, a[...]
it will die fr[...]
suffocati[...]

BIRDS BEWARE
Tree boas hunt birds by
creeping up on them as they
roost in the branches of trees;
mammals are also eaten. The emerald
tree boa lives in the lush rain forests
of the Amazon basin.

EMERALD TREE BOA

PRIMITIVE SNAKES
Scientists call pythons,
boas, and some other species
"primitive" because these
snakes have tiny claws where
the hind legs and hips of
their lizard ancestors once
were. The claws lie on either
side of the cloaca and are
said to play a part in mating.

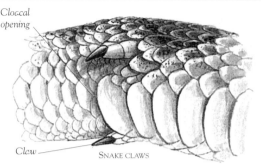

Cloacal opening

Claw

SNAKE CLAWS

HOW A CONSTRICTOR CONSUMES ITS PREY

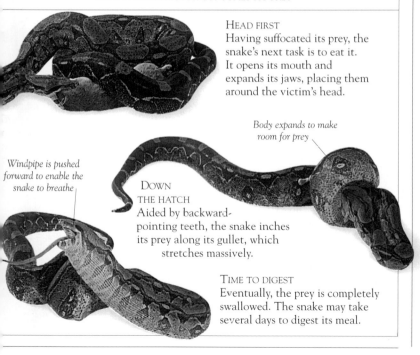

HEAD FIRST
Having suffocated its prey, the
snake's next task is to eat it.
It opens its mouth and
expands its jaws, placing them
around the victim's head.

*Body expands to make
room for prey*

*Windpipe is pushed
forward to enable the
snake to breathe*

DOWN
THE HATCH
Aided by backward-
pointing teeth, the snake inches
its prey along its gullet, which
stretches massively.

TIME TO DIGEST
Eventually, the prey is completely
swallowed. The snake may take
several days to digest its meal.

Boas

All but three species of boa are found in the tropical warmth of Central and South America. These constrictors have adapted to a wide variety of habitats, many spending their lives in trees, while a number of others live on the ground or burrow into it.

COOK'S TREE BOA

RAINBOW COLORS
The dazzlingly iridescent rainbow boa lives in the forests, woodlands, and grassy plains of northwestern South America. It feeds on small mammals and birds.

RAINBOW BOA

BOA CONSTRICTOR
The red-tailed boa is one of 11 subspecies of boa constrictor. It grows to an average of 10 ft (3 m) in length (although snakes over 13 ft [4 m] have been seen), and lives in the semidesert plains of northwestern Peru.

RED-TAILED BOA

COOK'S BO
Cook's tree boa is the large of several subspecies of tr or garden boa. It is four only on the Caribbea islands of Trinida Grenada, Carriaco Union, and St. Vincer

PACIFIC BOA

BOA FACTS

- When a rubber boa is threatened, it rolls itself into a ball, hides its head among its coils, and presents its tail toward the intruder.
- Boas do not hatch from eggs. Instead, females give birth to live young.

CUNNING IMPOSTER
The Pacific boa, native to the rain forests, marshes, and swamps of New Guinea and nearby islands, lives and hunts on the ground. To defend itself against attack, it mimics a venomous viper, hissing and striking at the intruder.

TREE OR GARDEN BOA

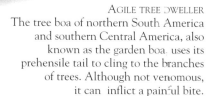

AGILE TREE DWELLER
The tree boa of northern South America and southern Central America, also known as the garden boa, uses its prehensile tail to cling to the branches of trees. Although not venomous, it can inflict a painful bite.

RUBBER ROBBER
The North American rubber boa lives in woodlands and meadows, where it hunts among fallen logs, in crevices, or down burrows. It also climbs trees to steal young birds from their nests. This snake looks and feels rubbery, hence its name.

RUBBER BOA

237

More constrictors

Pythons, from Australasia, Africa, and Asia, and anacondas, from South America, are some of the biggest snakes in the world. But despite tales of man-eating serpents, they are not large enough to devour people or any other large mammal. If a snake did eat such a meal, it would be defenseless for at least a week digesting it.

Tail acts as anchor

D'ALBERT'S WATER PYTHON

WATER PYTHON
D'Albert's water python lives in rain forests and swamps in southern New Guinea and on neighboring islands. Its dark body has no markings, except for some pale areas around the mouth. It eats mammals and birds.

LARGEST PYTHON
The reticulated python of Southeast Asia is well camouflaged for life on the forest floor. It may grow to 33 ft (10 m) in length, making it the longest snake in the world. It feeds on mammals, lizards and the occasional snake.

RETICULATED PYTHON

SHORT AND BLOODY
The blood python gets its name from its colorful camouflage markings. It is also known as the short python because its tail is much shorter than those of other species. It comes from wet places in the central and southern Malay peninsula and on neighboring islands.

BLOOD PYTHON

HUNTED FOR ITS SKIN

The Indian python lives in a wide range of habitats, feeding on mammals, birds, and reptiles. It is now an endangered species because people have slaughtered it for its skin and destroyed much of its natural habitat.

Skin is used to make belts and shoes

INDIAN PYTHON

ANACONDAS

YELLOW ANACONDA

SWAMP SNAKE

The yellow anaconda lives in swamps and marshes and on the banks of rivers and streams in Brazil, Bolivia, Paraguay, and Argentina. At 11½ ft (3.5 m) in length, it is about half the size of the common anaconda.

RECORD HOLDER

The common anaconda is probably the world's largest snake, being heavier than its rival for the title, the reticulated python. The average adult length is about 20 ft (6 m), although individuals of over 26 ft (8 m) have been seen. It is found in Trinidad and many parts of tropical South America.

COMMON ANACONDA

REPTILES

COLUBRID SNAKES

ABOUT THREE-QUARTERS of the world's snakes – over 2,000 species – belong to the colubrid family. Some are venomous, but a large number are completely harmless. Among the harmless ones are kingsnakes, water snakes, ratsnakes, the egg-eating snake, and the grass snake.

CALIFORN
KINGSNAK

VARIABLE PATTERNS
The colors and patterr
of California kingsnake
vary greatly – individua
may be cross-banded (
have stripes runnin
down the bod
Kingsnakes eat
wide range
small anima!
includin
venomou
snake

CALIFORNIA MOUNTAIN
KINGSNAKE

Markings loo
similar to a
coral snake's

COLUBRID FACTS

• A Japanese albino form of the yellow ratsnake is considered to be an earthly form of a fertility goddess called Benzai-ten.

• Scientists call colubrids "typical" snakes.

MOUNTAIN KINGS
California mountain kingsnakes prey on small animals, including rodents, lizards, and nestling birds. When not hunting, they often hide under stones, logs, or piles of leaves. They come from the west coast of the US.

240

MILK DRINKER?
The milk snake is a species of kingsnake; there are over 17 subspecies. The name comes from the popular but totally incorrect belief that they take milk from cows. This subspecies occurs in Mexico, where it preys mostly on rodents, killing them by constriction.

SINOLOAN MILK SNAKE

Colored bands mimic those of a poisonous coral snake

Markings resemble the patterns on an ear of corn

Iridescent colors give the sunbeam snake its name

SUNBEAM SNAKE

CORN SNAKE

NIGHT HUNTER
Like boas and pythons, the Asian sunbeam snake still has the remnants of hind limbs. It lives in burrows in areas where the soil is damp and emerges at night to prey on frogs, small mammals, and other snakes.

URBAN MYTH?
The corn snake, also called the red ratsnake, is said to be common in the sewers of cities in the southeastern US. Its natural surroundings are, in fact, woodlands, where it preys on rodents, bats, birds, and lizards. A shy snake, it uses logs and tree stumps for cover.

241

More colubrid snakes

Nonvenomous colubrid snakes kill either by constricting or by overpowering and swallowing the victim. For defense, they usually rely on camouflage and the ability to escape quickly. Ratsnakes, however, defend themselves by throwing the front end of their bodies into an S-shape and vibrating their tails, while bullsnakes puff themselves up to appear more formidable.

EUROPEAN
WATER SNAKE

Markings look like an adder's

HARMLESS VIPER
The European water snake, also called the viperine grass snake, has warning markings that resemble those of a venomous adder. It is actually completely harmless, like all other water snakes. A good swimmer, it feeds on fish and frogs.

MOELLENDORFF'S
RATSNAKE

HUNDRED FLOWERS
Moellendorff's ratsnake, known poetically as the "hundred flower snake" in Chinese, comes from southeastern China, where it feeds on rodents and birds.

Flowerlike patterns give this snake its Chinese name

COLUBRID FACTS

• Ratsnakes vibrate their tails when threatened and are often mistaken for rattlesnakes.

• In the US, farmers sometimes use bullsnakes to catch rats and mice in barns.

BAT CATCHER

The mangrove ratsnake lives in the forests of Southeast Asia. It preys on birds and small mammals, including bats, which it catches as they fly out to feed. If threatened, it inflates its body to look larger than normal.

Tail wrapped around a rock gives good anchorage

MANGROVE RATSNAKE

SPECIAL SPIKES

The egg-eating snake's backbone has about 30 ventral spikes, which are used for breaking up eggs inside the snake's body.

EGG-EATER'S SPINE   *Ventral spikes*

EGG-EATER

Egg-eating snakes are virtually toothless and have unusually elastic skins. This enables them to swallow a whole egg, which is crushed inside the body. About 5 minutes later, the snake ejects the shell remains from its mouth.

Egg may be up to three times the size of the snake's mouth

AFRICAN EGG-EATING SNAKE

243

VENOMOUS SNAKES

VENOM – a poisonous fluid produced by an animal – is widely used for killing or incapacitating prey. Snake venom, which is a very complex substance, serves two main purposes. First, the poison quickly subdues a prey animal, thus reducing the risk to the snake of injury from retaliation. At the same time, chemicals within the venom start to break down the prey's tissues, making digestion easier.

KING COBRA

Fangs are in forward position, ready to strike

Fangs normally lie flat inside the mouth

Rattle warns off predators

EASTERN DIAMONDBACK RATTLESNAKE

FIXED FANGS
Cobras have fixed fangs at the front of the mouth, as do kraits, sea snakes, coral snakes, the taipan, and the tiger snake.

WARNING RATTLE
A rattlesnake is a typical front-fanged snake. As it opens its mouth, the snake rotates its fangs forward, ready to inject venom. This species is the most venomous snake in North America and feeds mainly on rats and rabbits.

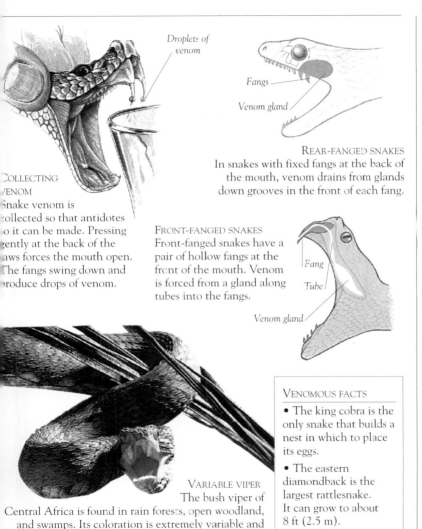

Droplets of venom

REAR-FANGED SNAKES
In snakes with fixed fangs at the back of the mouth, venom drains from glands down grooves in the front of each fang.

Fangs

Venom gland

COLLECTING VENOM
Snake venom is collected so that antidotes to it can be made. Pressing gently at the back of the jaws forces the mouth open. The fangs swing down and produce drops of venom.

FRONT-FANGED SNAKES
Front-fanged snakes have a pair of hollow fangs at the front of the mouth. Venom is forced from a gland along tubes into the fangs.

Fang

Tube

Venom gland

VENOMOUS FACTS
• The king cobra is the only snake that builds a nest in which to place its eggs.

• The eastern diamondback is the largest rattlesnake. It can grow to about 8 ft (2.5 m).

VARIABLE VIPER
The bush viper of Central Africa is found in rain forests, open woodland, and swamps. Its coloration is extremely variable and may be anything from pale green to reddish brown.

REAR-FANGED SNAKES

SNAKES WITH FANGS in the back of their mouth are found in both the Old and New Worlds, and, as with other groups of snakes, they vary greatly in color, size, and habitat. They are not as efficient as front-fanged snakes at injecting venom, and so most species are harmless to humans. Large rear-fanged snakes, however, can be dangerous.

CORAL MIMIC
The false coral snake preys on lizards, small mammals, and other small snakes. It is found in the forests of Central America, from Venezuela to Costa Rica.

FALSE CORAL SNAKE

Colors resemble those of a more dangerous snake

MANGROVE SNAKE
In the mangrove swamps of the Malay Peninsula this large snake – adults grow to over 6½ ft (2 m) – preys on a wide variety of small animals. The seven subspecies of mangrove snake have different numbers of yellow bands.

LIZARD HUNTER

The blunt-headed tree snake is found in trees and shrubs from southern Mexico to Bolivia and Paraguay. It is active by night and feeds mostly on lizards such as anoles and geckos.

PARROT SNAKE

Gaping mouth is a warning to enemies

BLUNT-HEADED TREE SNAKE

IDLE THREAT

When threatened, a parrot snake raises its head and opens its mouth, but rarely strikes. Slender and well camouflaged, it hunts lizards and amphibians in the dense foliage of the rain forests of Central and South America.

This snake often feeds on eggs laid on leaves by frogs

Camouflaged for life in the treetops

CAT EYES

The green cat-eyed snake lives in the forests of northeastern India, where it hunts at night for frogs, lizards, and small birds.

GREEN CAT-EYED SNAKE

247

More rear-fanged snakes

The venom produced by rear-fanged snakes is just as lethal as that of front-fanged snakes, and in some cases is specific to a particular prey. For example, the venom of a snake that usually eats frogs may be more toxic to frogs than to other animals, such as mice. The venom of both the boomslang and the twigsnake has occasionally killed people.

HOG-NOSED BURROWER
The Madagascan giant hognose snake eats birds and small mammals. It shelters in rock crevices, beneath debris, or in burrows that it digs. It lives in grassland and grows to about 5 ft (1.5 m) in length.

When threatened, this snake flattens its neck like a cobra and hisses loudly

MADAGASCAN GIANT HOGNOSE SNAKE

SONORAN LYRE SNAKE

REAR-FANGED FACTS

• The mussurana first constricts its prey, and then injects venom into it.

• The Australasian brown tree snake, introduced into Guam, has caused the decline of many native birds.

LYRE HEAD
Lyre snakes get their name from the lyre-shaped marking on the head. They live in rocky places in California, Arizona, and Mexico, feeding on lizards, small birds, and mammals. They are nocturnal.

FROG-EATER

The night snake, also known locally as the cat-eyed snake, is found in Mexico and Central America. It spends much of its time in trees and hunts at night for frogs and lizards.

NIGHT SNAKE
EATING FROGS' EGGS

Vine snake hangs from a branch, waiting for prey

VINE CREEPER

The vine snake's camouflage allows it to creep unseen among bushes and vines. Native to brush-covered hillsides in Mexico and Arizona, it preys mainly on lizards, and occasionally on small birds and nestlings.

MEXICAN
VINE SNAKE

BOOMSLANG

The African boomslang moves with speed and grace through woodland, scrub, savannah, and swamp. It eats birds' eggs and also uses its quick-acting venom to kill small mammals, frogs, and birds. Its name is Afrikaans for "tree snake."

249

FRONT FANGS

FRONT-FANGED SNAKES, such as cobras, can inject venom into almost any animal, making them among the most dangerous of all reptiles. As with all venomous snakes, their venom is normally used for killing or disabling prey, but it is equally effective as a defense. However, most snakes usually prefer to escape rather than attack a predator.

HORUS
The Egyptian sky god, Horus, demonstrates his dominion over reptiles by grasping snakes and standing on a crocodile.

COBRA FACTS

• Every year, thousands of Asian cobras are killed for their skins.

• The king cobra is the world's largest venomous snake – individuals exceeding 16 ft (5 m) in length have been recorded.

Cobra rears up before spitting

RED SPITTING COBRA

VENOM SPITTER
A spitting cobra has a very effective method of defense. When threatened, and with no means of escape, it rears up and squirts a jet of poison into the attacker's eyes, causing severe pain and even permanent blindness.

MARK OF BUDDHA
The Asian cobra has a characteristic "eye" or "monocle" on its hood. This is said to be the fingerprint of Buddha, who blessed this snake after it had shaded him as he slept in the desert.

MONOCLED COBRA

Some snake charmers remove the cobra's fangs

Cobras follow the instrument's movements

"Eye" is meant to frighten aggressors

Cobras are active at dawn and dusk

SNAKE CHARMER
AND COBRAS

HOODED MENACE
Most cobras have a hood, created by spreading the neck ribs as the front of the body is raised off the ground. This characteristic is particularly well developed in Asian species, such as the Ceylonese cobra.

A cobra can move forward while keeping its front raised

CHARMED SNAKES
Snake charmers in Asia and North Africa have long induced cobras to "dance" to their tunes. The snakes, however, are deaf and are probably reacting to the swaying movements of the instrument, not to the music.

The hood is spread as the body is raised

CEYLONESE COBRA

251

Vipers

With their long, hollow fangs, vipers and their close relatives, the pit vipers and rattlesnakes, are among the most dangerous snakes in the world. When one of these snakes opens its mouth to bite, it swings its fangs downward and forward, ready to stab the victim. The snake has absolute control over the movement of its fangs – it can even choose to erect them one at a time.

RECORD RANGE
The adder has the greatest range of any living snake. It is found throughout Europe and Asia, as far north as the Arctic Circle and eastward through northern China to the Pacific coast.

This viper's venom is very toxic

Blunt nose gives the snake its alternative name

Depending on the climatic conditions, this viper lays eggs or gives birth to live young

LEVANT VIPER

AVICENNA VIPER

SAND VIPER
The Avicenna viper is a sidewinder that lives in sandy places from Lebanon, through Israel westward to the northwestern coast of Africa. It is closely related to the horned viper.

BLUNT-NOSED VIPER
Levant, or blunt-nosed vipers, of which there are seven subspecies, are found in dry, rocky places southward from Georgia to northern Israel, Iraq, Iran, and a few of the Greek islands

YELLOW PERIL
The eyelash viper has
tiny scales above its eyes
that resemble eyelashes.
This tree-dwelling pit
viper is found in rain
forests from southern
Mexico southward to
Ecuador and western
Venezuela. It varies in
color from brown or
green to lemon yellow.

EYELASH VIPER

LOOKS LIKE A VIPER . . .
The death, or deaf, adder
looks and behaves like
a viper, but is related
to the cobras, coral
snakes, and kraits.
It lives in dry, sandy
places in Australia,
New Guinea, and
nearby islands.

DEATH ADDER

*Grey and brown
coloring for
camouflage in
dry grass*

ALL PUFFED UP
A good climber and swimmer, the puff
adder is found in all habitats except
deserts in Africa south of the
Sahara. It preys on a wide
variety of animals and, like
all vipers, prefers to lie in
wait for its victims. The puff
adder's venom is highly toxic.

PUFF ADDER

253

Rattlesnakes

The distinctive feature of these well-known, front-fanged snakes is the rattle at the end of the tail, which is made of a series of special, ringlike scales. Rattlesnakes, all of which are found in the southern half of North America, are under threat, mainly from excessive slaughter by hunters, together with the continued spread of agriculture and urban development. All rattlesnakes give birth to live young.

SOUTHERN PACIFIC
RATTLESNAKE

ADAPTABLE
The southern Pacific rattlesnake is found in rocky and sandy environments. An adaptable species, it can also survive in urban and agricultural areas. It preys mainly on rodents.

EASTERN
DIAMONDBACK
RATTLESNAKE

RATTLESNAKE FACTS

• Organized hunts called "rattlesnake roundups" in the US have wiped out many local populations.

• Western diamondbacks always return to the same den to hibernate.

LARGE – BUT SECRETIVE
The eastern diamondback is a secretive reptile found in pine and oak woods and abandoned agricultural areas. It is a large, heavy-bodied snake that preys on small mammals, particularly rabbits and rats.

VARIED HABITATS

Black-tailed rattlesnakes are found in Mexico, Arizona, and Texas, usually in rocky places and sometimes in woodland and open grassland. They may be active at any time of the day, and they prey on small rodents.

BLACK-TAILED RATTLESNAKE

Diamond-shaped, pale-bordered blotches

LARGE GATHERINGS

Western diamondbacks can be found in a variety of dry habitats in Mexico and the southern US. They hibernate in the autumn, gathering in large numbers in suitable den sites. They feed on small mammals and birds.

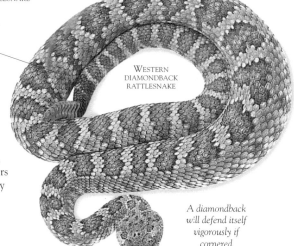

WESTERN DIAMONDBACK RATTLESNAKE

A diamondback will defend itself vigorously if cornered

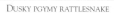

DUSKY PYGMY RATTLESNAKE

PYGMY RATTLER

The dusky pygmy rattlesnake lives in dry, sandy places near water. It is active at any time of the day or night, and it preys on small animals, including small snakes and large insects. It grows to only about 20 in (50 cm) in length.

255

Other front-fanged snakes

Front-fanged snakes that have fixed fangs include the tiger snake, the taipan, kraits, and sea snakes. Unlike true vipers and rattlesnakes, these snakes cannot stab their prey with their fangs and must actually bite. The cottonmouth and its close relatives, the moccasin and the copperhead, are pit vipers and are thus members of the Crotalinae, the viper subfamily that includes the rattlesnakes.

BANDED SEA SNAKE

TIGER SNAKE

SEA SERPENT
Sea snakes include the world's most venomous snakes. Luckily, the banded sea snakes, of which five species live in coastal waters around New Guinea and Pacific islands, seldom bite in defense.

TOXIC TIGER
The venom of southern Australia's tiger snake is highly toxic – just 3 mg is enough to kill a human. It feeds mainly on frogs, but also kills small mammals and lizards. The tiger snake is quick to attack if disturbed.

NEVER FATAL
The American copperhead is found in open woodland, where it feeds on mice, birds, frogs, and insects. Contrary to popular belief, its bite is never fatal, although this has not stopped the widespread killing of these snakes.

Copperhead's hibernate in communal den

COPPERHEAD

URTLE EATER
he cottonmouth, also called the
ater moccasin, is an impressive-
oking, heavy-bodied snake that
es in swamps and marshes in
abama, Georgia, and Virginia.
Its prey includes
small turtles and
young alligators.

COTTONMOUTH

*Taipans shelter in
mammal burrows and
rock crevices, or under
piles of forest litter*

TAIPAN

DO NOT DISTURB
The taipan is a large, slender snake found
in northern Australia. When not hunting,
it seeks shelter and,
whenever possible,
will retreat when
disturbed. If cornered,
however, it becomes
fearsomely aggressive.

*Prey consists of
small mammals*

*Taipan is one of
Australia's most
dangerous snakes*

COMMON KRAIT
The common, or blue,
krait is a highly venomous
snake found in the dry
woodland plains and
meadows of Bangladesh,
dia, and Sri Lanka. It hides during the day and at
ght hunts rodents, lizards, and other snakes.

FRONT-FANGED FACTS

• A cottonmouth uses
its bright yellow tail as
a lure to attract prey.

• A bite from a krait is
fatal in over 75 percent
of cases.

• Some species of sea
snake are considered
to be a delicacy in the
Far East.

257

BIRDS

WHAT IS A BIRD?

BIRDS ARE DIFFERENT from all the other animals in the world because they have feathers – at least a thousand of them. They also have two wings, a strong bill, no teeth, scaly legs and feet, and three or four toes with claws. Most birds can fly and they are the largest, fastest, and most powerful flying animals. Like us, birds breathe air, have a skeleton inside their bodies, and are warm-blooded. Unlike us, birds lay eggs.

JUVENILE
STARLING
FEATHER

ADULT
STARLING
FEATHER

FEATHERS

Birds' feathers are light, yet strong and flexible. The feathers of young birds are often a different color from those of the adults.

STARLING
EGGS

EGGS

A bird's egg is a survival capsule which protects and nourishes a baby bird while it develops inside. When the bird is ready to hatch, it has to force its way out.

Secondary flight feathers

Primary flight feathers

Rump

Uppertail coverts

Wing coverts

Undertail coverts

Ankle

Tail

EUROPEAN
STARLING

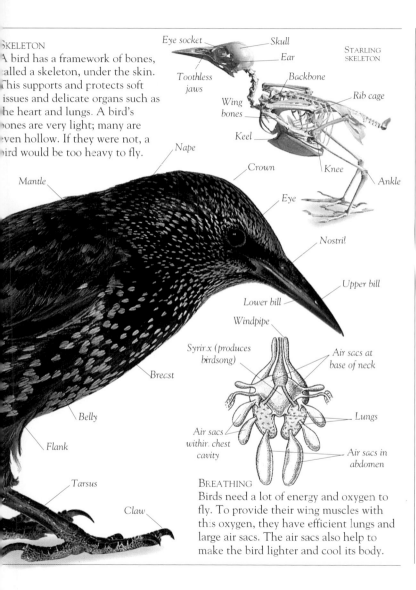

SKELETON

A bird has a framework of bones, called a skeleton, under the skin. This supports and protects soft tissues and delicate organs such as the heart and lungs. A bird's bones are very light; many are even hollow. If they were not, a bird would be too heavy to fly.

Eye socket

Skull

Ear

STARLING SKELETON

Toothless jaws

Backbone

Wing bones

Rib cage

Keel

Crown

Knee

Ankle

Eye

Nape

Mantle

Nostril

Upper bill

Lower bill

Windpipe

Syrinx (produces birdsong)

Air sacs at base of neck

Breast

Lungs

Belly

Air sacs within chest cavity

Flank

Air sacs in abdomen

Tarsus

BREATHING

Birds need a lot of energy and oxygen to fly. To provide their wing muscles with this oxygen, they have efficient lungs and large air sacs. The air sacs also help to make the bird lighter and cool its body.

Claw

261

Types of birds

The huge variety of birds alive today – over 9,000 species – evolved from reptilelike creatures that climbed trees about 150 million years ago. Reptile scales developed into bird feathers, although there are still scales on a bird's legs. Now, there are birds of all shapes and sizes, from huge ostriches to tiny wrens. Some of the main types of birds are shown here.

PIGEON

PIGEONS
Most pigeons and doves have rather small heads, plump bodies, dense, soft feathers, and a powerful straight flight. They live all over the world.

ARCHAEOPTERYX
The first bird we know of lived about 150 million years ago. It is called *Archaeopteryx*, meaning ancient wing. It had feathers but could not fly well.

ANCIENT BIRD FACTS

• Birds may be living descendants of the dinosaurs.

• *Archaeopteryx* had teeth.

• The first flying bird was a ternlike seabird called *Ichthyornis*.

• The heaviest bird, *Dromornis stirtoni*, was four times heavier than an ostrich.

ZEBRA FINCHES

PERCHING BIRD
Over half of the birds alive today are perching landbirds. Most are strong fliers and many sing well.

PARROTS
Colorful, noisy, tree-
living birds of the
tropics, parrots
have powerful,
hooked bills.

RED-AND-
GREEN
MACAW

DUCKS
These are broad-bodied
waterbirds with a wide, flat
bill, webbed feet, and
short legs set well
back on the body.

WOOD
DUCK

KING
PENGUIN

GOLDEN
EAGLE

PENGUINS
These flightless
seabirds of the
Southern
Hemisphere
have wings
like flippers.

EAGLES
Powerful
birds of prey,
eagles have
broad, rounded
wings, strong
talons, and a
hooked bill.

JUVENILE
BLACK-
HEADED
GULL

GULLS
These stocky seabirds have a
heavy bill, long, pointed
wings, and webbed feet.

263

Bird senses

OSTRICH

Birds rely mainly on their eyes and ears to find food or a mate, to fly, and to escape from danger. Their eyes are so large that there is not much room for them to move in the skull. Instead, birds have a flexible neck and move their whole head to see things. Most birds have a poor sense of smell.

SIGHT

A bird's huge eyes are often as big as its brain. Much of the brain deals with the information picked up by the eyes. Like us, birds see in color, but they may have better eyesight than we have.

Large eyes to spot danger coming

PIED AVOCET

The avocet uses its sense of touch to catch small water creatures.

TOUCH

Some birds, such as the avocet, have a well-developed sense of touch in the tongue and bill tip. Nightjars have bristles around their broad bills to help them sweep moths into their mouths as they fly at night.

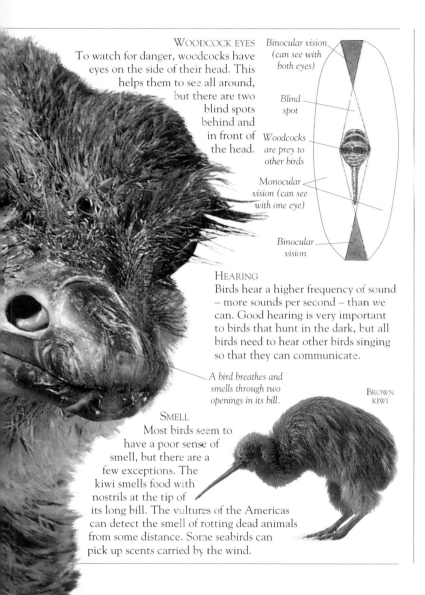

WOODCOCK EYES

To watch for danger, woodcocks have eyes on the side of their head. This helps them to see all around, but there are two blind spots behind and in front of the head.

Binocular vision (can see with both eyes)

Blind spot

Woodcocks are prey to other birds

Monocular vision (can see with one eye)

Binocular vision

HEARING

Birds hear a higher frequency of sound – more sounds per second – than we can. Good hearing is very important to birds that hunt in the dark, but all birds need to hear other birds singing so that they can communicate.

A bird breathes and smells through two openings in its bill.

BROWN KIWI

SMELL

Most birds seem to have a poor sense of smell, but there are a few exceptions. The kiwi smells food with nostrils at the tip of its long bill. The vultures of the Americas can detect the smell of rotting dead animals from some distance. Some seabirds can pick up scents carried by the wind.

265

FEATHERS

A BIRD'S BODY is almost completely covered with feathers, although some birds have bare legs. Feathers keep the bird warm, give it shape, color and pattern, and help most birds to fly. Some birds have special display feathers. Feathers carry out many important jobs, so they need to be kept in good condition.

What is a feather?

There are three main types of feather – flight, body, and down. Feathers grow out of pits or follicles in a bird's skin, like the hairs all over our bodies. They can be easily repaired because of the way the parts of the feather hook together.

Web or vane

Smooth, curved shaft for flight

Shaft or rachis

Macaw flight feather

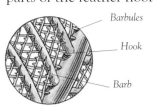

Barbules

Hook

Barb

BARBS AND BARBULES
Each side of a feather consists of parallel barbs, held in place by tiny hooks on side branches called barbules. There are many thousands of barbules on a flight feather.

FEATHER STRUCTURE
Feathers have a central shaft with a web or vane on either side. They are made of a strong, flexible material called keratin, which also forms our hair and nails.

FLIGHT FEATHERS

Found in the wings and tail, flight feathers provide a large area to push the bird through the air. Their special airfoil shape lifts the bird in the air, and controls the way it twists and turns in flight.

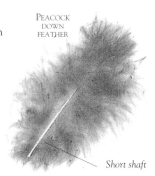

PEACOCK DOWN FEATHER

Short shaft

DOWN FEATHERS

The soft down feathers trap warm air next to the body and are important in young birds. The barbs are long and soft and the barbules do not hook up so the feather stays fluffy.

REGENT PARROT FLIGHT FEATHERS

Long shaft

AFRICAN GRAY PARROT BODY FEATHER

Inner fluffy part to keep bird warm

Quill

BODY FEATHERS

Overlapping like tiles on a roof, body feathers act as a weatherproof jacket. The inner part has softer barbs and the barbules have no hooks.

FEATHER FACTS

• Swans have 25,000 feathers, sparrows 3,500, and hummingbirds less than 1,000.

• The male crested argus pheasant has the largest tail feathers at 5¼ ft (173cm) long, 5in (13cm) wide.

• Feathers evolved from reptile scales.

• Grebes eat their feathers to help digestion.

Feather color

The colors of bird feathers are produced in two ways. One is by chemical pigments laid down in the feather when it is being formed. The other is by the structure of feathers and the way they reflect light. Bird colors help individuals of the same species to recognize each other. They also help birds attract a mate, threaten a rival, or camouflage themselves.

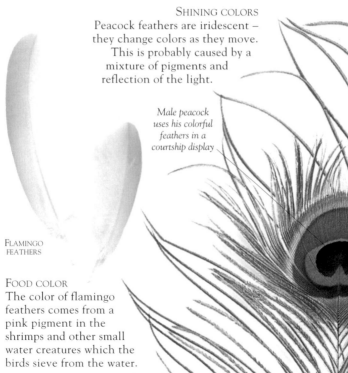

SHINING COLORS
Peacock feathers are iridescent – they change colors as they move. This is probably caused by a mixture of pigments and reflection of the light.

Male peacock uses his colorful feathers in a courtship display

FLAMINGO FEATHERS

FOOD COLOR
The color of flamingo feathers comes from a pink pigment in the shrimps and other small water creatures which the birds sieve from the water.

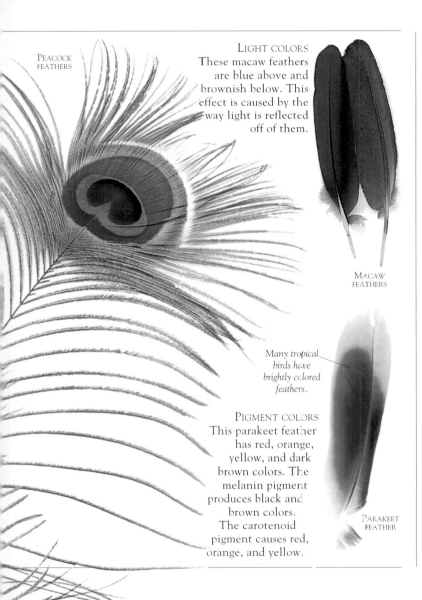

PEACOCK
FEATHERS

LIGHT COLORS
These macaw feathers
are blue above and
brownish below. This
effect is caused by the
way light is reflected
off of them.

MACAW
FEATHERS

*Many tropical
birds have
brightly colored
feathers.*

PIGMENT COLORS
This parakeet feather
has red, orange,
yellow, and dark
brown colors. The
melanin pigment
produces black and
brown colors.
The carotenoid
pigment causes red,
orange, and yellow.

PARAKEET
FEATHER

269

Looking after feathers

Birds must take great care of their feathers
and spend a few hours each day cleaning
and tidying their plumage.
They use the bill to
pull ruffled feathers
into shape, and
may also take
water or dust
baths. Many
birds spread
an oily liquid
over their
feathers to
keep them
waterproof.

YELLOW
CANARY
PREENING

PREENING
To preen its feathers, a bird draws
each one carefully through its bill.
This fits the barbs and barbules back
into place – like pulling up a zipper –
and cleans and smooths the feathers.
Preening also removes parasites, such
as feather lice, which live on feathers
and eat them.

*Most birds use
their feet to
preen their head
feathers.*

*The oil used for preening
comes from a special
gland at the base of the
tail, on the rump.*

BIRD BATH

Many birds, like the blue tit below, bathe in water. They clean their feathers and skin, and get ready for preening. Most birds bathe and preen regularly. Some also take dust baths, perhaps to get rid of parasites.

NEW FEATHERS

A new feather is rolled up as a cylinder inside a thin, horny sheath. When it is fully developed, the sheath splits open and flakes away. The feather can then unroll and begin to grow to its full length.

Emerging adult feather

Fully grown tail feather

Young penguins lose their fluffy feathers

MOLTING KING PENGUINS

Horny sheath

ADULT KESTREL FEATHER

YOUNG KESTREL FEATHER

GROWING FEATHERS

At least once a year, most birds molt their feathers and new feathers grow to replace old ones. Molting allows birds to replace worn or damaged feathers, and to change color as they grow up or the seasons change.

HOW BIRDS MOVE

TO FIND FOOD and escape danger, birds walk, run, hop, swim, and wade. Most birds can also fly. They have light bones, powerful flight muscles, and an efficients respiratory system. A few birds cannot fly. Some of these flightless birds run very fast indeed.

Flight

Most birds fly by flapping their wings up and down. As the wings beat down, they push the air back, making the bird move forward.

LIFT
Birds have curved wings covered with feathers to push and steer them through the air. The inner part of a bird's wing can stay still to provide lift.

TAKEOFF
A heavy bird, such as a swan, has to run while flapping its wings to get enough lift for take-off. Smaller birds take off by jumping into the air and then flapping their wings to create lift.

TAWNY OWL

COMING IN TO LAND

To land, birds slow down in midair, then drop gently to the ground, onto a perch. or the surface of the water, spreading out their wings and tail like brakes. Heavy birds land into the wind to help slow themselves down.

Strong legs to absorb impact of landing

Wings and tail spread to increase air resistance and drag

BLUE-AND-WHITE FLYCATCHER

CURVED WINGS

A bird's wing is an airfoil shape – curved on top and slightly hollow underneath. The air flows faster over the top, creating low air pressure, while air pressure underneath stays much the same. The difference in pressure produces lift.

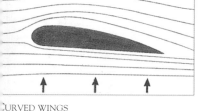

Fingerlike feathers to push and steer through the air

MUTE SWAN

Neck stretched out and feet tucked up to streamline bird's body

FLIGHT FACTS

- Common swifts may stay in the air for three years at a time without landing.

- Some hummingbirds beat their wings up to 90 times a second.

- Swans have been recorded flying as high as 29,500 ft (8,230 m).

- Peregrine falcons can reach speeds of 112 mph (180 km/h) when diving after prey.

273

Flight patterns

Different kinds of birds have differently shaped wings which they flap in patterns that suit their lifestyle. To save energy, some birds like gulls and vultures soar on rising air, while smaller birds glide between flaps of the wings. Ducks and other heavy birds flap their wings all the time they are in the air. A few, such as hummingbirds and kestrels, can hover in one spot.

Feathers spread apart on upstroke for air to slip through wing

UP AND DOWN FLIGHT
Small birds, like this red-tailed minla, have a bouncing, undulating flight. Bigger birds such as cranes, ducks, and geese tend to fly in straight lines.

RED-TAILED
MINLA

Eagles thermaling

Hot air rising

Seabirds have powerful flight muscles.

GLIDING AND SOARING
Seabirds glide upward on air currents rising from waves or over cliffs. Large birds of prey, such as eagles or vultures, also use natural currents of rising hot air to lift them higher into the air. These currents are called thermals.

GLIDING IN A THERMAL

HOVERING

Hummingbirds can hover, move straight up or down, and even fly backward. They do this by turning each wing in a circle, and using up and down wingbeats for extra power.

HUMMINGBIRD

Unlike other birds, hummingbirds have rigid wings with a swivel joint at the shoulder.

Between flaps, wings fold against body so bird can glide and rest

GLIDING
HERRING GULL

Feathers closed together on downstroke to push against the air

Tail used for steering and changing direction

Long, narrow wings for gliding

Feathers hug the body, creating a streamlined shape so air can flow past more easily

WING SHAPE

The size and shape of wings give clues to how a bird lives and helps with identification, especially if the bird is high in the sky.

Long and wide for soaring – vultures and some hawks

Long and narrow for gliding – fulmars and albatrosses

Wide and rounded for short, fast flight – pheasants

Narrow and pointed for fast flight – swallows and swifts

275

CASSOWARY AND CHICK

Flightless birds

A few birds do not fly at all. Some of them swim or run so well that they do not need to fly. Many flightless birds, such as ostriches, rheas, or emus, are very large birds that can run faster than their enemies, or can win a fight so easily that they do not need to fly away. Other flightless birds live on remote islands where there are few enemies from which they need to escape.

DEFENSE
With powerful legs and daggerlike claws, birds such as cassowaries do not need to fly away. Cassowaries even attack people, lashing out with strong feet and sharp nails.

GALAPAGOS CORMORANT

WING
Flightless birds usually have small, weak wing which are not strong enoug for flight. The Galapago cormorant uses its wings t help it balance on land

FLIGHTLESS FACTS

• The heaviest bird of all time was *Dromornis stirtoni*, a flightless bird that died out about 25,000 years ago.

• Ostriches are nearly seven times too heavy to fly. They have the biggest legs of any bird, over 4 ft (1.2 m) long.

• The Inaccessible Island rail is the world's smallest flightless bird, about the size of a chick.

BIRDS IN DANGER
Many flightless birds, such as this kakapo, are threatened by the cats and rats introduce to their island homes by settlers. Kakapos are too heavy to fly.

KAKAPO

GREATER
RHEA

FAST RUNNERS

Running away from danger can be just as good as
flying. Rheas can sprint faster than a horse,
reaching speeds of 31 mph (50 km/h), and are also
good swimmers. Rheas are related to ostriches and
emus and follow a similar lifestyle, but they live on
the South American grasslands, rather than on the
grasslands of Africa or Australia.

*Fluffy wings
used for display,
not flight*

*Long neck to
see over tall
grasses*

HUMBOLDT
PENGUIN

FAST SWIMMERS

Penguins are well
suited to their life
in the sea – they are
even a different
shape from most
birds. They use their
wings as flippers for
swimming, while
their feet and tail
steer like a rudder.

*Large leg
muscles
provide power
for running*

*Three strong toes
on each foot for
defense and for
running fast*

277

LEGS AND FEET

BIRDS USE their legs and feet for preening their feathers, as well as for moving around. The size and shape of their feet depends on where they live and how they feed.

Three toes point forward and one back.

Stringlike tendons

PERCHING
Birds that perch can sleep without falling off a branch. They bend their legs, pulling the tendons tight and drawing in the toes. This locks their feet tightly around the perch.

TAWNY
OWL
TALON

TALONS
Birds of prey, such as owls and eagles, have strong, sharp, curved claws called talons. They use these to catch and carry their prey.

Long toes are spread wide

WATTLED
JACANA

Scaly skin along each toe

WIDE TOES
Some water birds, such as coots, have lobes of skin on each toe. These push aside the water for faster swimming and help to stop the coot from sinking into mud.

COOT
TOES

LONG TOES
Jacanas, or lily trotters, have very long, thin toes. These spread the weight of the bird over a bigger area so it can "trot" across lily pads on the ponds and lakes where it lives.

278

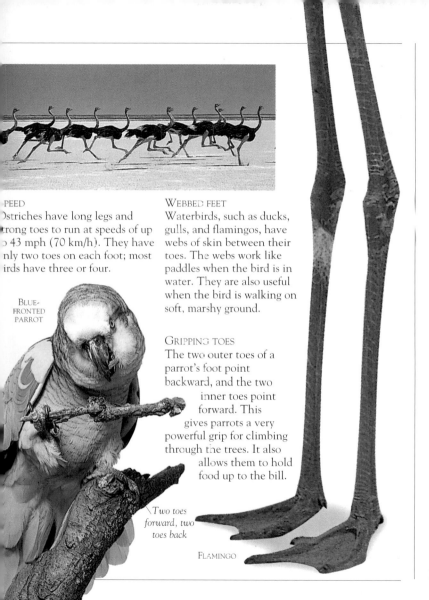

SPEED
Ostriches have long legs and strong toes to run at speeds of up to 43 mph (70 km/h). They have only two toes on each foot; most birds have three or four.

BLUE-FRONTED PARROT

WEBBED FEET
Waterbirds, such as ducks, gulls, and flamingos, have webs of skin between their toes. The webs work like paddles when the bird is in water. They are also useful when the bird is walking on soft, marshy ground.

GRIPPING TOES
The two outer toes of a parrot's foot point backward, and the two inner toes point forward. This gives parrots a very powerful grip for climbing through the trees. It also allows them to hold food up to the bill.

Two toes forward, two toes back

FLAMINGO

279

COLLARED
SUNBIRD SIPPING
NECTAR

FOOD AND FEEDING

BIRDS SPEND MUCH of their time finding food, whether pecking at berries and nuts, or snapping up fish or small mammals. They rely mainly on their eyes and ears to find food, and their bill or claws to catch it. A few birds steal their food from other birds. Some birds eat plants; others eat animals or have a mixed diet.

Hunting and fishing

Meat-eating birds usually catch weak or unfit prey. They may lie in wait to ambush their quarry, or chase after it through air or water. Most of these birds hunt by day; a few, such as owls, hunt at night.

GREAT WHITE
PELICAN

GOLDEN
EAGLE

BIRDS OF PREY
Most birds of prey, such as this golden eagle, soar high in the sky to search for food, then swoop down to seize and crush prey in their sharp talons. However, nine out of ten attacks are unsuccessful and the prey manages to escape.

A pelican's bill can hold more food than its stomach

UMBRELLA FISHING
Some birds have developed their own special techniques for catching food. The black heron shades the water with its wings. This cuts out reflections and makes it easier for the bird to see fish.

SNAKE HUNTERS
Secretary-birds are unusual because they search for their prey mainly on foot. They have tough scales on their legs for protection from snakebites. They pin prey to the ground with sharp claws.

SECRETARY-BIRDS

Great white pelicans eat about ½ lb (1.2 kg) of fish a day

Sharp, hooked bill to pull and tear at food

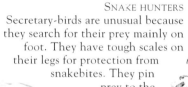

EGYPTIAN VULTURE

FISHING IN GROUPS
Great white pelicans usually fish in groups. The birds gather in a circle on the water, lifting their wings and plunging their bills into the water to drive the fish into the middle of the circle. Then they scoop up the fish.

USING TOOLS
A few birds use tools to find and obtain their food. Egyptian vultures throw or drop stones onto ostrich eggs to break open the thick shells.

281

What birds eat

Birds have healthy appetites. They need to eat large amounts of food to give them enough energy to fly, keep warm, build nests, and lay eggs. Some birds eat only one kind of food, while others, such as starlings, crows, and jays, eat almost anything. Vultures eat carcasses, the dead bodies of animals.

HELMET BIRD

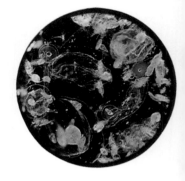

MICROSCOPIC SEAFOOD
A drop of seawater teems with tiny organisms such as diatoms, plankton, and crab larvae. This plankton floats about the oceans and is a vital part of the diet of many seabirds.

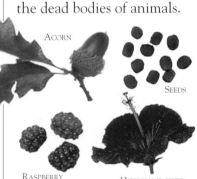

ACORN

SEEDS

RASPBERRY

HIBISCUS FLOWER

FLOWERS, FRUITS, AND SEEDS
For hummingbirds, the sweet liquid called nectar produced by flowers is a high-energy food. Many birds eat the fruits and seeds that develop when the flowers are pollinated.

GRASS

CABBAGE LEAF

CONIFER

GRASS AND LEAVES
A few birds, like geese, ducks, and grouse, eat grass and leaves. These ca be hard to digest and poor in nutrien so the birds have to eat a lot of this s of food to get the energy they need.

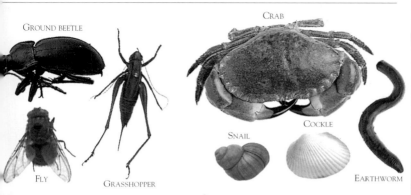

GROUND BEETLE

FLY

GRASSHOPPER

CRAB

SNAIL

COCKLE

EARTHWORM

INSECTS

dult insects are more abundant in armer weather, but caterpillars and ubs survive colder periods buried in il or under bark. Insects are a body-ilding food, vital for young birds.

INVERTEBRATES

Invertebrates such as crabs and shellfish are an important source of food on the seashore, where there are few insects. Garden and woodland birds, such as thrushes, eat juicy earthworms.

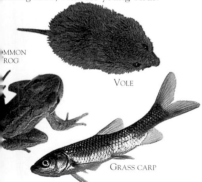

COMMON FROG

VOLE

GRASS CARP

VERTEBRATES

rds that feed on vertebrates (animals th backbones) have to work hard for als. The animals they hunt can run, im, or slither away, and often succeed escaping.

NEST AND YOUNG

EGGS AND YOUNG

Some birds eat the eggs and helpless young of other birds. For example, skuas pounce on puffin and penguin chicks, and magpies often take eggs and young birds from the nest.

Bird bills

A bird uses its bill like a hand to carry out all sorts of tasks, from catching and holding food to preening its feathers and building a nest. Parrots also use their bills to help them climb. The size and shape of a bird's bill depends mainly on what it eats and where it finds its food.

YELLOW-HEA[D]
PARROT

FRUIT-AND-NUT EATERS
A parrot's bill deals wit[h] two different kinds of food. The hook at the t[ip] pulls out the soft parts [of] fruit, while the strong nutcracker at the base opens seeds. Parrots use their feet to hold food.

Bee-eaters beat sting[ing] insects against a bra[nch] to get rid of the sting

WHITE
THROATED
BEE-EATER

INSECT EATERS
Birds that feed on insects have thin, pointed bills to probe und[er] bark and stones. Birds that eat flying insects have wide, gaping bills to scoop them up as they f[ly]

FLAMINGO

A flamingo dips its bill in the shallow water upside-down

FILTER-FEEDER
The flamingo has a very special bill. Sieve-like edges on the top bill filter out tiny plants, shrimps, and other invertebrates from the water. The bottom bill and the tongue move up and down to pump water through comblike fringes on the sides of the top bill.

BLACK-CROWNED
NIGHT-HERON

*Bill used to
stab fish*

GOULDIAN
FINCH

*Powerful bill that is
broad at the base and
pointed at the tip.*

FISH EATERS
A dagger-shaped bill is characteristic of fish-eating birds, such as herons. Others, such as ospreys, have a hooked bill with which to tear the fish into pieces.

SEED EATERS
To crack open seeds, seed-eating birds such as finches have pyramid-shaped bills. The hawfinch's bill is so strong it can even crush cherry stones.

SCARLET-CHESTED
SUNBIRD

*Flaps over
nostrils keep out
flower pollen*

NECTAR EATERS
Nearly one-fifth of all the world's birds feed on nectar. Sunbirds and hummingbirds push their needlelike bills into flowers and lick up the sweet nectar.

*Powerful
hooked bill to
tear up food*

GOLDEN
EAGLE

MEAT EATERS
Often called birds of prey, these include eagles, owls, and falcons. They use their bills to pull apart animals they kill into bite-sized chunks. Owls swallow small animals, such as voles and mice, whole.

COURTSHIP

BEFORE MATING, male birds usually
court the females. Some males grow
more colorful or elaborate feathers for
the breeding season. They may give
singing or dancing displays. Some
show off nest-building
or hunting skills.

YELLOW-
THROATED
LAUGHING-
THRUSH

TERRITORY
Many birds nest in an area, or territory,
which has enough food for their young
when they hatch out. Male birds sing in
their territory to attract a mate and keep
away other males.

*Laughing-thrushes
make loud,
cackling sounds*

MALE
PIN-TAILED
WHYDAH

MALES AND FEMALES
Male and female birds of
the same species often
look different. The
male is usually more
colorful, but the
dull colors of the
female help
camouflage
her on the
nest.

*Female bird
duller, with
short tail*

*Long tail
feathers used in
display flight to
impress females*

FEMALE
PIN-TAILED
WHYDAH

MALE
PEACOCK

*Male's long
feathers make
flight difficult*

DISPLAY
The male peacock
erects his long,
colorful feathers in
a shimmering fan to
impress a female. After the
breeding season, the long tail
feathers fall out.

RED-CROWNED
CRANES

*The "eyes"
may hypnotize
the female.*

DANCING
Some birds dance together
before they mate. Cranes jump
up and down in the air with
their partners. Great crested
grebes perform a series of
dances, including head-shaking.

287

NESTS AND EGGS

ALL BIRDS LAY EGGS and most build nests
to keep eggs and young safe and warm.
Birds know instinctively how to
build a nest, and female birds
usually do most of the work. Nests
vary from a shallow scrape in the
ground and simple cup shapes, to
more elaborate constructions.

NEST BOX

Building a nest

Birds use a wide range of
nesting materials and may
make hundreds of trips to
collect material. Nest materials must both
support the nest and keep the young warm.
Nest boxes encourage birds to nest in
gardens or woods with few
natural tree holes.

WAGTAIL
NEST

PEBBLE
NEST
Oystercatchers lay their
eggs in a shallow dip, or
scrape, on the shoreline.
Their eggs are difficult to

TWIGS
Most hedgerow and
woodland birds use twigs
and sticks to support
their nests since these
are readily available.

FEATHERS
Birds use feathers as a
warm lining for a nest.
Hundreds of feathers li
a long-tailed tit's nest.

To make the cup shape, birds turn around and around.

MOSS
Moss traps warm air in the nest and stops heat loss. It helps to keep both eggs and young birds warm.

STRING
Birds often collect household materials when nest-building. Pieces of string have been found in many nests.

MUD
Some nests are lined with wet mud mixed with saliva and droppings. When it dries, it forms a hard and strong lining.

MUD NEST
Swallows and martins collect mud with their bills, and build nests with pieces of mud stuck together with saliva.

Woodpeckers have chisellike bills.

TREE NEST
Woodpeckers dig nest holes in rotten trees with their strong beaks. Many other birds use existing tree holes. The nests inside the holes are usually lined with grass or feathers.

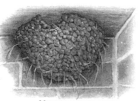

HOUSE MARTIN NEST

GRASS
Grass is a flexible nest material. It is used by many birds because it is easy to weave into differently shaped nests.

289

Unusual nests

From woven purses and saliva cups to mud ovens and compost heaps, some birds' nests are quite unusual, while others are very elaborate. They may be a strange shape, such as the trumpetlike weaverbird nests, or made with unusual materials, such as the bird's own saliva.

PENDULINE TIT NEST

Strong and lightweight basket

False entrance

WOVEN NEST
A male West African weaver knotted grasses to weave this nest. The entrance tunnel stops snakes and other enemies from getting inside.

PURSE NEST
The penduline-tit weaves hanging nest from grasses, leaves, and moss. A false entrance leads to an empty chamber and dead end.

THATCHED COTTAGE
Each colony of the social weaverbirds of South Africa builds a huge "haystack" that is up to 13 ft (4 m) deep and 24 ft (7.2 m) across. Up to 300 pairs then build their nests under the protection of this thatched roof.

WEAVER NEST

NEST FACTS

- Biggest nest ever found: a bald eagle's which was 9½ ft (2.9 m) wide and 20 ft (6 m) deep.

- A bee hummingbird's nest is no bigger than a thimble.

- A malleefowl's nest is a "compost heap" of rotting vegetation.

- A hamerkop nest may consist of over 10,000 sticks.

BASKET NEST

Reed warblers join their nest to several reed stems. This helps to hold the nest steady as the wind blows. The nest is made from grass, reed fibers, and feathers.

Nest is joined to reeds

REED WARBLER NEST

TAILORBIRD NEST

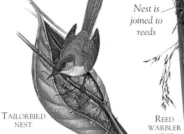

SEWING BIRD

The tailorbird sews a pocket of leaves to support its nest. Its sharp bill makes a row of holes along the edges of the leaves. Then the bird pulls spider or insect silk or plant material through the holes to stitch the leaves.

NORTHERN ORIOLE NEST

STRING NEST

Many birds that nest near people make use of artificial materials. This northern oriole has used pieces of string in its baglike nest, and has even joined the nest to a twig with string.

291

All kinds of eggs

Like dinosaurs and other reptiles, birds lay eggs in which the embryos grow and are nourished. Some birds lay one large clutch (set of eggs) in a season, while others lay several smaller clutches. Some birds, such as snowy owls, lay extra clutches if there is plenty of food. No two eggs have exactly the same markings. The color and shape depend on where the eggs are laid and how much camouflage they need.

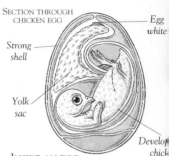

SECTION THROUGH CHICKEN EGG

Egg white

Strong shell

Yolk sac

Developing chick

INSIDE AN EGG
A bird's egg contains a developing bird – an embryo – plus a store of food and a supply of air. Pores in the shell allow air to pass through from outside. The egg white supplies proteins, water, and vitamins.

EGG FACTS

• One ostrich egg has the same volume as 24 hens' eggs.

• Cuckoos can lay eggs in a few seconds; some birds take 1-3 minutes.

• Nearly 80 species of bird lay eggs in the nests of other species.

• Gray partridges lay the largest clutches – up to 16 eggs.

• Most small eggs take under an hour to hatch.

BARN OWL EGG

WHITE EGGS
Birds that nest in holes or burrows, such as owls or kingfishers, usually lay white eggs. They do not need to be camouflaged because they are hidden.

CURLEW EGG

SPECKLED EGGS
Birds that nest in the open, where there is little cover, usually lay patterned eggs. The camouflage colors hide the eggs from predators.

PALE EGG

SPECKLED EGG

DARK EGG

DISGUISE
Female cuckoos lay their eggs in the nests of other birds such as catbirds, robins, wrens, or meadow pipits. The foster parents raise the cuckoo chick as their own. The cuckoo's egg looks similar to those of the foster parents.

COLORS IN A CLUTCH
The three eggs above were laid by a single snipe but come from different clutches. In one clutch, the eggs usually look similar.

CUCKOO EGG

Pear shape to roll in a circle

EURASIAN ROBIN EGGS

PATTERNS
Common murre eggs show a variety of patterns and colors, possibly to help parent birds recognize them. The pear shape stops it from rolling off cliff ledges.

BIG AND SMALL
Ostriches lay the largest eggs of any living bird. Each egg weighs about 3½ lb (1.7 kg), and is as long as an adult human's hand. Hummingbirds' eggs, however, are only as big as peas.

HUMMINGBIRD EGGS

OSTRICH EGG

293

BIRTH AND GROWTH

PARENT BIRDS SIT on their eggs to keep them warm so that the chicks inside can develop properly. This is called incubation. After the chicks hatch, the parents work hard feeding the chicks, keeping them warm and clean, and protecting them from enemies.

Egg to chick

SWAN INCUBATING
EGGS IN NEST

In order to incubate, most birds develop patches of bare skin, brood patches, to let body warmth through to the eggs. Small birds incubate for about two weeks, eagles for five to seven weeks, and albatrosses for up to 11 weeks. Some baby birds are helpless when they hatch. Others can soon run around.

First the chick pecks at shell to make a hole

Then chick cuts a circle

Chick pushes to widen crack

HATCHING
To break out of its shell, a baby bird chips away with a pointed "egg tooth" on top of its bill. This egg tooth disappears soon after hatching. Some chicks, such as quail, can walk about immediately after hatching out of their shells.

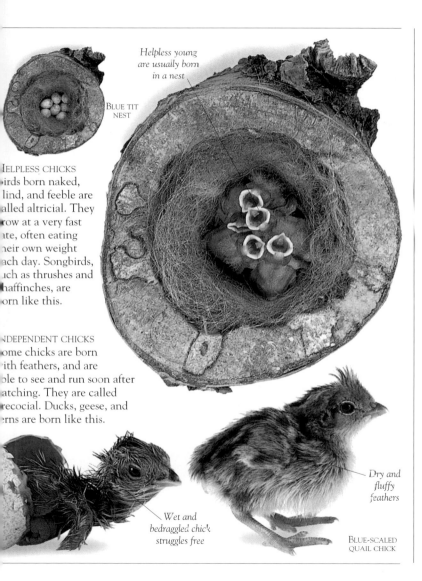

Helpless young are usually born in a nest

BLUE TIT NEST

HELPLESS CHICKS
Birds born naked, blind, and feeble are called altricial. They grow at a very fast rate, often eating their own weight each day. Songbirds, such as thrushes and chaffinches, are born like this.

INDEPENDENT CHICKS
Some chicks are born with feathers, and are able to see and run soon after hatching. They are called precocial. Ducks, geese, and terns are born like this.

Wet and bedraggled chick struggles free

Dry and fluffy feathers

BLUE-SCALED QUAIL CHICK

295

Growing up

Baby birds take a few weeks or a few months to grow up. They all rely on their parents to keep them warm and out of danger, and most chicks are fed by their parents as well. Small birds may make hundreds of feeding trips in a day; larger birds only two or three. Chicks that are born helpless grow faster than chicks that hatch fluffy and alert.

EAGLE AND CHICKS

HEN AND CHICKS

BIRDS OF PREY
Eagles and other birds of prey tear up food for their chicks at first. As the chicks grow bigger, they learn to tear it up for themselves.

INDEPENDENT FEEDERS
Some baby birds, such as chicks, ducklings, and goslings, can feed themselves soon after hatching. At first, they peck at anything, then they watch their parents to find out what to eat.

PECKING SPOT
A herring gull chick pecks at a red spot on its parent's bill to make the parent cough up food. Herring gulls feed out at sea, so they swallow food rather than carry it long distances.

HERRING GULL

CRECHE OF YOUNG
KING PENGUINS

Young penguins huddle together for warmth and protection while their parents are away.

SAFETY IN NUMBERS
Young penguins cannot join their parents in the water until they have grown waterproof adult feathers. The parent birds leave them behind when they go to sea to feed. When they return, the adults cough up partly digested fish for the chicks, but there may be a wait of days or even weeks between meals.

JUVENILE
STARLING

A young starling takes off unsteadily for its first flight

FIRST FLIGHT
Baby birds have to learn how to fly as quickly as possible to avoid predators and other dangers. They flap their wings while they are in the nest to exercise their muscles and make them strong. Taking off and landing is not easy – many young birds crash-land.

MIGRATION

NEARLY HALF the world's birds migrate to find food and water, to nest, or to avoid bad weather. They navigate by instinct, but use familiar landmarks, the Sun, Moon, and stars, and the Earth's magnetic field to find their way. Migration journeys are often dangerous for birds and use up a lot of energy. Some small birds double their weight to provide enough fuel for traveling.

RED-BREASTED GOOSE

NESTING
This goose is one of many birds that migrate to arctic tundra to nest in the brief summer when there is plenty of food available.

MIGRATION ROUTES

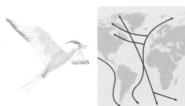

ARCTIC TERN
This is the champion bird migrant, flying from the Arctic to Antarctica and back each year. It spends summer in both polar regions.

AMERICAN GOLDEN-PLOVER
This plover has the longest migration of any land bird. It breeds in northern Canada and flies to the Argentinian pampas for the winter

...-FORMATION

...lying in a V-shaped formation helps birds to
...ve energy on a long journey. The birds
...llowing the leader fly in the slipstream of
the bird in front. When the leader
tires, another bird
takes over.

SNOW GEESE
MIGRATING

*Snow geese breed in
the arctic tundra and
migrate to the Gulf of
Mexico for the winter.*

HIMALAYAN
MONAL
PHEASANTS

MOUNTAIN MIGRATION
Some birds migrate short
distances. The Himalayan
monal, a pheasant, migrates up
and down the mountains with
the seasons, moving to warmer,
lower slopes in winter.

MIGRATION FACTS

• American golden-
plovers are fast
migrants, flying
2,050 miles (3,300 km)
in 35 hours.

• The ruby-throated
hummingbird travels
2,000 miles (3,200 km)
across the Americas

• Most migrating birds
fly below 300 ft (91 m).

...HORT-TAILED SHEARWATER
...etween breeding seasons off
...outhern Australia, this bird flies
... a figure-eight route from Australia
... the North Pacific and back again.

GREATER WHITETHROAT
This small warbler breeds in Europe
in spring and summer, and then
migrates to Africa just south of the
Sahara Desert for the winter.

WHERE BIRDS LIVE

FROM BUSY CITIES to frozen polar regions, birds have adapted to a range of habitats on every continent. Where birds live depends on the food they eat and their nesting requirements, as well as their competitors and predators. In many parts of the world, people have had a destructive influence on the distribution of birds.

NORTH
AMERICA

SOUTH
AMERICA

SEAS, CLIFFS, AND SHORES
Marine habitats are a huge feeding ground for many birds. They nest on islands and continental shores.

DESERTS AND GRASSLAND
These dry, mainly hot habitats provide little shelter for birds. Food and water may be hard to find.

POLAR AND TUNDRA
In the Antarctic, Arctic, and tundra, it is cold and windy. Birds breed there in summer.

RIVERS, LAKES, AND SWAMPS
Lakes and rivers are freshwater, while marshes and swamps are fresh- or saltwater.

FOREST AND WOODLAND
Conifers and broad-leaved trees grow in temperate climates where there is usually rain all year.

ARCTIC

EUROPE

ASIA

AFRICA

AUSTRALASIA

NTARCTICA

CTIES AND FARMLAND
Birds that have adapted to live near people can take advantage of the extra food and the less severe climate.

RAINFOREST
These are mostly hot, wet habitats near the Equator in the Americas, Africa, southeast Asia, and northeast Australia.

MOUNTAINS AND MOORLANDS
Moorlands occur in cool, wet uplands. Mountains have a variety of habitats.

301

CITIES AND FARMLAND

BIRDS HAVE LEARNED to live close to people, and eat the food we give them, as well as insects, plants, and crops around our homes. Birds that used to nest on cliffs or in caves, nest in buildings or under bridges. Woodland birds nest in hedgerows.

EURASIAN KESTREL

HUNTING BIRDS
Most birds of prey do not like living near people, but kestrels and sparrowhawks hunt along roadsides and in parks.

HABITAT FACTS

• At night, a city is as much as 9°F (5°C) warmer than the surrounding countryside.

• Some starling roosts in cities may contain over one million birds.

• Of every 10 birds caught in the wild, only 1 reaches the pet shop alive.

• The African red-billed quelea is the world's worst agricultural bird pest.

BLUE BUDGERIGAR

CITY BIRDS
Birds such as geese fly over cities on migration routes, or land to feed and roost in city parks. Starlings roost in city centers at night because it is warmer than the countryside.

CAGED BIRDS
Many people keep birds such as budgerigars, canaries, and parrots in cages. They like their colors, their company, and their songs. People breed birds to create colors never seen in the wild.

BARN
WALLOW
FEEDING
YOUNG

SONG THRUSH

NESTS IN BUILDINGS
Attics, barns, and
even chimney pots make
ideal nesting places for birds
used to nesting on cliffs, rocky
hillsides, or trees. Swallows used
to nest in caves, but now many
nest inside buildings.

NESTS IN HEDGEROWS
Hedgerows are small strips of
woodland where birds such as
the song thrush can nest safely.
Birds roost and feed in hedgerows.
They are an important refuge in
open areas of crops and grass.

SONG THRUSH NEST

303

HOMES AND STREETS

MANY BIRDS HAVE LOST their natural fear of people and live near our homes and in our cities, despite all the noise and pollution. These urban birds change their diet or the places they nest to take advantage of our leftover food scraps, the artificial habitats we build, and the warm climates we create.

HOUSE SPARROW
By following people from country to country, the fearless house sparrow has spread from Europe and Asia over two-thirds of the world's land surface. It nests in buildings close to people.

This is a male with a gray crown and black bib.

CAGED BIRDS
Every year, people take thousands of birds from the wild, often illegally. This has critically reduced the numbers of some wild birds, especially parrots.

The house sparrow is friendly and intelligent.

WHITE STORKS
In many parts of Europe, white storks are believed to bring good luck. They often nest on roofs, and people may put up platforms to encourage them.

Red streak below eye and upright black crest

HOUSE CROW
The aggressive house crow is always ready to grasp a tasty morsel of food. It lives near busy towns and small villages in India, as well as in other parts of Asia, often swarming in large, busy groups.

Likes to perch on a high branch to sing

RED-WHISKERED BULBUL
The inquisitive red-whiskered bulbul is not frightened of people and is a common species around the villages of Asia. It has a pleasant and varied song and is often kept as a pet.

Pigeons are tame enough to be fed by hand.

PIGEON
The city pigeons of today are descended from the wild rock doves that people originally kept for food and, later, for racing. Pigeons are the only bird group to feed their young with a secretion called pigeon's milk.

City pigeons even travel on subways.

305

PARKS AND GARDENS

FROM TREES AND FLOWERBEDS to grassy lawns and garden ponds, parks and gardens contain a great variety of habitats for birds. People put up feeding tables, birdbaths, and nesting boxes to encourage birds to live near houses. Unfortunately, pets such as cats often catch and kill garden birds.

BLACK-BILLED MAGPIE
This adaptable magpie visits surburban gardens. It eats a range of food, especially insects and small rodents, but also steals eggs and young from the nests of other birds.

Pale gray border

Orange breast and face typical of robins

EUROPEAN ROBIN
These birds are aggressive. Males often set up territories in gardens and sing loudly to keep away other male robins. In winter, both males and females defend feeding territories.

BLUE TITS
These bold, lively birds often visit gardens in winter to feed on nuts, seeds, and leftover food scraps put out by people. They can easily land on nut feeders and often use the nest boxes that people build and put up for them.

Blue tits are agile, acrobatic birds.

Cone-shaped bill typical of a seed eater

WATERFOWL IN PARKS
The artificial lakes in parks make a welcome feeding, resting, and nesting area for swans, ducks, and grebes. Islands in the middle of lakes provide safe nesting places.

NORTHERN CARDINAL
These cardinals are frequent visitors to feeders in the backyards of North America. They often move around in pairs or family groups to feed on seeds that people leave out for them.

SUPERB STARLING
A common visitor to campsites and hotels in East Africa, the superb starling is a tame bird, not frightened of people. It feeds mainly on the ground, pecking up seeds, fruit, and insects.

FIELDS AND HEDGEROWS

FARMLAND HAS TAKEN the place of woodlands, grasslands, and wetlands, but some birds have adapted to this habitat. They feed on the crops and nest in the animal pastures, hedges, orchards, and farm buildings. However, numbers of farmland birds have been reduced by the removal of hedgerows and the use of poisonous pesticides.

EUROPEAN GOLDFINCH
Flocks of goldfinches feed on weeds along the edges of fields. They are light enough to perch on thistle heads and eat the seeds.

FOLLOWING THE PLOW
Large flocks of birds, such as black-headed gulls, often follow a tractor plowing a field. The birds feed on the insects and other invertebrates, such as worms, exposed by the plow.

Gulls feed on newly plowed land.

RING-NECKED PHEASANT
The female pheasant may nest in hedgerows, making a shallow scrape in the ground in which she lays her eggs. Pheasants wander over farmland, feeding mainly on grains, seeds, berries, and insects.

HOOPOE
In the Mediterranean the reeds and grasses under the olive groves teem with invertebrates. Hoopoes probe the ground with long curved bills for worms and insects.

DUNNOCK
Sometimes called the hedge sparrow, the dunnock is not related to a sparrow at all – it just looks like one. Dunnocks nest in hedgerows, where they build cup-shaped nests.

The chicks are well camouflaged, like their mother.

The gray head and underparts help to tell the dunnock from a sparrow

FOREST AND WOODLAND

WITH PLENTY OF FOOD and safe nesting places, forests and woodlands provide a rich habitat for birds, from the treetops right down to the forest floor. A greater variety of birds live in the deciduous and eucalyptus woodlands than in the dark coniferous forests, because of the more favorable climates.

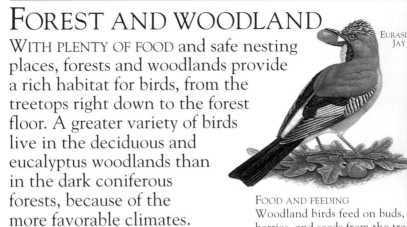

EURASIAN JAY

FOOD AND FEEDING
Woodland birds feed on buds, berries, and seeds from the tree and shrubs. Some eat insects and small animals. Diets may vary with changes in season.

BIRDSONG
Most woodland birds, such as the nightingale, have loud songs and calls to attract mates, and establish breeding territories in the thick undergrowth.

RING-NECKED PHEASANT WING

NIGHTINGALE

WINGS
Many woodland birds have short, broad, rounded wings to help them rise quickly into the air and avoid twigs and branches. Pheasants can fly quickly for short distances.

NESTS IN HOLES
Holes in trees are safe and warm places for birds such as redstarts to raise a family. In the nesting season, the adults frequently fly in and out with food for the growing young.

MALE
REDSTART

CAMOUFLAGED
WOODCOCK

CAMOUFLAGE
Many woodland and forest birds are well camouflaged to protect them from predators. The dull, mottled colors of this woodcock hide it against the decaying leaf litter of the woodland floor.

DECIDUOUS WOODLAND

IN THESE WARM, moist woodlands, a great variety of birds can live together by feeding at different levels, sharing the available food. In warm weather, the birds nest, raise young, and eat as much as they can. In cold weather, leaves fall off the trees and some birds migrate to warmer places.

Thick skull

Two toes facing forward and two backward

WOODPECKER SKULL

YELLOW-FRONTED WOODPECKER
This thrush-sized woodpecker of South America hammers into decaying tree trunks to find insect larvae and make nesting holes. It licks up insects with its long, sticky tongue.

Strong, stiff tail feathers for support

LONG-TAILED TITS

Long-tailed tits flit about on the edges of woodlands pecking insects and spiders off the leaves and bark. Outside the breeding season, the tits huddle in small groups at night to keep warm.

GREEN WOODHOOPOE

These birds probe tree trunks with their long, curved bills searching for food. They live in noisy family groups in African woodlands.

Long bill is used to find insect grubs or eggs and spiders.

The bill is broad at the base to catch insects.

SPOTTED FLYCATCHER

Perching on exposed branches, spotted flycatchers dart out to snap up passing insects. In cold weather, they migrate to warmer places, such as Africa, to find food.

Green woodhoopoes have high, cackling calls

WHIP-POOR-WILL

During the day, this well-camouflaged bird sleeps on the woodland floor. At night, it flies near the ground catching insects.

313

CAPERCAILLIE
The capercaillie is able to eat pine needles to help it survive through the winter. Comblike fringes on its toes keep it from sinking into snow.

CONIFEROUS FOREST

DARK CONIFEROUS FORESTS – the taiga – stretch across the top of the Northern Hemisphere from the tundra in the north to the more open deciduous woodlands in the south. The leaves stay on the trees all year round, but winters are bitterly cold and most birds leave for warmer places. In the short summer, they feed on berries, seeds, or insects.

EURASIAN SISKIN
The restless and acrobatic siskin often hangs upside-down to pull the seeds out of pine and larch cones. Siskins are social birds and build nests high in conifer trees, where predators cannot easily reach the young birds.

The siskin feeds on the seeds of pine, larch, alder, and birch trees.

ED CROSSBILL
Crossbills use their scissor-like bill to lever apart the scales on the cones of pine, spruce, larch, and other conifers to reach the seeds. Parent crossbills cough up partly digested pine seeds to feed to their young.

PINE CONES

Scales
levered apart
by a crossbill

JAPANESE WAXWING
These birds are named for the red waxlike tips on some of their flight feathers. Waxwings eat berries or fruit, but will also catch insects when they can. They migrate south in the autumn in large numbers.

Waxwings
live in
large flocks

Male and
female birds
are similar
in color

JUVENILE BALD EAGLE
Bald eagles live in forests near water, where they hunt for fish and waterbirds. They do not grow the white feathers on the head and tail until they are four years old.

315

EUCALYPTUS WOODLAND

IN THE EVERGREEN eucalyptus woodlands of
Australia, there is food and shelter for a variety
of unique birds all year. The birds
help to pollinate the trees and
shrubs and spread their seeds.
In the rainy season, waterbirds
gather in marshy areas on the
border of these woodlands.

*Strong, hooked
beak characteristic
of parrot family*

MALLEEFOWL
These birds build a huge moun
of rotting vegetation covered
with sand to keep their eggs
warm. The male checks the
temperature with his bill.

*Two toes in
front and two
toes behind*

RAINBOW LORIKEETS
Noisy flocks of rainbow lorikeets feed
high in the trees. They crush the flowers
of eucalyptus and other flowering trees to
soak up the sticky mixture of nectar and
pollen with their fringe-tipped tongues.

Large, broad-based bill to catch and swallow prey

Large head and bill with brown ear patch

LAUGHING KOOKABURRA
Named for its very noisy, chuckling calls, the laughing kookaburra is a giant kingfisher that rarely eats fish. Instead, it pounces on reptiles such as snakes, small mammals, birds, and invertebrates.

317

Feathers are fanned out to make owl look frightening.

OWLS

MOST OWLS SLEEP by day and hunt by night. Their sharp hearing and keen eyesight help them catch prey such as mice and small birds. Many owls roost in trees and have brown feathers for camouflage.

SCOPS-OWL
Almost impossible to spot because of its superb camouflage, the scops-owl eats large insects. Here, it is seen defending itself from an enemy.

In a complete pellet, animal fur and bones are all stuck together.

Owl mucus binds pellet together

OWL FACTS
- Order *Strigiformes*
- About 174 species
- Mainly nocturnal
- Birds of prey
- Eat birds, insects, and small mammals
- Habitat: mainly woodland
- Nest in tree holes or other bird's nests
- Eggs: white

OWL PELLETS
Once or twice a day, owls cough up pellets containing indigestible bits of their last meal, such as fur or bones. Pulling a pellet apart reveals what an owl has eaten.

SOUTHERN BOOBOOK
This small Australian owl gets its name from its double hoot. It feeds mainly on insects.

Large feet with hooked talons

318

BARN OWL

A heart-shaped face is the trademark of the barn owl, a bird so different from other owls that it is in a separate family. The disk of feathers on the face collects sounds like a radar dish. Barn owls make a haunting shrieking sound.

Owls catch and kill prey with their sharp talons.

"Ears" are only tufts of feathers.

EURASIAN EAGLE-OWL

The largest of all owls, eagle owls are powerful hunters, strong enough to attack hares and mallards. They have very loud hoots: male eagle owls can be heard hooting over ½ mile (1 km) away.

BARN OWL FEATHER

TAWNY OWL FEATHER

OWL FEATHERS

Soft, velvety feathers with fringes on the flight feathers muffle the sound made by the wings in flight.

Thick covering of soft feathers

319

RAINFOREST

TROPICAL RAINFORESTS are the richest bird habitats. They provide a wealth of food and safe nesting places, and a warm, wet climate throughout the year. Rainforest birds usually have short, broad wings to twist and turn easily when flying through the trees. This unique habitat is under threat from forestry, mining, dams, and farming.

BIRDS-OF-PARADISE
Male birds-of-paradise have ornate and colorful feathers to attract females. They live only in the dense rainforests of northeastern Australia and Papua New Guinea.

CANOPY

UNDERSTORY

FOREST FLOOR

LAYERS OF LIFE
The birds live at different levels in the trees. In this way, they share the available food and nesting places, so a huge variety of birds live close together.

SPREADING SEEDS
Fruit-eating birds such as aracaris and parrots help to spread the seeds of rainforest trees. They feed on fruits and pass the seeds in their droppings.

Wide tail helps the aracari to balance on branches

CHESTNUT-EARED
ARACARI

Long bill with
serrated edge

Groups of crested
oropendolas hang
their woven nests
from tree branches.

NESTING

To keep their nests
out of sight and out of
reach of predators, rainforest birds nest
high in the trees or in dense thickets above
the ground. Some, such as parrots and
hornbills, nest in tree holes.

COLOR

The bright colors of rainforest
birds like these macaws are
surprisingly hard to see among the
leafy trees. These birds are feeding
on mineral-rich soil.

HABITAT FACTS

• Since 1945, over half
the rainforests have been
destroyed; an area the
size of a soccer field is
cut down every second.

• Rainforests contain
over 50 percent of all
plant and animal species.

• One-fifth of all the
kinds of birds in the
world live in the
Amazon rainforest.

UNDER THE CANOPY

BENEATH THE GREEN ROOF of the forest is the dark, cool understory of smaller trees, shrubs, and climbing plants, and below this, the leafy forest floor. There is less food and warmth at these lower levels than up in the canopy, so there are fewer birds. Large birds such as trumpeters and cassowaries stalk across the forest floor. In the understory, hummingbirds and jacamars flit through the branches.

HOATZIN CHICK

HOATZIN
Groups of hoatzins live along riverbanks in the rainforests of South America. They are poor fliers and make short, noisy flights through the trees.

Chick has claws on its wings for climbing

DOUBLE-WATTLED CASSOWARY
This huge cassowary melts into the forest if it senses danger. Males make loud, booming calls during courtship. The horny casque on its head is used to push aside forest undergrowth.

SUNBITTERN
This bird is named fo the sunset colors on i wings, visible during its courtship display. At other times, it is well camouflaged by the mottled gray and brown colors of its feathers.

Male not displaying

Courtship display of male

BLUE BIRDS-OF-PARADISE

The male blue bird-of-paradise performs a dramatic upside-down display to show off his iridescent feathers to a female. He also makes a series of loud, vibrating notes. Females look after the young on their own.

These birds live in the middle or upper levels of the rainforest, rarely coming down to the ground.

ASIAN FAIRY-BLUEBIRDS

Noisy fairy-bluebirds move busily through the trees searching for fruit, such as figs. The metallic blue of the male is not easy to see in the shade of the trees.

...airy-bluebirds ...n make sharp, ...histling calls.

IN THE TREETOPS

HIGH UP IN THE RAINFOREST CANOPY it is light and warm and there is plenty of food, especially fruits, seeds, and insect life. Bird life includes large bird predators such as eagles which patrol the treetops looking for prey. Canopy bird such as parrots and toucans, climb well and have strong feet for grasping branches.

Bare, orange-yellow face and bill

HARPY EAGLE
The huge harpy eagle is one of the most powerful birds of prey. It swoops into the canopy to seize monkeys (like this capuchin), birds, sloths, a reptiles. It can fly very fas through the branches.

LADY ROSS'S TURACO
This African turaco lives in small, noi groups, usually high in the canopy. Although clumsy fliers, turacos are good at running along tree branche They make a great variety of cackling and croaking calls.

OCO TOUCAN

his is the largest toucan, with
bill up to 7½ in (19 cm) long. The bill
hollow with supporting struts, so it is
ot as heavy as it looks. The colors
elp it to recognize other toucans
nd find a mate.

ORANGE-BELLIED LEAFBIRD

This Asian leafbird helps to
ollinate the forest trees as it
eeds on nectar. It also
preads the seeds of
lants in the
istletoe family
y eating the
erries.

*This leafbird is
good at
mimicking other
birds' songs*

*The casque is a thin layer
of skin and bone over
a honeycomb structure.*

GREAT HORNBILL

The hornbills of Southeast Asia and
Africa look like the toucans of South
America because they live and feed in
a similar way. They are named for the
horny casques on their bills. No-one
knows how these bony growths are used.

325

BIRDS

PARROTS

MOST PARROTS are brightly
colored and live in
tropical forests. They
tend to fly about in
flocks, making
harsh, screeching
calls. Many
species are threatened by
habitat destruction.
There are three main
groups: the lories, the
cockatoos, and the parrots.

Narrow, tapering
wings to fly fast
through the trees

CANARY-
WINGED PARAKEET
This small parrot's
long tail helps
balance as it flies. Large
parrots usually have broad,
rounded wings and fly more
slowly. One parrot, the
kakapo, cannot fly at all.

CHATTERING LORY
The chattering lory spends most
of its time high in the trees
feeding mainly on pollen
and nectar. Lories have a
long tongue with a
brushlike tip which
picks up pollen as
they drink.

YELLOW-CRESTED
COCKATOO
Cockatoos raise and lower their
head crests when they are
excited, frightened, or
angry. They
also do this
when landing
on a perch.

PARROT FACTS

- Family: *Psittacidae*
- About 330 species
- Diurnal
- Tropical land birds
- Eat fruits, seeds,
nuts, and other
plant parts; also some
invertebrates
- Habitat: forest,
scrub, grassland, and
mountains
- Nest: usually tree
hole, hole in bank or
among rocks.

ECLECTUS PARROTS
These parrots are unusual because the bright
red female is such a different color from
the green male. Males
and females mostly
look alike.
Eclectus parrots
feed
on fruits,
nuts, and
leaf
buds.

*Nutcracker
bill to crush
seeds and nuts*

SKULL AND BILL
Parrots have large, broad skulls
with a fairly big space for the
brain – they are intelligent
birds. The top bill curves
sharply down, fitting neatly
over the broad bottom bill,
which curves upward.

*Many parrots
have green feathers
to camouflage
them in the leaves
of the trees.*

*Two toes point
forward and two
backward to give
a powerful grip.*

RIVERS, LAKES, AND SWAMPS

WATERY HABITATS are home to a rich variety of birds. There are plenty of plants, invertebrates, and fish for birds to eat, and safe nesting places in reeds and on riverbanks. Many birds rest and feed on lakes, marshes, and swamps during migration. But drainage schemes, dams, acid rain, and pollution from farms and factories threaten these habitats.

KINGFISHER DIVING

WEBBED FEET

Many waterbirds, such as Canada geese, have webbed feet to push the water aside as they swim. Long legs to wade in deep water and long toes to walk over soft mud are other common features of waterbirds.

HUNTING FOR FISH

To catch fish, birds like this kingfisher dive into the water to seize their prey. Others, such as herons, stand still and catch fish that swim past. Another technique is to scoop up fish from the surface.

CATCHING FISH

Birds need strong bills and feet to hold slippery prey. Mergansers' bills have serrated edges to help them keep a strong grip on fish they catch.

CANADA GOOSE FOOT

HOODED MERGANSER SKULL

NORTHERN
SHOVELER

FILTER FEEDING
Birds like the shoveler filter tiny floating plants and animals from water. The shoveler has "combs" on its bill to trap food.

CAMOUFLAGE
The dark, mottled colors of some birds, such as the buff-banded rail, help to camouflage them as they skulk noiselessly through the reed beds of marshes and swamps.

BUFF-
BANDED
RAIL

NESTING
Hiding a nest from predators is a relatively easy task in these habitats. Nesting materials such as dried reeds are also easy to find. Some birds even build floating platforms of vegetation for extra security.

HABITAT FACTS

• Lake Baikal in Siberia is the oldest freshwater lake – 25 million years old.

• About six percent of the Earth's surface is covered by marshes, bogs, and swamps.

• One-fifth of all the freshwater on Earth flows through the Amazon River daily.

COOT
NESTING IN
REEDS

RIVERS AND LAKES

THESE FRESHWATER habitats are important for birds, especially in undisturbed areas free of pollution. Some birds prefer the still waters of ponds and lakes while others, such as dippers, are adapted to move in fast-flowing waters. Around the edge of the water are many places to nest and a variety of food for the young, including water insects.

GRAY WAGTAIL
The busy gray wagtail patrols mountain streams, darting out to snap up flying insects in its long bill. It has sharp claws to grip slippery rocks and wet branches.

CLARK'S GREBES
The courtship dance, like that of the Western grebe, is elaborate. In it, a pair of grebes stands up tall and races fast across the water with heads tilted forward.

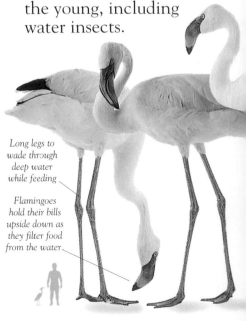

Long legs to wade through deep water while feeding

Flamingoes hold their bills upside down as they filter food from the water.

At the last moment, the feet swing forward to grasp the fish.

OSPREY

The osprey is a powerful hunter, lunging feet first into water to snatch fish from near the surface. It sometimes goes right under before pulling up into the air again. Stong claws and spines under the toes help it hold slippery fish.

All flamingos have some black feathers in their wings.

Crop

WHITE-CROWNED FORKTAIL
These Asian birds live by rocky streams, perching on boulders wagging their long tails. They have a loud, high-pitched whistle to communicate above the noise of the water.

Lesser flamingos are the smallest of the six species of flamingo.

LESSER FLAMINGOS
Flamingos live in noisy colonies, sometimes containing thousands of birds. They nest on mounds of mud, and both parents feed the young on a rich "milk" produced in the crop.

RIVERS, LAKES, & SWAMPS

331

SWAMPS AND MARSHES

WET, TREELESS GRASSLANDS, called marshes, and waterlogged forests, called swamps, are often given the name "wetlands." They can be fresh- or saltwater habitats. Fish-eating birds, such as egrets and pelicans, are common, but a lot of birds can feed together by eating different kinds of food at different levels in the water. Rare birds often find refuge in wetlands since large mammal predators cannot easily hunt there.

SCARLET IBIS
Spectacular flocks of scarlet ibis feed, roost, and nest together in the tropical swamps of South America. Scarlet ibises feel in soft mud or under plants for insects, crabs, shellfish, frogs, and fish. Young scarlet ibises have gray-brown backs for a year while they mature into adults.

Long, thin, down-curved bill to probe for food

Slim body to slide easily through dense vegetation

BLACK CRAKES
These East African birds have long, widely-spaced toes to keep them from sinking into the mud and help them walk over floating water plants. Their thick bills are too short to probe in mud, so they peck small invertebrates and seeds off the surface.

BEARDED PARROTBILL

Active and acrobatic bearded parrotbills fly low over reed beds on their rounded wings. They feed on insects in warm weather, and seeds in cold weather. Both parents build the nest in the reeds and share the care of their young.

WHOOPING CRANES

Among the world's rarest birds, the whooping crane spends the winter on the coastal marshes of Texas. In spring, it migrates to Canada to breed.

Male has black mustaches

A bird's "knee" is really its ankle, so it bends backward, just like a person's ankle.

BIRDS

DUCKS

WEBBED FEET and broad, flat bills are distinctive features of ducks. These birds are good swimmers and strong fliers. There are two main types of duck – dabbling ducks, such as the mallard, that feed on the surface, and diving ducks, such as the pochard. Many ducks migrate to avoid cold weather.

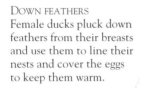

FEMALE

MALE

DOWN FEATHERS
Female ducks pluck down feathers from their breasts and use them to line their nests and cover the eggs to keep them warm.

Short legs set well back on body

MANDARIN DUCKS
These ducks live near ponds and lakes surrounded by woods, and nest in tree holes. The male is more colorful than the female, except when he molts his feathers once a year.

WOOD DUCK
Found in North America, wood ducks are related to Asian mandarin ducks. The females look after the nest, eggs, and ducklings on their own.

The ducklings swim soon after hatching

DIVING DUCKS
These ducks have shorter, rounder bodies than ducks that feed on the surface. Diving ducks, such as this pochard, can stay underwater for 30 seconds or more.

MALE MALLARD

DUCK FACTS
- Family: *Anatidae* includes ducks, swans, and geese
- About 150 species
- Diurnal
- Waterfowl
- Eat water plants and small water animals
- Habitat: ponds, lakes, rivers, or the sea
- Nest: built near water, or in tree holes
- Eggs: white or pale

PLUMED WHISTLING-DUCK
Whistling-ducks live in the tropics and look more like geese than ducks. They feed mainly on the surface.

Webbed feet used like paddles for swimming

MALLARD
These dabblers feed on the surface of the water or upend themselves to reach plant and animal food a little way below the surface. Mallards are the ancestors of most domestic ducks.

Wide, flat bill to sift food out of water

SEAS, CLIFFS, AND SHORES

SOME SPECIALLY adapted birds spend most of their lives gliding over the open oceans. But they nest on shores and in the safety of cliff ledges, usually in large colonies. The rich feeding grounds of estuaries attract huge numbers of waders and wildfowl, especially on migration.

FLIGHT
Seabirds such as the fulmar have long, narrow wings to glide fast over the waves for long distances. However, they are not very good at walking, and are clumsy and ungainly on land.

FULMAR IN FLIGHT

Fulmars have tube-shaped nostrils above the bill. Albatrosses and petrels are also tube-nosed birds.

Fulmars have a stiff-winged flight, hardly bending their wings at all.

CURLEW   REDSHANK   LITTLE STINT   RINGED PLOVER

FEEDING
Finding food out at sea is not always easy, and seabirds spend most of their time looking for the next meal. Terns dive to take fish at or near the surface. Other seabirds, such as puffins, dive underwater.

PUFFIN WITH CATCH

SHARING FEEDING PLACES
Some shorebirds can feed close together without competing because their bills are different lengths. The curlew's long bill reaches worms in deep burrows, while the ringed plover picks insects off the surface.

HERRING
GULL EGGS

Most seabird
eggs are more
pointed at one
end than the
other.

CAMOUFLAGED EGGS
Birds such as gulls or terns
that nest in the open on
beaches or dunes have
camouflaged eggs. The
spots and other
markings help the
eggs to blend into
the background so
predators find it
hard to see them.

GANNET
ON NEST

NESTING
Many seabirds nest in
tightly-packed colonies
of thousands or even
millions of birds. The
vast numbers stimulate
them to breed at the
same time. Gannets
nest close together
in noisy, smelly
colonies.

HABITAT FACTS

• Oceans cover about
70 percent of the
Earth's surface.

• The sea cools more
slowly than the land,
keeping coastal areas
warmer in winter.

• The tidal range in
open oceans is only
about 20 in (50 cm).

• In 10 sq ft (1 sq m) of
estuary there may be
over 1,000 worms.

337

ESTUARIES AND SHORES

APART FROM CLIFFS, other areas along the shoreline, such as dunes and beaches, provide nesting areas for seabirds. Where rivers meet the sea, the shallow, muddy waters of estuaries teem with a wealth of food such as fish, worms, and shellfish. Estuaries are particularly important in cold weather, when inland feeding areas are frozen.

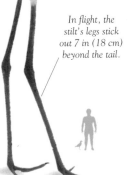

PURPLE SANDPIPER
Stocky purple sandpipers migrate south in colder weather to feed on rocky shores. They search the shoreline for food, finding their prey by sight rather than by touch.

BLACK-NECKED STILT
This stilt has extremely long legs that allow it to feed in deeper water than other shorebirds. However, it prefers to feed in shallow water and on muddy shores, using its long bill to catch insects and small aquatic creatures.

In flight, the stilt's legs stick out 7 in (18 cm) beyond the tail.

SLEEPING
On an estuary, shorebirds such as this dunlin feed when they can, and sleep when the tide comes in and covers their feeding grounds. They flock to the safety of high-tide roosts, like small islands

INCA TERN

This South American tern often gathers in flocks of many thousands, and roosts on sandy beaches. Inca terns are graceful fliers, hovering over the sea and dipping down to snatch food from the surface.

Inca terns may follow whales and seals to seize scraps of food.

GREAT BLACK-BACKED GULL

These huge gulls are fierce predators of seabird colonies on the coast. They have long, powerful wings for gliding.

RINGED PLOVER

As soon as the ringed plover stops moving, its colors make it hard to see among the pebbles on the beach. Females may pretend to be injured to draw predators away from eggs and young.

SEA AND CLIFFS

OVER THE OPEN OCEAN, seabirds search for food, also landing on the surface to rest and preen. Seabirds have waterproofed feathers, webbed feet for swimming, and sharp bills to catch slippery prey. Many nest on cliffs where eggs and young are safe from predators.

NESTING SPACE
To share the nesting sites on a cliff, the birds nest at different levels. Alcids, such as razorbills and murres, gannets, and kittiwakes nest near the top.

After fishing, cormorants hold their wings open to dry.

GANNET SKULL
To catch fish, gannets plunge into the sea like torpedos from heights of up to 100 ft (30 m). They have a strong skull to withstand the impact when they hit the water with such a great force.

GREAT CORMORANT
With feathers that trap very little air and heavy bones, the great cormorant sinks in water more easily than other seab and can feed on bottom-dwelling creature

A frigatebird robs a tropicbird of its fishy meal.

PIRACY AT SEA
Frigatebirds steal much of their food from other birds such as pelicans and gulls. They are speedy fliers and can swoop, dart, soar, and hover better than most other seabirds.

Nests of grass, seaweeds, and mud sit snugly on narrow ledges

KITTIWAKES
These small gulls nest close together in colonies consisting of hundreds of birds. They are named after their call. Unlike other gulls they are rarely found on land.

DESERTS AND GRASSLAND

IN THESE MAINLY HOT, dry habitats, birds may have to travel long distances to find food and water, or migrate to avoid dry seasons. Seeds and insects are the main sources of food, but some larger birds also feed on reptiles, small mammals and dead animals. In the heat of the day, most birds are less active and rest in the shade.

Bee-eaters feed mainly on honeybees.

INSECT EATERS
Birds such as bee-eaters and warblers feed on the insects that are most abundant during a rainy season. In the dry season, insect eaters often have to migrate to find enough to eat.

ROADRUNNER

VARIED DIET
Food is often hard to find, so birds survive by eating any food they come across. Reptiles are a common source of food. This roadrunner has caught a lizard.

White-throat[e] bee-eaters f[ly] to wett[er] grasslan[d] in the d[ry] seas[on].

WHITE-
THROATED
BEE-EATER

These birds are threatened by the caged bird trade.

SEED EATERS

Grass seeds are a vital source of food for many birds, such as these Australian Gouldian finches. When the grasses die back in the dry season, the finches migrate toward wetter areas on the coast.

GOULDIAN FINCHES

GARBAGE CLEAN-UP

The carcasses of large ~ing animals and human ~s provide food for birds ~ such as marabou storks. ~spite the harsh habitat, there is plenty to eat.

BURROWING OWLS

~NDERGROUND SHELTERS

~o keep out of the heat of ~e Sun, burrowing owls rest ~d nest safe from enemies ~side burrows dug by small ~mmals like prairie dogs.

MARABOU STORK

HABITAT FACTS

• More than a quarter of all the land on Earth is covered in grass.

• Deserts have less than 10 in (25 mm) rain a year.

• In Death Valley, in the Southwest, temperatures reach 131°F (55°C).

• The African ostrich is the heaviest, tallest, and fastest-running bird in the world.

DESERTS

BIRDS THAT LIVE in deserts have to get most of their water either from their food or by flying long distances. By day, they may rest in the shade of rocks, or inside cacti or underground burrows. Some come out to feed at night, when it is cooler. Many birds of prey survive in deserts on a diet of reptiles and small mammals.

SANDGROUSE
These birds are strong flie and travel many miles to find water. The males carr water back to their chicks their belly feathers.

Hooked beak typical of bird of prey

ELF OWL
The sparrow-sized elf owl nests in holes dug out by woodpeckers inside giant saguaro cacti. The spines of the cactus protect the eggs and young from predators. Elf owls hunt for insects in the cool of the night.

It is much cooler inside the cactus.

HARRIS'S HAWK
A fearless hunter of birds, lizards, and small mammals, Harris's hawk sometimes feeds on carcasses, alongside vultures and caracaras. It is often found near roadsides in the desert regions of the Americas.

The female does not have orange cheek patches and her bill is a duller red.

The male has zebralike stripes on the chest.

ZEBRA FINCHES
These lively little birds are common in the Australian outback. They nest after the rains when there are plenty of seeds and insects to feed to their young. They live in flocks of up to 100 birds, and several may nest together.

SCRUB AND BUSH

THE BIRDS OF these warm, dry, dusty habitats may roam widely in search of food, or follow the rains. The thorny bushes and shrubs often form dense thickets and these make safe nesting places. The berries that grow on the shrubs can be a useful source of food in colder weather for many species.

Males have brighter markings on the face than the females.

COCKATIELS
These small cockatoo wander over the Australian bush count looking for fruits and grass seeds. They usually nest after rainfall at any time of year.

BLUE-CAPPED CORDONBLEU
Small groups of cordonbleus search the ground for grass seeds and insects in the thorn scrub of East Africa. They feed their young mainly on a protein-rich diet of insects.

Short, stubby bill to crush seeds

RAY FRANCOLIN

These birds are common in southern Asia because they are able to survive dry conditions. They usually live in small family groups, and feed on weed seeds and grain crops. In warm weather, they also eat insects.

Francolins try to escape danger by running.

EMU

Small flocks of flightless emus roam widely through the Australian bush in search of seeds, berries, and insects. The male looks after the chicks for up to 18 months.

SCRUBLAND

The scrubland habitats of small trees and thorny shrubs are halfway between grassland and woodland. They include the Mediterranean scrublands, the Californian chaparral, and the bush, or outback, of Australia.

WHITE HELMETSHRIKE

Tame and active white helmetshrikes live in small flocks of two to 20 birds. They hop through the African bush snapping up insects and spiders with their strong, hooked bills.

GRASSLAND

A VARIETY OF seed- and insect-eating birds live in grasslands, especially those birds that can adapt to living near people. Some birds follow herds of grazing animals to snap up the insects disturbed by their feet. Other birds feed on the animals when they die. Long legs enable birds such as ostriches and rheas to see over tall grasses and watch for danger.

Oxpeckers and giraffe

OXPECKERS
Using their sharp claws to cling to the skin of large mammals such as giraffes and zebras. Oxpeckers pick off ticks and insects living in their fur.

In breeding plumage, male is bright chestnut, with black head and throat

This weaver is a shy bird with a fast, dashing flight.

CHESNUT WEAVER
These weavers nest in dense colonies in the African grasslands. Out of the breeding season, both male and female are dull brown.

OSTRICH
Able to survive in very dry conditions, ostriches stride over the African savannah or their long legs, searching for leaves, seeds, and insects. Th are threatened by hunting and habitat destruction.

348

Bare head
and neck

HOODED VULTURE
The bare head
and neck of the
hooded vulture allow
it to reach right inside an animal
carcass to feed without getting
its feathers dirty. Vultures fly
high, using their sharp eyesight
to spot carrion.

*It is sometimes called
the "ovenbird"
because its nest looks
like an old-fashioned
baker's oven*

*Strong talons
cling onto branch*

RUFOUS HORNERO
There are few trees on the South
American pampas grasslands, so the
rufous hornero builds a huge nest of mud
and straw. The nest dries, forming a hard
"birdhouse" to protect the eggs and young.

MOUNTAINS AND MOORLANDS

MOORLANDS TEND TO BE wet, boggy places while mountains can be very cold and windy. Only a few hardy birds live on mountains and moorland because of the harsh climate and lack of food, especially in the cold seasons. However, these habitats are important breeding areas for birds.

This shy, secretive bird rarely emerges from the bamboo thickets and dense forest where it lives.

SEASONAL MIGRATION
Hardy pheasants such as this Lady Amherst's pheasant live in the mountain forests of Asia. They move up and down the mountains with the seasons. Many pheasants are threatened by hunting.

Feathered feet to insulate against the cold

Colorful feathers and neck ruff

LADY AMHERST'S PHEASANT

CAMOUFLAGE
In autumn, ptarmigans grow new white feathers for camouflage. These tough birds bury themselves in snow to keep out cold, biting winds. In summer, their plumage is mottled gray-brown.

NESTING
CURLEW

MOUNTAIN FORESTS
The warmer forests on the lower slopes of mountains provide many birds with plenty of food and nesting places. In colder weather, birds may move down to these forests from the upper slopes.

RUFOUS-
BELLIED
NILTAVA

These Asian flycatchers live in mountain forest above 3,000 ft (1,000 m).

ESTING PLACES
horebirds such as this curlew est on windswept moorlands in immer. They hide their nests nong grasses and bushes. heir young feed on insects, orms, frogs, and snails. In inter, they move to the coast.

ROUSE
EGG

MOORLAND EGGS
Heavy blotches of color help to camouflage the eggs of moorland nesters such as grouse and shorebirds among the heather and bracken. The eggs are laid in a shallow scrape on the ground.

CURLEW
EGG

Male has long tail for display

HABITAT FACTS

• The Appalachians were formed over 250 million years ago; the Himalayas formed only 40 million years ago.

• The world's longest mountain chain is the Andes at 4,500 miles (7,250 km) long.

• Some moorlands are created by a change to a wetter climate; others by people clearing trees for farmland.

MOUNTAINS

IN COLD WEATHER food is scarce on mountains, but these areas are undisturbed breeding areas for birds. Birds' feathers keep them warm when it is freezing cold, and efficient lungs enable them to get enough oxygen from the thin air. Many mountain birds are large and powerful fliers.

RAVEN
These powerful birds are among the largest members of the crow family. They patrol mountain slopes searching for food with their sharp eyes.

WALLCREEPER
This nimble bird clings onto rock faces with its sharp claws, probing for insects with its slender bill. In cold weather, it moves to lower slopes where there are more insects for it to eat.

SWORD-BILLED HUMMINGBIRD
This hummingbird lives high in the Andes. It has a very long bill, which it uses to sip nectar from flowers.

SNOW, ICE AND ROCK

GRASSY MEADOWS

CONIFEROUS FOREST

TEMPERATE FOREST

HABITAT ZONES
Mountains have a variety of habitats. There are warm, deciduous forests on the lower slopes, cooler coniferous forests higher up, and, just below the snow covered peaks, grasslands and scrub.

The lammergeier is also called the bearded vulture

LAMMERGEIER

Soaring over the mountain slopes on rising warm air currents, the lammergeier searches the steep slopes for animals killed by the harsh climate. It drops the skeleton bones on rocks to smash them, then scoops out the marrow with its long tongue.

...mmergeiers fly to ...t heights and drop ...nes onto rocks to ...reak them apart.

...DEAN CONDOR

...e world's heaviest bird of ...y, the Andean condor has ...y keen eyesight. It has ...longest wingspan of ...land bird and soars ...r the Andes looking ...dead, sick, or wounded ...mals to feed on. ...ere is a ready supply ...ood because ...he difficult ...ng ...ditions.

MOORLANDS

THIS WATERLOGGED, tundralike habitat is found
in cool, upland areas with lots of rain. It is an
important breeding ground for shorebirds and
grouse. Predators such as harriers and golden eagles
find many small birds and mammals to eat here,
and there are plenty
of insects
breeding in the
peaty bogs.

*Golden-plovers
feed on
insects, worms,
and seeds.*

*The upperparts
of this species
have golden
color all year.*

EURASIAN GOLDEN-PLOVER
In late spring, golden-
plovers migrate to
moorlands to breed. They
lay their well-camouflaged
eggs in a shallow scrape
in the ground.

STONECHAT
The restless stonechat perches on bushes and posts to watch for insects, worms, and spiders. It builds a nest of moss, grass, and hair, well hidden in bushes or thick grass.

PEREGRINE FALCON
These falcons stoop at an incredible speed to kill prey such as golden-plovers or pigeons with their talons. They pluck the feathers from prey before eating the flesh.

RED GROUSE
This bird is a distinctive subspecies of the willow ptarmigan. Many moorlands are carefully managed to keep a stock of these birds for shooting in the autumn grouse season.

Birds such as red grouse shelter, hide, and nest in heather.

Some stonechats migrate to warmer places in cold weather.

BIRDS

EAGLES

WITH THEIR SHARP eyes, huge wings, and strong legs and feet, eagles are the most powerful of the birds of prey. Females are larger than males. Many species of eagle are threatened by people hunting them, poisoning them, and destroying their habitat.

Light-colored crown and neck feathers

Strong ta to grip a crush pr

COURTSHIP

During courtship, many eagles show off their amazing flying skills. A pair of bald eagles will tumble and spin through the sky, while trying to touch or grip one another's talons.

Courtship display of bald eagles

IMPERIAL EAGLE
Feathered legs are a characteristic of the imperial eagle, which belongs to a group called the booted eagles. It is widespread in parts of Asia, but rare in Europe.

GOLDEN EAGLE
These eagles are strong fliers, soaring high on outstretched wings to search for prey. They are named for the golden feathers on the top of the head and the back of the neck.

Large primaries for power and steering

ATELEUR
This eagle's name comes
from the French word
for "juggler" because
of its aerial courtship
display. It has long
wings and a short
tail. When it is
excited or angry, it
raises its crest.

Raised crest

A bald eagle's eyrie

EYRIE
Eagle nests are called eyries
and bald eagles have made
some of the biggest eyries in
the world. They use the same
nest year after year, adding
more and more twigs and
sticks each time they nest.

EAGLE FACTS

• Family: *Accipitridae* –
includes hawks and
kites as well

• About 63 species

• Diurnal

• Birds of prey

• Eat a variety of
animals, alive and dead

• Habitat: wide range

• Nest: mass of sticks
in tree or on cliff ledge

• Eggs: white or
marked with brown

357

POLAR AND TUNDRA REGIONS

THE FROZEN POLAR REGIONS are the coldest and windiest places on Earth. Few birds can survive there all year around. Most migrate there to breed in the short summer months, when the Sun shines 24 hours day and there is plenty of food. These unique habitats are threatened by mining, tourism, and pollution.

TUNDRA LANDSCAPES

Around the edge of the Arctic Ocean lie the flat tundra lands, which have a frozen layer called permafrost under the ground. In summer, the soil above the permafrost thaws out, and lakes and marshes form on the surface.

Tundra means "barren land" in Finnish

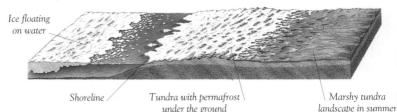

Ice floating on water

Shoreline

Tundra with permafrost under the ground

Marshy tundra landscape in summer

MIGRATION

In summer, millions of ducks, swans, and geese, such as the barnacle goose, migrate to the tundra lands to feed and nest there. They eat new vegetation sprouting from the warm, moist ground.

Do...

ADAPTATIONS

The Arctic alcids, such as dovekies look like the Antarctic penguins. They have flipperlike wings for swimming, but can fly.

KEEPING WARM
Birds such as the eider duck cover their eggs with soft down which the female plucks from her own breast. This helps to keep the eggs warm until they are ready to hatch.

PENGUIN
FLIPPER

EIDER NEST

LAPLAND
LONGSPUR

SWIMMING
Many birds of these habitats are good swimmers. Penguins have stiff, densely packed scalelike feathers on their wings to reduce the drag of the water against them when swimming.

FACTS

• Antarctica has 90 percent of all the ice on Earth and 70 percent of all the water.

• Permafrost under the tundra can be up to 3,840 ft (1,400 m) thick.

• The Arctic is an ice-covered ocean surrounded by land – Antarctica is frozen and surrounded by ocean.

FOOD
The tundra summer is brief, but thousands of insects swarm over marshy pools. So birds like the Lapland longspur have plenty of food to collect for their young.

ARCTIC AND TUNDRA

AROUND THE NORTH POLE is a huge ice-covered ocean surrounded by tundra landscape. This region is called the Arctic. In summer months, gulls, auks, and terns feed on the fish at sea, and nest on the coast. The insects and seeds on the tundra are food for shorebirds, ducks, geese, and small songbirds. Before winter, the birds fly south to warmer regions.

Male giving his mate a fishy gift during courtship

ARCTIC TERNS
After courtship, terns raise their young in the Arctic summer, then fly all the way to Antarctica for the summer there. They do an incredible round trip of 22,000 miles (35,400 km)

SNOWY OWL FOOT

SNOWY OWL
The plumage of the snowy owl camouflages it against the Arctic landscape, as it glides over the ground looking for prey. Feathers on its legs and feet help it to keep warm.

COMMON REDPOLL

This little bird can survive low temperatures. It eats a lot of seeds, and some small insects and their larvae in summer. Some redpolls nest in dwarf birches near the ground in tundra habitats.

Redpolls are named after their red forehead, or "poll."

EMPEROR GOOSE

This handsome gray goose breeds along marshy shores in Alaska. Some birds may migrate south to northern California in winter.

Adults have orange legs.

In winter, the male snow bunting turns browner and looks more like the female.

SNOW BUNTING

Hardy snow buntings breed in the Arctic – farther north than any other perching bird. They usually hide their nest from predators in crannies in the rocks.

Snow buntings may burrow in the snow to escape intense cold.

361

ANTARCTICA

THIS VAST AREA of frozen land surrounded by ocean has little rain or snow, so the birds have little fresh water to drink, apart from melted snow. The only two landbirds are sheathbills. All the others are seabirds, including albatrosses, petrels, and penguins, millions of which nest around Antarctic coasts in summer. The seabirds have dense feathers or layers of fat to keep warm, and are strong swimmers or fliers.

BROWN SKUA
With their hooked bills and strong claws, skuas are fierce predators of penguin eggs and chicks. In summer, they regularly invade penguin colonies in Antarctica.

ADELIE PENGUINS
Adelies are one of the two species of penguin that nest on the rocky coasts of Antarctica itself. In spring, they march inland from the sea to nest on the ground in huge rookeries.

BLACK-BROWED ALBATROSSES
Albatrosses mate for life and reinforce the pair bond each year when they return to the nest. This pair are bill-touching and preening each other.

The only bird found in Antarctica that does not have webbed feet

SNOWY SHEATHBILL
A relative of shorebirds, this bird scavenges around seal and penguin colonies as well as searching the shoreline for fish, invertebrates, and shellfish. Sheathbills live in small flocks, except in the breeding season.

IMPERIAL SHAGS
These cormorants nest in large colonies on coastal ledges or among rocks. They have strong, hooked bills to grasp slippery fish. In the breeding season, they grow wispy crests.

Nest is a big heap of mud and grass about 24 in (60 cm) high

BLACK-BROWED ALBATROSSES

BIRDS

PENGUINS

WITH THEIR SMOOTH, streamlined shape, and stiff, strong wings, penguins are expert swimmers. They dive to catch fish and squid with their spiky tongues. Dense, oily feathers and thick fat under the skin keep them warm in the cold southern oceans.

Penguins only come out of the water to molt and breed, some in colonies of 500,000.

EMPEROR PENGUINS
These are the biggest penguins. They never come on land, but breed on the ice that floats around Antarctica in winter. Males incubate the single egg for about nine weeks.

Powerful, narrow wings for swimming

KING PENGUINS
The striking golden orange ear patches of these birds are used for display during courtship. The markings also help them to recognize other king penguins. These large birds can dive down as deep as 850 ft (250 m).

Stiff tail feathers used to support body on land

Male king penguin incubates egg against bare patch of warm skin

In the water, penguins look dark from above and pale from below – this helps to camouflage them

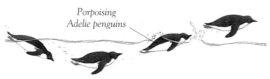

Porpoising
Adelie penguins

SWIMMING AND DIVING

In order to breathe while swimming fast, penguins leap in and out of the water. This technique is called porpoising. They can travel through water in this way at over 20 mph (30 km/h), using their stiff wings to push themselves along.

MACARONI PENGUIN

During their courtship displays, these birds shake their bright yellow head crests. The crests also help them to recognize other macaronis.

Spread flippers cool bird down

CHINSTRAP PENGUIN

These penguins are named because of the black line under their chin. They are noisy and quarrelsome birds.

Feet well back on body to act as rudder

PENGUIN FACTS

- Family: *Spheniscidae*
- About 17 species
- Diurnal and nocturnal
- Flightless seabirds
- Eat fish, squid, and small sea creatures
- Habitat: southern oceans, cool temperate islands, tropical shores
- Nest: stones, grass, mud, caves, or burrows
- Eggs: whitish

365

MAMMALS

MAMMALS

WHAT IS A MAMMAL?

ALL MAMMALS HAVE FUR or hair and a backbone for support, and they are all warm-blooded. Females give birth to live young and feed them with milk from their mammary glands – from which the word *mammal* derives. The most intelligent and adaptable of all animals, they have come to dominate the animal world. There are over 4,000 different kinds of mammals, from enormous whales to tiny bats and shrews.

It takes just less than a year for a foal to grow inside its mother.

Foal, or baby horse, drinks milk from teats between its mother's hind legs

YOUNG MAMMAL
Female mammal
feed their young b
producing milk ir
mammary glands
For a long time, a
their young grow an
develop, parents tak
care of them, passin
on survival skills

368

HORSE AND FOAL

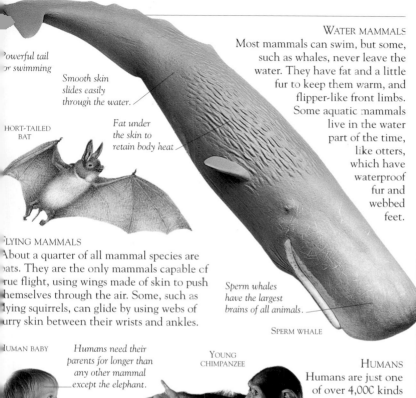

Powerful tail for swimming

Smooth skin slides easily through the water.

Fat under the skin to retain body heat

SHORT-TAILED BAT

WATER MAMMALS

Most mammals can swim, but some, such as whales, never leave the water. They have fat and a little fur to keep them warm, and flipper-like front limbs. Some aquatic mammals live in the water part of the time, like otters, which have waterproof fur and webbed feet.

FLYING MAMMALS

About a quarter of all mammal species are bats. They are the only mammals capable of true flight, using wings made of skin to push themselves through the air. Some, such as flying squirrels, can glide by using webs of furry skin between their wrists and ankles.

Sperm whales have the largest brains of all animals.

SPERM WHALE

HUMAN BABY

Humans need their parents for longer than any other mammal except the elephant.

YOUNG CHIMPANZEE

Humans are closely related to chimps, gorillas, and orang utans.

HUMANS

Humans are just one of over 4,000 kinds of mammals. Chimpanzees are our closest living relatives. Their body structure and behavior is similar and we share 99 percent of the same genes.

369

REPRODUCTION

MAMMALS FALL INTO THREE categories of reproduction
Most, including humans, are placental: through an
organ called a placenta, mothers nourish their unborn
young inside the womb. Marsupial mammal
begin developing in the womb but, when
still tiny, crawl out to finish growing in
their mother's pouch, called a marsupium.
The rarest kind are monotremes, the only
mammals to lay eggs. Though these three
types of mammals reproduce differently,
they all feed their young on milk.

Baby
develops in
mother's
uterus.

Baby, or fetus,
facing head-down,
ready to be born

Muscles of uter
will contract
push baby ou

Placenta

Blood reaches placenta
through umbilical cord.

PREGNANT
WOMAN

PLACENTAL MAMMALS
The placenta is a disk-
shaped organ that forms
in the lining of the uterus
after fertilization. The
umbilical cord is attached
to the placenta. This allows
the baby to receive food,
oxygen, and antibodies
from its mother, and to
pass waste products
back into her blood.

Amniotic sac i
filled with fluid t
cushion the baby

Mucous plug blocks
cervix during pregnancy.

FETUS AT 36 WEEKS

370

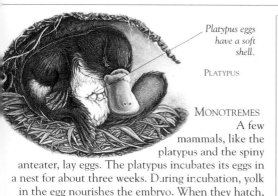

Platypus eggs
have a soft
shell.

PLATYPUS

MONOTREMES
A few
mammals, like the
platypus and the spiny
anteater, lay eggs. The platypus incubates its eggs in
a nest for about three weeks. During incubation, yolk
in the egg nourishes the embryo. When they hatch,
young monotremes suck milk from their mother.

Mother's teat swells in
the baby's mouth,
keeping it attached
for 1–2 months.

Baby kangaroo,
or joey, stays in
the pouch for
about six
months.

KANGAROO
AND JOEY

MARSUPIALS
Young marsupials, like kangaroos,
spend only 12–30 days in the mother's
uterus and are born in an immature
stage of development. They then
crawl into the pouch to reach the
mother's teats, and feed on her
milk, staying there until fully
developed.

BIRTH AND GROWTH

MOST MAMMALS are born live. Seals, whales, and monkeys and apes have one or two young at a time. On the other hand, some mammals bear 10 or 15 babies in a single pregnancy. Mice can have a litter of 18! Most tropical mammals are born at various times of the year; in temperate and cold climates, however, births usually take place in spring and summer. Mammals tend to spend a lot of time caring for and teaching their young.

Nesting material helps keep mice warm

NEWBORN MICE

HAIRLESS BABIES

Baby mice are born without hair or fur. Unable to see or hear, they are totally dependent on their mother. Fur starts to appear when they are one week old; and after ten days, their eyes open. The young are ready to leave the nest after two or three weeks.

HAIRY BABIES

Kittens are born with all their fur. The mother licks the fur, making it dry and fluffy, so it traps body heat and keeps the kitten warm. Though newborn kittens are active, their eyes and ears are sealed, leaving them temporarily blind and deaf. But they're ready to leave their mother in eight weeks.

Mother cuts through umbilical cord with her teeth

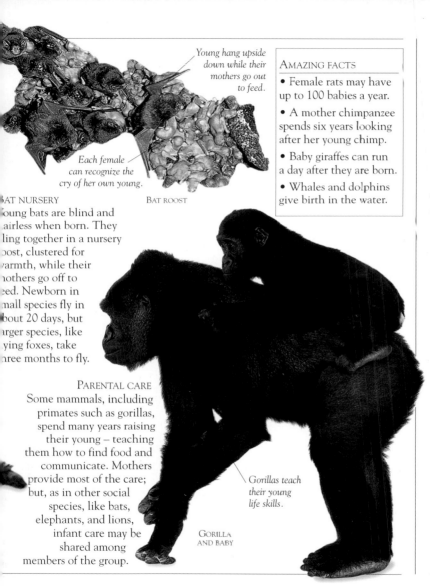

Young hang upside down while their mothers go out to feed.

Each female can recognize the cry of her own young.

BAT ROOST

BAT NURSERY
Young bats are blind and hairless when born. They cling together in a nursery roost, clustered for warmth, while their mothers go off to feed. Newborn in small species fly in about 20 days, but larger species, like flying foxes, take three months to fly.

AMAZING FACTS

• Female rats may have up to 100 babies a year.

• A mother chimpanzee spends six years looking after her young chimp.

• Baby giraffes can run a day after they are born.

• Whales and dolphins give birth in the water.

PARENTAL CARE
Some mammals, including primates such as gorillas, spend many years raising their young – teaching them how to find food and communicate. Mothers provide most of the care; but, as in other social species, like bats, elephants, and lions, infant care may be shared among members of the group.

Gorillas teach their young life skills.

GORILLA AND BABY

373

SKIN AND HAIR

A MAMMAL'S SKIN forms a protective outer layer that, aided by hair, regulates body temperature. Among all animals, only mammals have hair, which grows as fur, whiskers, wool, prickles, and spines. It retains body heat and keeps out cold, heat, wind, and rain. Some mammals, like chinchillas, have thick, dense fur coats. Others, like whales, have very little hair.

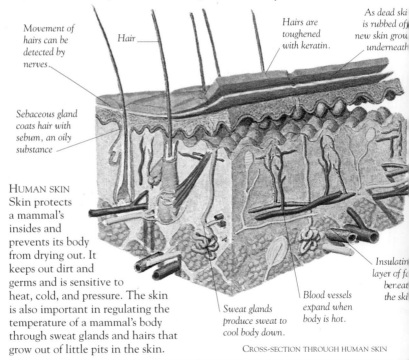

Movement of hairs can be detected by nerves.

Hair

Hairs are toughened with keratin.

As dead skin is rubbed off, new skin grows underneath.

Sebaceous gland coats hair with sebum, an oily substance

HUMAN SKIN
Skin protects a mammal's insides and prevents its body from drying out. It keeps out dirt and germs and is sensitive to heat, cold, and pressure. The skin is also important in regulating the temperature of a mammal's body through sweat glands and hairs that grow out of little pits in the skin.

Sweat glands produce sweat to cool body down.

Blood vessels expand when body is hot.

Insulating layer of fat beneath the skin

CROSS-SECTION THROUGH HUMAN SKIN

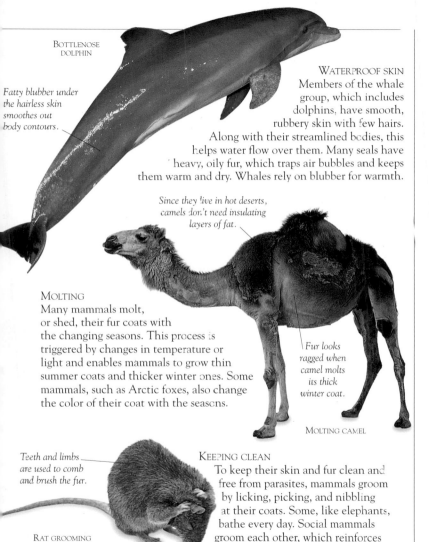

BOTTLENOSE
DOLPHIN

*Fatty blubber under
the hairless skin
smoothes out
body contours.*

WATERPROOF SKIN
Members of the whale
group, which includes
dolphins, have smooth,
rubbery skin with few hairs.
Along with their streamlined bodies, this
helps water flow over them. Many seals have
heavy, oily fur, which traps air bubbles and keeps
them warm and dry. Whales rely on blubber for warmth.

*Since they live in hot deserts,
camels don't need insulating
layers of fat.*

MOLTING
Many mammals molt,
or shed, their fur coats with
the changing seasons. This process is
triggered by changes in temperature or
light and enables mammals to grow thin
summer coats and thicker winter ones. Some
mammals, such as Arctic foxes, also change
the color of their coat with the seasons.

*Fur looks
ragged when
camel molts
its thick
winter coat.*

MOLTING CAMEL

*Teeth and limbs
are used to comb
and brush the fur.*

KEEPING CLEAN
To keep their skin and fur clean and
free from parasites, mammals groom
by licking, picking, and nibbling
at their coats. Some, like elephants,
bathe every day. Social mammals
groom each other, which reinforces
the bonds between individuals.

RAT GROOMING

375

SENSES

TO PICK UP INFORMATION about their surroundings, and to communicate with each other, mammals use their senses of sight, hearing, smell, taste, and touch. They are the only animals that have external ear flaps. Most mammals see the world in black and white.

Some dogs are trained to sniff out drugs and explosives.

SMELL

Vital for identifying individuals and food, along with possible predators or mates, the sense of smell is highly developed in some insectivores, carnivores, (such as dogs) and rodents. In whales and higher primates, such as humans, it is much less developed.

BLACK LEOPARD, OR PANTHER

BEAGLE

A dog's sense of smell is a million times more sensitive than our own.

Wet nose helps identify scents

CATS WHISKERS

Whiskers are long hairs that usually grow on the face. Some mammals, however, have whiskers on their legs, feet, or back. Whiskers respond when they are touched, helping mammals to feel objects in the dark and gauge the width of narrow spaces

Long, sensitive whiskers

Horseshoe
bat

Sound echoes
bouncing off
prey

Insect prey

Bats can detect
insects as small
as midges from
a distance of
65.5 ft (20 m)

Large ears to
pick up sound
echoes

HOW A BAT USES ECHOLOCATION

Large ear flaps
funnel sound.

Large eyes to spot prey.

ECHOLOCATION
Some bats and dolphins
have a special sense called
echolocation. They make
high-pitched sounds that
bounce off objects in
their environment
and return as echoes,
which can reveal
the location of
the objects.

BUSHBABY

NIGHT SENSES
Many mammals
are nocturnal and
have sensitive eyes
and ears to navigate
and locate food in the dark.
Bushbabies have huge eyes with
pupils that open wide to let in as
much light as possible. Their large
ears swivel to track small flying insects.

377

FEEDING AND DIET

MAMMALS MUST EAT regularly to maintain a constant body temperature, particularly small mammals, which need to eat more often than large ones. Most are plant eaters; however, some eat meat, and others have a diet that combines both. Most mammals have three kinds of teeth: incisors and canines for biting and tearing, and molars for grinding. These develop from two sets of teeth – milk teeth in young, and adult teeth that grow as the jaws become larger.

PLANT EATERS

Herbivores, such as cows, horses, camels, sheep, goats, and deer eat only plants. They have long jaws to hold rows of molar teeth, which grind and crush tough plant material. Many have a hard pad instead of top front teeth.

Deep lower jaw to anchor large chewing muscles

GOAT SKULL

Gap for tongue to curl around bulky plant food

Horny pad

Jaws move sideways, as well as up and down.

Carnassial teeth work together like shears

JACKAL SKULL

Powerful canine teeth

MEAT EATERS

Carnivores, like lions, tigers, and wolves eat meat. Their jaws are shorter and more powerful than those of herbivores. Carnivores have special cheek teeth called carnassials, which have pointed edges that can slice meat or crack bones.

BEAVER

ack part of
oth wears away
ore easily than
e front, forming
sloping, chisel-
ke edge

VERGROWING TEETH
odents, such as beavers, have four strong front teeth
alled incisors, which keep growing. Continually worn
own, they are kept sharp by constant use. The teeth
f pet rodents can grow too
ong if they lack hard
aterials to gnaw on.

urved upper jaw to hold
ng lengths of baleen

Section cut away to show
baleen plates with fringes
facing inside the mouth

OOD STRAINER
ome whales, like the
umpback, the gray,
nd the blue whale,
ave no teeth. Instead,
ney have long, fringed
lates hanging from their jaws.
hey draw sea water into their mouths
nd spit it back out through the baleen
inges, which trap food like a sieve.

BALEEN WHALE

BONES AND MUSCLES

ALL MAMMALS HAVE a skeleton, an internal
framework of bones that supports the body and
protects its delicate internal organs. Bones cannot
move on their own. They are pulled into different
positions by firmly attached groups of powerful
muscles, enabling mammals to move. Some mammals
have especially strong bones and muscles, and can run
and swim faster than other animals.

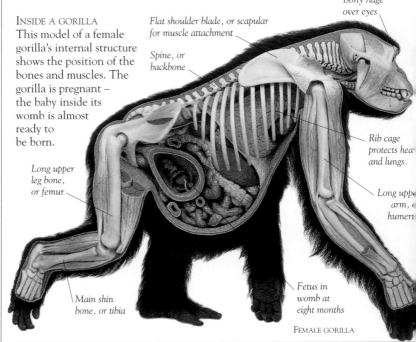

INSIDE A GORILLA
This model of a female
gorilla's internal structure
shows the position of the
bones and muscles. The
gorilla is pregnant –
the baby inside its
womb is almost
ready to
be born.

*Bony ridge
over eyes*

*Flat shoulder blade, or scapular
for muscle attachment*

*Spine, or
backbone*

*Rib cage
protects hea
and lungs.*

*Long upp
arm, (
humeri*

*Long upper
leg bone,
or femur*

*Main shin
bone, or tibia*

*Fetus in
womb at
eight months*

FEMALE GORILLA

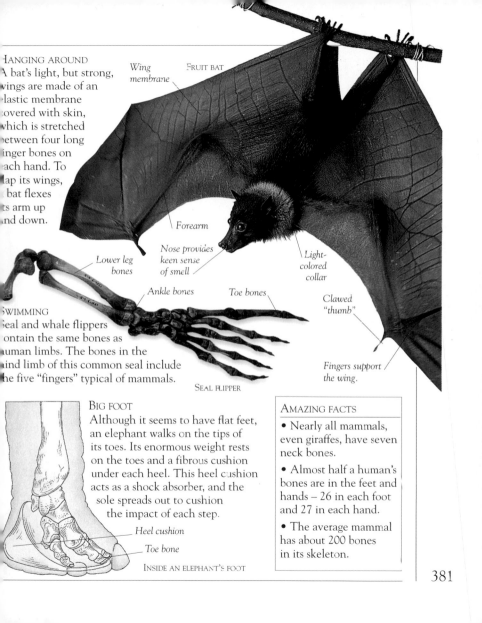

HANGING AROUND
A bat's light, but strong, wings are made of an elastic membrane covered with skin, which is stretched between four long finger bones on each hand. To flap its wings, a bat flexes its arm up and down.

Wing membrane

FRUIT BAT

Forearm

Nose provides keen sense of smell

Light-colored collar

Clawed "thumb"

Fingers support the wing.

Lower leg bones

Ankle bones

Toe bones

SWIMMING
Seal and whale flippers contain the same bones as human limbs. The bones in the hind limb of this common seal include the five "fingers" typical of mammals.

SEAL FLIPPER

BIG FOOT
Although it seems to have flat feet, an elephant walks on the tips of its toes. Its enormous weight rests on the toes and a fibrous cushion under each heel. This heel cushion acts as a shock absorber, and the sole spreads out to cushion the impact of each step.

Heel cushion

Toe bone

INSIDE AN ELEPHANT'S FOOT

AMAZING FACTS
• Nearly all mammals, even giraffes, have seven neck bones.

• Almost half a human's bones are in the feet and hands – 26 in each foot and 27 in each hand.

• The average mammal has about 200 bones in its skeleton.

DEFENSE

PLANT-EATING MAMMALS, especially small ones, have many enemies. Among these predators are meat-eating mammals, snakes, and birds. To avoid detection, some herbivores are camouflaged. Others bear weapons – from claws and spiky coats to horns, armor, and terrible smells.

Horns are not shed each year, like a deer's antlers.

Pointed tips of horns could injure a predator.

ANTELOPE SKULL

Curved (annulated) horn

Joints between bones

Unlike antlers, horns are never branched but are curved and twisted.

PORCUPINE

SPIKE ATTACK
If threatened, a porcupine will turn its back, rattle its quills, grunt, and stamp its feet. If the enemy won't retreat, the porcupine charges it in reverse, sticking quills into its skin.

HORNS, ANTLERS AND TUSKS
Used mainly to fight other males in competition for a mate or territory, horns, antlers, and tusks are also useful in defense. The horns of antelope, cattle, and sheep are hollow structures made of bone that has a slightly softer covering.

ODOR POWER

The striking color of the skunk alerts enemies to stay away. If they don't, the skunk will turn its back, stamp its feet, and raise its tail. Then it squirts its enemy with foul-smelling liquid, which takes a long time to wear off.

Skunk can spray smelly liquid 12 ft (3.6 m)

Body armor is impossible to penetrate.

ARMADILLO

ARMOR-PLATING

The body of an armadillo is encased in bony plates, or scutes. Some of the 20 armadillo species roll up into a ball when attacked, to protect their soft underparts.

Handstand warns enemy to watch out!

SPOTTED SKUNK

OKAPI

CAMOUFLAGE

Stripes or spots on a mammal's fur break up its outline, so it is less visible to enemies. The okapi lives in rainforests.

DEFENSE FACTS

• Opossums play dead if attacked – predators prefer live animals.

• Zebra stallions kick lions, sometimes smashing their teeth.

• Only two mammals are poisonous: the male platypus has poison spurs on its back legs, and the water shrew has poisonous saliva.

383

MAMMAL HOMES

BUILT IN TREES, under the soil, in riverbanks and lakes, or even in people's houses, mammal homes provide a safe, warm shelter that protects them and their young from the weather and from enemies. To construct their dwellings, mammals use natural materials, such as grass, leaves, sticks, and fur and use their teeth and limbs to shape them. Many of these homes, such as badger setts, are permanent while others are built daily or seasonally.

Outer layer of twigs and leaves

Cozy lining of grass, moss, leaves, bark, feathers, and sheep's wool

GRAY SQUIRREL IN NEST

TREE HOUSES
As trees are exposed, they are battered by wind and rain. For protection, squirrels build round tree-nests, in which they rest, sleep, and raise their young. Most nests are built in a new tree each year. Winter nests are stronger than summer ones, and special nurseries are built for the young.

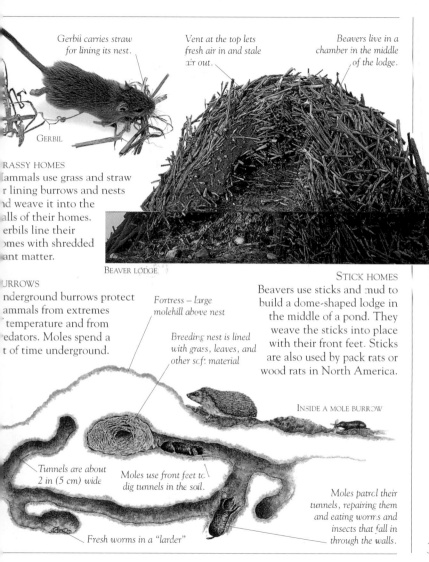

Gerbil carries straw for lining its nest.

Vent at the top lets fresh air in and stale air out.

Beavers live in a chamber in the middle of the lodge.

GERBIL

GRASSY HOMES

Mammals use grass and straw for lining burrows and nests and weave it into the walls of their homes. Gerbils line their homes with shredded plant matter.

BEAVER LODGE

BURROWS

Underground burrows protect mammals from extremes of temperature and from predators. Moles spend a lot of time underground.

Fortress – large molehill above nest

Breeding nest is lined with grass, leaves, and other soft material

STICK HOMES

Beavers use sticks and mud to build a dome-shaped lodge in the middle of a pond. They weave the sticks into place with their front feet. Sticks are also used by pack rats or wood rats in North America.

INSIDE A MOLE BURROW

Tunnels are about 2 in (5 cm) wide

Moles use front feet to dig tunnels in the soil.

Moles patrol their tunnels, repairing them and eating worms and insects that fall in through the walls.

Fresh worms in a "larder"

WHERE MAMMALS LIVE

MAMMALS LIVE all over the world, from mountaintop and the icy poles to baking hot deserts. They can do this because they are warm-blooded, which enables them to keep a constant body temperature – even when their surroundings are extremely hot or very cold.

WOODLAND AND FOREST
There is plenty of food and shelter in these habitats, but mammals have to cope with seasonal changes that bring cold weather and less food.

NORTH AMERICA

ATLANTIC OCEAN

PACIFIC OCEAN

SOUTH AMERICA

AFRICA

- Woodland and forest
- Rainforest
- Grassland
- Deserts
- Mountains and polar
- Oceans and seas
- Freshwater bodies

RAINFOREST
The year-round warm, wet climate encourages a variety of mammals that live in the trees and on the forest floor.

FRESHWATER BODIES
Mammals in rivers, lakes, and swamps are often strong swimmers with waterproof fur and webbed feet.

OCEANS AND SEAS
These habitats form 70 percent of the earth's surface. Some mammals breed on land; others never leave the water.

MOUNTAINS AND POLAR
With cold temperatures, strong winds, and little moisture, these habitats are home to some of the hardiest mammals.

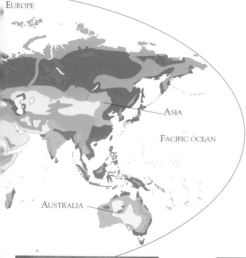

EUROPE

ASIA

PACIFIC OCEAN

AUSTRALIA

GRASSLAND
Small burrowers and herds of grazers live in both hot and cool grasslands, which occur where it is too dry for trees.

DESERTS
Desert mammals are specially adapted to survive dry conditions and extreme temperatures. Many store food and rarely drink.

WOODLAND AND FOREST

PLENTY OF FOOD, shelter, and nesting places are to be found in woodlands and forests. The main large herbivores are deer. Many small herbivores, such as mice and voles, live in the undergrowth away from predators such as stoats and wolverines. Much of this habitat is protected, but some is still threatened by logging and pollution.

Powerful legs help pine martens climb

Long, bushy tail helps provide balance.

Chipmunks crack nuts with their strong front teeth.

FOOD AND FEEDIN
From nuts and berries to leaves and bar
food for plant eaters like chipmunks
adundant here and varies with th
seasons. Small mamma
scurrying through falle
leaves are a major sourc
of food f
predatc

NIGHT HUNTERS
Many woodland mammals rest during the day and become active at night, especially at dusk or dawn. The pine marten is a swift and agile hunter of birds and rodents in trees and on the ground.

CF

MOVING THROUGH THE FOREST

Some woodland mammals climb, glide, or fly up into the trees to find food or places to shelter and nest. Climbers, such as squirrels and koalas, have sharp claws for gripping, while gliding mammals can parachute from tree to tree. Only bats fly freely though the branches.

SUGAR GLIDER

Flaps of skin are spread along sides of body to glide between trees.

WINTER SURVIVAL

Mammals survive the winter in many ways. Some, such as the sable, have a thick fur coat to keep warm, while others build up food stores for the hard times ahead. Larger mammals hibernate, or rest, during cold periods.

Sable is up to 18 in (45 cm) long.

Thick fur coat

Even the soles of the feet are furry.

Hedgehogs have up to 5,000 sharp, stiff spines.

HEDGEHOG

HIBERNATING HEDGEHOGS

When a mammal such as a hedgehog or a dormouse hibernates, its body processes slow down, keeping it barely alive. In this deep sleep, there is no need to waste energy finding food or keeping warm. A hibernating mammal relies on stores of food or body fat and a protected den to help it survive.

No spines underneath body

DECIDUOUS WOODLAND

IN TEMPERATE WOODLANDS, mammal lifestyles change with the seasons. Young are born in spring, so they can grow strong by the time winter comes. In summer and autumn, mammals feed as much as possible to gain stores of fat for winter's lean months. While larger mammals spend the winter resting in their burrows, many small ones stay active to keep warm.

Meadow vole is hard to see among dead leaves.

UNDER COVER
Hidden in vegetation and leaf litter, small mammals, such as voles, depend on camouflage for survival. As they must feed frequently, many climb trees to collect nuts and other food for storage in underground chambers

SKILLED CLIMBERS
Leaping nimbly from branch to branch, gray squirrels are masters of life in the trees. They can balance on the thinnest twigs and run up and down tree trunks by climbing with their sharp claws. Food is kept in their twiggy nests, which are built high above ground in trees.

Squirrels eat nuts and seeds.

Bush tail used for balance

Badgers have keen senses of smell and hearing but poor eyesight.

Black-and-white face markings break up the outline of the badger, so it is hard to see in twilight.

Long, strong claws for digging underground homes

Whiskers brush against surroundings to help the weasel navigate in the dark.

BURROWING BADGERS
A family of badgers lives in a system of underground burrows which may be hundreds of years old. Signs of occupied burrows include well-marked paths, piles of old bedding material, and dung pits.

AMAZING FACTS

• The largest system of badger burrows had 50 underground chambers and 178 entrances.

• Gray squirrels carry acorns up to 100 ft (30 m) from an oak tree before burying them.

• Dormice in some countries hibernate for as long as nine months.

WOODLAND PREDATOR
Ferocious hunters of small animals, weasels are slim enough to chase mice or voles right into their burrows. During the winter months in cold, snowy climates, weasels may grow a white coat, making it hard for both prey and predators to see them.

Sharp claws

Weasels often stand up on their hind legs to look for signs of food and danger.

391

CONIFEROUS FOREST

STRETCHING ACROSS northern Europe, Asia, and Nort
America, coniferous forests provide year-round shelter
for mammals. In the bitter winters, some mammals
hibernate and others turn white for camouflage. To
conserve heat, mammals that live here have thick
fur coats and are larger than their southern relatives.

*Powerful
muscles give
bears great
strength.*

SLEEPY BEAR
In autumn, brown
bears eat as much as
possible to build up fat
stores that keep them
alive during the winter.
In winter, females give
birth to cubs, while
males have periods of
inactivity. Bears are not
true hibernators – if it
turns warm, they wake
up and begin feeding.

*Powerful jaws and
teeth allow the bear to
eat a variety of foods*

*Thick fur coat
protects the bear
against freezing
temperatures.*

*Strong claws for
killing prey or digging
for plant food*

Fur is molted in summer

Long ears pick up sounds clearly

BIG EARS!

Long-eared bats hover in the trees where they catch insects. They feed at night, navigating by making high-pitched sounds and picking up the echoes as they bounce back off nearby objects.

Powerful jaws give a crushing bite.

Thick fur keeps in heat.

PERSISTENT PREDATOR

As the largest member of the weasel family, the fierce wolverine can catch animals as large as caribou (reindeer), pursuing them for up to 40 miles (65 km). Inuit peoples once prized wolverine fur for making coats because it can shed ice crystals.

Widespread toes help the wolverine to travel over snow without sinking

Young have more distinct stripes than adults.

WILD THING

The striped coat of the wildcat provides good camouflage for stalking the forest. Wildcats live a solitary life, hunting at night. They are closely related to domestic cats.

EUCALYPTUS WOODLAND

AUSTRALIA'S HOT, DRY woodland provides food and shelter all year round. Most mammals here are marsupials (pouched mammals) that come out at night, using their sharp senses of smell and hearing to find their way around. Some, such as koalas, live in the trees, while others, including bandicoots, live on the forest floor.

POUCHED JUMPER

During the day, groups, or mobs, of gray kangaroos rest under the trees, but at night they search for plants to eat. Young kangaroos stay in the pouch for up to 11 months, longer than any other marsupial, and suckle until they are 18 months old.

Large ears and eyes and keen sense of smell to detect signs of danger.

AMAZING FACTS

• A baby kangaroo, or joey, is the fastest-growing animal. When born, it is thimble-sized, but it grows by 30,000 times in its lifetime.

• The common wombat is the largest burrowing marsupial. It burrows at 10 ft (3 m) an hour.

Fro lim have fi claw digi:

Kangaro graze wi all four fe on the grou

Powerful back legs f bounding away fro enemi

Tail helps keep balance.

FUSSY EATERS

The tree-dwelling koala seldom comes to the ground, clinging to branches with its strong limbs and sharp claws. Koalas spend about 18 hours a day snoozing in the trees. When awake, they feed only on the leaves of 12 out of the 100 species of eucalyptus tree, eating about 3 lb (1.5 kg) of leaves each day.

A baby koala lives in its mother's pouch for six months, then spends another six months carried on her back.

Koalas have a long intestine to help digest tough leaves.

Numbats have about 50 teeth.

Tail can grow 8 in (20 cm) long

Striped coat camouflages numbat from predators such as eagles.

NUMBAT

TERMITE HUNGRY

One of the few mammals in these woodland to be active during the day, numbats eat thousands of termites, which they collect with their long, narrow tongue.

The name "devil" comes from its black color and eerie call.

Sensitive nose to sniff out prey

LETHAL PREDATOR

The huge head and strong jaws of the Tasmanian devil allow it to crush and eat its prey, bones and all. Tasmanian devils live in dens under rocks or tree stumps and are mainly nocturnal. Their young stay in the pouch for about 15 weeks and then are left in the nest or carried around on the mother's back until 20 weeks of age, when they are weaned.

DEER

WOODS AND FORESTS, home to many kinds of deer, provide ample food and shelter. In this habitat, deer are hard to spot, with their camouflaged coat and shy nature. They use their sharp senses to detect danger, and long legs to nimbly leap away.

Sharp incisors to tear grass

MALE MUNTJAC SKULL

GRINDING TEETH
The narrow snout of the deer allows it to reach into small space to find food. Molar teeth grind and mash tough plant matter.

Long legs and broad hooves to move through swamps or deep snow

Males have broad, flat antlers, which they use to joust with each other in competition for a mate.

Overhanging top lip tears off leaves and branches.

Flap of skin is known as the bell.

Strong neck and shoulder muscles support heavy head and antlers.

LARGEST DEER
Moose, or elk, are the largest deer, weighing up to 1,000 lb (450 kg) and standing 6.5 ft (2 m) tall at the shoulder. Unlike most deer, moose do not live in groups and excluding the autumn breeding season, are usually alone or with their young. In winter, moose eat woody plants, but in summer, they wade into water for more tender vegetation.

ANTLER GROWTH

1. Antlers start to grow.

2. Antlers are covered in soft skin, called velvet.

3. Velvet dries up and peels off.

4. Fallow deer have flat (palmate) antlers.

RED DEER AND FAWN

DEER ANTLERS

All male deer, apart from Chinese water deer, have, on their head, a set of bony antlers which serve as a sign of strength and dominance. They shed and grow a new set of antlers each year. In the autumn rutting (mating) season, male deer use their antlers in pushing contests to win females.

ROE DEER

The reddish brown coat of the roe deer blends in well with the summer colors of woods and forests. In winter, it grows a thick, gray-brown coat for warmth and camouflage.

Antlers no more than 12 in (30 cm) long

Roe deer feed on grasses at dusk and dawn.

MALE ROE DEER

AMAZING DEER FACTS

• Deer are the only animals in the world to have antlers.

• The American wapiti and the caribou have the longest antlers, at about 5 ft (1.5 m) in length!

• The South American pudu is the smallest deer, at 15 in (38 cm) tall!

• Red deer are likely to live for over 30 years.

397

RAINFOREST

THE WORLD'S RICHEST habitat, rainforests provide a year-round warm, wet climate and a variety of food and resting places. Most mammals here are agile climbers that live in trees, but large predators stalk the forest floor. Rainforests are being destroyed at an alarming rate.

Thin "wings" of skin run along the sides of the body.

COLUGO, ALSO CALLED FLYING LEMUR

GLIDING IN THE TREES
Gripping with long toes, claws, or tails; gliding on skin flaps; or flying with wings, mammals move easily from branch to branch in search of food or mates or to escape danger.

Canopy: monkeys, fruit bats, sloths, gliders

Understory: jungle cats, tree kangaroos, lorises

Forest floor: peccaries, tapirs, okapis, elephants

LAYERS OF THE RAINFOREST
Mammals share the rich resources of the rainforest by living at various levels. In the trees, there are leaves, flowers, insects, fruits, and nuts on which to feed. The forest floor provides a feast of millions more insects, spiders, worms, and other invertebrates, as well as plant roots, shoots, and fungi

FOREST ECHOES
Visual communication is difficult among thick tangles of vegetation, so many mammals, especially monkeys and apes, rely on sound or scent signals instead. They mark territorial boundaries by scent or shrill cries, sounding alarms and remaining in contact with one another by calling.

Tail can be 3 ft (90 cm) long

HOWLER MONKEY

A tiger's stripes help it stalk its prey without being seen.

Every tiger has a different pattern of black stripes on its face.

Calls of the howler monkey can be heard up to 2 miles (3 km) away.

Tigers live in the forests of South and Southeast Asia and mark their territories with scent and droppings.

WELL CAMOUFLAGED
Spots, stripes, and other markings on rainforest mammals help to camouflage them in the dappled forest light. They break up the animal's outline and blend it in with the background. Both predators, such as tigers, and their prey, such as deer, use camouflage. Young mammals are often better camouflaged than their parents.

TIGER

399

IN THE TREES

HIGH UP IN the rainforest, tangled tree branches form tricky walkways. Mammals living here may be swift-moving climbers or flyers, or slow movers that can grasp branches well. Many tree-dwelling mammals come out at night to avoid predators such as cats, hawks, eagles, and snakes.

SPIDER MONKEY

Gripping tail

Long fingers to catch onto branches

JUNGLE ACROBAT
The spider monkey's strong tail helps support its weight and provides an extra "hand," to reach fruit and leaves. These monkeys can make acrobatic leaps of more than 30 ft (10 m) through the branches.

LAZING IN THE TREES
Hanging upside down from branches in the rainforests of Central and South America, sloths spend 20 hours a day snoozing in the canopy. Their fur grows toward the spine so that rain runs straight off their backs. Green algae grow in the hair, camouflaging the sloth.

The sloth hooks its claws around branches and moves only one limb at a time

*Nir
nec
vertebra
allow the sloth
turn its head farth
than other mamma*

SLOTH

Bats roost in trees, holding their wings around their body and gripping tightly with their strong claws

Fruit bats have excellent eyesight and a fine sense of smell for detecting ripe fruit.

Because their faces look like those of foxes, fruit bats are sometimes called flying foxes.

Figs and mangoes are easily crushed with strong teeth and tongues.

FRUIT BAT

NECTAR SPREADER
The flowering and fruiting trees of the rainforest make ideal homes for bats that eat pollen, nectar, or fruit. These bats are useful in spreading the pollen and seeds of rainforest plants. Long, bristly tongues help pollen- and nectar-eaters to scoop up food.

TREE
KANGAROO

Sharp claws for climbing

Feet are strong and wide, with rough pads for gripping branches.

The tree kangaroo lives in the cooler forests of New Guinea and has a warm fur coat.

IN THE TREES FACTS
• Three-toed sloths are slow movers, with an average ground speed of just 6–8 ft (1.83–2.44 m) a minute.

• The tail of a spider monkey can grow to 3 ft (90 cm) – a third longer than its body length!

• Fruit bats are the largest of all bats, with wing spans as great as 7 ft (2 m)!

KEEPING A BALANCE
Living in northeast Australia and New Guinea, tree kangaroos have long tails that help them to balance on branches. They do not hop like other kangaroos. Small groups of tree kangaroos live and sleep together in the same tree, but they usually come down to feed.

401

ON THE FOREST FLOOR

THE RAINFOREST FLOOR is home to larger mammals. Peaceful herbivores, such as okapis, elephants, and gorillas, feed on leaves, while anteaters, pangolins, and armadillos eat termites and other invertebrates. Peccaries dig out roots, keeping a lookout for predators, such as jaguars and ocelots.

STURDY HERBIVORE
Consuming around 375 lb (170 kg) of fibrous plant matter a day, elephants need to have tough stomachs. Their trunks are vital for reaching understory vegetation.

FOREST FLOOR FACTS

• The armadillo's front claws, used for digging up prey, are larger than any other animal's.

• You can tell an Asian elephant from an African one by its smaller ears and shorter tusks. Its dome-shaped forehead also contrasts with the African elephant's rounded one.

Long trunk reaches up to pick fruit or tear down branches

Trunk is a long nose and top lip joined together

Teeth have sharp ridges for grinding up tough plants

Adult bull elephant stands 10 ft (3 m) tall

Flat sole spreads out to help distribute the massive weight

AFRICAN ELEPHANT

SHY ANTELOPE

Rabbit-sized royal antelope, which live in African rainforests, are one of the smallest hoofed mammals. They are timid, coming out at night to feed on leaves. Royal antelope can slip away silently or leap as high as 10 ft (3 m) into the air to escape predators such as birds and snakes.

Females do not have horns.

ROYAL ANTELOPE

CHAMPION DIGGER

Massive claws on its front feet enable the giant armadillo to smash its way inside rock-hard termite mounds. It also digs for other insects, worms, and spiders, and eats snakes.

Protective horny plates

GIANT ARMADILLO

Each ocelot has different fur markings.

RARE PAINTED LEOPARD

The ocelot, or painted leopard, lives in the rainforests of Central and South America. Hunting at night, the ocelot has large, keen eyes for navigating the dark forest, and its spotted coat gives camouflage as it creeps up on prey. Ocelots are rare because of forest destruction and hunting for their fur.

403

JUNGLE APES

TROPICAL RAINFORESTS are home to all the world's apes, including gibbons, chimpanzees, gorillas, and orangutans. Unlike monkeys, apes do not have tails. Gorillas and chimpanzees spend much of their time on the ground, while gibbons and orangutans swing through the trees. Apes usually live in families and feed by day.

HANGING AROUND
Gibbons are mainly vegetarian and live in small groups in Asian rainforests. Confident, skilled climbers, gibbons can run upright along large branches and swing effortlessly through the trees.

Lower spine is short and inflexible, and rib cage is solid to avoid distorting the trunk while swinging.

Arms are longer than legs.

OUR CLOSEST RELATIVES?
This chimp is investigating a toy block. Chimps are intelligent, communicating by sound and gesture.

AMAZING APE FACTS

• Male gorillas usually weigh 300–400 lb (135–175 kg), but a zoo gorilla once weighed in at 683 lb (310 kg)!

• Some apes can live to be over 50 years old.

• About 99 percent of human genes are the same as a chimpanzee's.

GIBBON SWINGING
THROUGH TREES

*Arms are twice as
long as legs, at a
span of about
6 ft (2 m).*

*Flexible hooklike
hands quickly grasp
branches or prey.*

*Hand-over-
hand swinging
movement is
called brachiation.*

*Making "rowing"
movements with its legs
helps the gibbon propel
itself through the air.*

*Mature male
gorillas have
silvery gray hair
on their backs
and are called
"silver-backs."*

GENTLE GIANT

This male gorilla is the head of
a family group that wanders
through the forest, eating fruit and
ferns. Females and young climb trees,
but males rarely
do because
they are so
big and
heavy.

*Fatty
throat
pouch*

*Long,
powerful
arms*

FIVE-YEAR-
OLD MALE

MALE GORILLA

KING OF THE SWINGERS

In the forests of
Borneo and Sumatra, shy
orangutans live a solitary
life, except in breeding
season. Males are much
heavier and larger than
females, and mature males have
wide cheek flaps on their faces.

405

GRASSLAND

LYING BETWEEN wet forests and dry deserts, grasslands fall into two categories– tropical, such as the African savanna, and temperate, such as the prairies or steppes. Grassland mammals include plant-eating herds, small burrowers, and the predators that feed on both groups.

Prairie dogs live in colonies of thousands in underground tunnels

PRAIRIE DOG

Horns measure up to 16 in (40 cm)

Strong, grinding teeth to reduce tough grasses and leaves.

Long legs and sharp hooves to run swiftly away from danger

THOMSON'S GAZELLE

BURROWERS

To avoid the heat and cold, and to escape predators and fires, many small mammals burrow underground. Their burrowing, meanwhile, mixes the soil and encourages plant growth.

GRAZERS

The most common large grassland herbivores are grazers – grass-eating mammals like antelope, bison, and horses. Grasses, which sprout again when the tops are bitten off, produce a continuous supply of food. Grazers, such as Thomson's gazelle, live in herds of up to 100 for protection against predators.

HUNTERS

Most large hunters – like lions, cheetahs, leopards, and hyenas– are found on the African savanna. Since they hunt in groups, lions and hyenas can prey on animals much bigger than themselves. Cheetahs hunt alone but can run fast enough to catch swift antelopes.

CHEETAH → THOMSON'S GAZELLE

LION → WILDEBEEST

HYENA → ZEBRA

Fur tufts on ears can be 1¾ in (4.5 cm) long.

Caracal is a Turkish word meaning "black ears."

GRASSLAND CATS

Cats, big and small, are common grassland hunters. Small cats, like caracals and servals, have longer legs than forest cats and rely on speed and surprise to catch their prey. Cats overpower prey with a vicious bite from their powerful jaws, which are armed with sharp, dagger-like teeth.

Sharp teeth for tearing prey apart

A swipe of the paw can kill a bird in mid-air.

Short, dense fur keeps caracal warm at night and cool by day.

CARACAL

407

PAMPAS AND STEPPES

THE VAST PLAINS known as
pampas in South America
and steppes in Europe and
central Asia have hot
summers and cold winters.
Many small mammals, such
as cavies on the pampas and
mole rats on the steppes, live
underground. Herds of wild
grazers have mostly been
replaced by domesticated
cattle and horses.

*Coat turns white
and thickens in
winter*

*Nostrils can
be closed
during sand
storms*

SAIGA
ANTELOPE

STEPPE GRAZERS
The saiga antelope's long nose helps
to warm the air it inhales during cold
winters on the steppes. Huge herds of
saigas once roamed the steppes; they
are now a protected species.

*As anteaters have no teeth, food
is mashed up by hard ridges in
the mouth and a muscular
stomach.*

*Tongue pushes
out 150 times
a minute.*

MANED WOLF

GIANT PREDATOR
Insects are the main grazers of the pampas,
and make a tasty meal for the giant anteater.
Anteaters feed mostly on ants and termites,
ripping open nests with their big claws and
licking the insects with their sticky tongues.

To escape danger, maras or Patagonian hares can use their back legs to leap 6½ ft (2 m) into the air.

Cavies are wild relatives of the pet guinea pig.

[vi]scachas dig with their strong [fro]nt legs and can close their [no]strils to stop soil from getting in.

BUSY BURROWERS
Underground burrows provide safe shelter for small mammals of the [p]ampas, such as the mara, [c]avy, and viscacha. Maras [an]d cavies may live in old viscacha burrows in groups of up to 40.

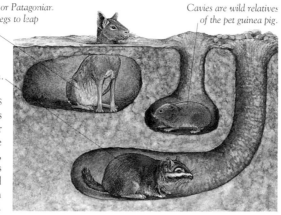

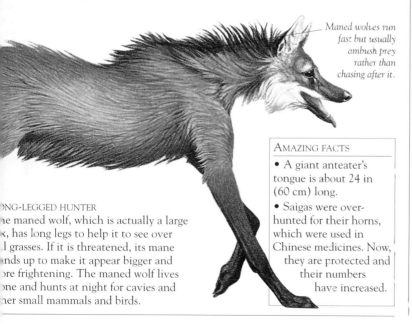

Maned wolves run fast but usually ambush prey rather than chasing after it.

LONG-LEGGED HUNTER
[Th]e maned wolf, which is actually a large [fo]x, has long legs to help it to see over [tall] grasses. If it is threatened, its mane [sta]nds up to make it appear bigger and [mo]re frightening. The maned wolf lives [alo]ne and hunts at night for cavies and [oth]er small mammals and birds.

AMAZING FACTS
• A giant anteater's tongue is about 24 in (60 cm) long.
• Saigas were over-hunted for their horns, which were used in Chinese medicines. Now, they are protected and their numbers have increased.

MAMMALS

AFRICAN SAVANNAS

THE HUGE GRASSLANDS of Africa are called savannas. They are home to the last great herds of mammals, such as elephants and antelope, and their predators, including hyenas and large cats. There are two main seasons – wet and dry – and many grazers migrate regularly in search of fresh grass to eat.

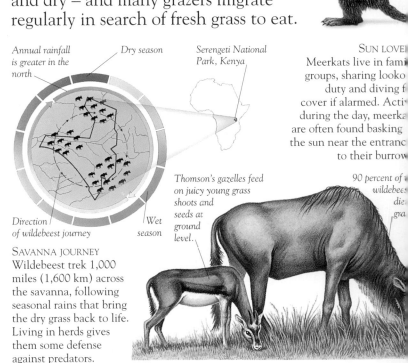

Meerk
sit up
their hi
legs
watch
dang

Annual rainfall is greater in the north

Dry season

Serengeti National Park, Kenya

Direction of wildebeest journey

Wet season

SUN LOVE
Meerkats live in fami
groups, sharing looko
duty and diving f
cover if alarmed. Acti
during the day, meerka
are often found basking
the sun near the entranc
to their burrow

Thomson's gazelles feed on juicy young grass shoots and seeds at ground level.

90 percent of
wildebees
dia
gra

SAVANNA JOURNEY
Wildebeest trek 1,000 miles (1,600 km) across the savanna, following seasonal rains that bring the dry grass back to life. Living in herds gives them some defense against predators.

Large, rounded ears

Giraffes can reach leaves up to 20 ft (6 m) above the ground

Only four toes on front foot

FFICIENT PREDATORS

ving in packs of 6 to 30, African
nting dogs are nomadic animals,
aming a wide area in search of
ey. By hunting together, the
gs can bring down prey
rger than themselves,
en wildebeest. The
ck shares a kill.

*any savanna
imals have
ttterned skin for
mouflage.*

Zebras feed on tough, grass tops and also dig for roots.

SHARING FOOD
Various mammals live
together on the savanna,
sharing resources. Giraffes
feed on the highest leaves;
zebras crop the top of the
grasses; wildebeest eat the
medium-length grasses; and
Thomson's gazelles nibble
grass close to the ground.

AMAZING FACTS

• Hyenas have jaws so
strong that they can
crunch through bones.

• Young wildebeest can
run very soon after they
are born.

• African hunting dogs
may start to feed on
their prey while it
is still alive.

411

GRASSLAND CATS

INTELLIGENT, POWERFUL hunters with sharp senses, grassland cats, both big and small, have strong claws and teeth and a rasping tongue to scrape meat off bones. The spotted coats of leopards, cheetahs, and servals, and the tawny-colored fur of caracals and lions, provide camouflage in the golden grasses. Lions are the only big cats to live in social groups

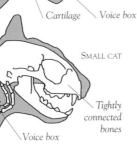

Loose bones

BIG CAT

Cartilage \ *Voice box*

SMALL CAT

Tightly connected bones

Voice box

Male lion's mane makes him look fiercer and protects his neck during fights

MALE

TO PURR OR ROAR?
Most big cats can roar, but little cats are unable to. The skull and voice box of a big cat, such as a lion or tiger, are loosely connected, allowing them to roar. In cheetahs and mountain lions, these connections are tighter, so the bones cannot vibrate.

reamlined body   _Flexible spine_

Tail helps the cheetah balance when sprinting

At top speed, all four feet are lifted between strides.

Claws are made of keratin, like human nails.

AST CAT

heetahs hunt by
ay, stalking and attacking prey
ith a short burst of speed. They
an reach 60 mph (96 km/h) in
just three seconds.

Long legs for fast running

Exposed claws grip the ground.

RELAXED

EXTENDED

KING OF THE CATS

Lions live in groups called prides,
made up of 5 to 15 related adult
females and their young and 1
to 6 adult males. Males defend
the pride while females hunt and
care for the young. Lions are the
only cats to hunt together, share
prey, and help rear one another's cubs.

CAT CLAWS

All cats, except cheetahs,
can draw in their claws.
This allows the cat to
creep up on prey. A cat
has four claws on its back
paws and five on its front.

_Male and female lions look
more different than the two
sexes of any other cat._

FEMALE

AMAZING CAT FACTS

- Lions sleep or doze for
up to 20 hours every day.

- A lion's roar can be
heard up to 3 miles
(5 km) away.

- A cheetah can only
run at top speed for 60
seconds, or it overheats.

- Adult lions eat as
much as 40 lb (18 kg)
of meat in one meal.

DESERTS

VERY LITTLE RAIN falls on the world's deserts. Most of them, such as the Sahara, are scorching hot all year round, although they get very cold at night. Some, such as the Gobi, have freezing winters. Many small desert mammals are nocturnal, burrowing by day to protect themselves from the extreme heat. Most desert mammals can survive with very little water. Their fur keeps out heat as well as cold.

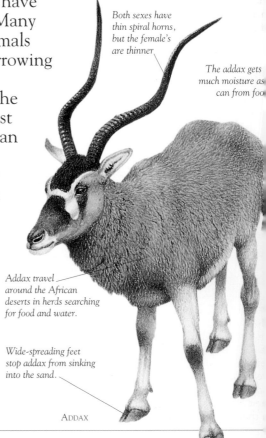

Both sexes have thin spiral horns, but the female's are thinner

The addax gets much moisture as can from foo

Addax travel around the African deserts in herds searching for food and water.

Wide-spreading feet stop addax from sinking into the sand.

ADDAX

LARGE MAMMALS
There are few large desert mammals because there is not enough food and water to keep them alive. Only a few kinds of specialized mammals, such as addax, camels, gazelle, antelopes, and kangaroos, manage to survive. They often have to travel long distances in search of water.

DESERT DEFENSE

By coming out at night, small mammals avoid predators as well as the heat of the day. The light color of their fur helps them to blend in with the sand and rocks. Small mammals often leap out of the way of predators.

EGYPTIAN SPINY MOUSE

Tail can be shed if grabbed by predator.

Hair in ears keeps out dust and sand.

Fur has stiff hairs to put off predators.

soles of feet are covered with long hair for walking on scorching sand.

ARABIAN SPINY MOUSE

BIG EARS

Some desert mammals, such as fennec foxes and jackrabbits, have large ears that work like radiators to give off heat and keep them cool. The African fennec fox looks like the North American kit fox, because they have both adapted to survive in the same habitat.

FENNEC FOX

DESERT BURROWERS

Most burrowing mammals, such as mulgaras, stay underground until the heat of the day has passed. The sand is much cooler slightly below the surface. The mammals' breath creates a moist atmosphere in the burrow, reducing the amount of water evaporating from their bodies. Many small mammals store food in their burrows to last them through lean times.

MULGARA

Mulgaras never drink and excrete concentrated urine to preserve water.

HOT DESERTS

TEMPERATURES IN THE deserts of western North America, Australia, and the African Sahara are scorching during the day. Because there are no clouds to retain the heat, however, they drop to freezing at night. There are few plants to provide shelter from the extreme temperatures. Most mammals avoid the daytime sun. Others have large ears or light coats to lose heat, and some pant to cool down. The dew that forms at night may provide much needed moisture.

Blood flow in ears is regulated to control heat loss or gain.

COOLING SYSTEM
The long ears of the North American jackrabbit have many blood vessels close to the skin's surface. Heat passes from the blood to the air around the ears, helping to cool the jackrabbit down.

Streamlined shape and smooth, silky fur help the mole slide easily through the sand.

MARSUPIAL MOLE

Marsupial moles are blind.

BLIND TUNNELLE
The Australian marsupial mole use its long claws to tunnel through san Its nose is protected by a horny shiel The burrows are not permanent – th sand is soft and tunnels collapse quickl

*Large ears to
listen for prey
and keep cool*

UNSINKABLE CAT
Thick fur on the
soles of the sand
cat's feet prevent it
from sinking into
the soft sand. Sand
cats shelter in a
burrow or under scrub
vegetation during the
day and hunt at
night. They don't
drink, getting all
the water they
need from
their prey.

*low-brown coat
nds into desert
kground.*

SAND CAT

SWEAT
ke all rodents, kangaroo rats conserve
ter by not sweating and by producing
ly a small amount of urine and dry
oppings. Kangaroo rats are nocturnal
d travel long distances looking for
od. When they find seeds,
ey carry them
their cheek
uches.

*Long tail helps the
kangaroo rat balance while
hopping and running.*

ears to
en for
ger*

*Strong back
legs for leaping
away from
predators*

KANGAROO
RAT

AMAZING FACTS

• Jackrabbits can bound
at 35 mph (56 km/h).

• The kidneys of a
kangaroo rat are four
times more efficient
than those of a person.

• Lions once lived in
the Sahara but died out
due to hunting by man
and increasing dryness.

417

COLD DESERTS

CENTRAL ASIA'S COLD DESERTS, such as the Gobi desert, are harsh habitats for mammals. Besides great swings in temperature between day and night, there are freezing winters of -42°F (-40°C). Some mammals such as Bactrian camels and dwarf hamsters, rely on their thick coats to keep warm. Small mammals survive desert conditions by spending a lot of time in burrows. Many have long legs to escape from predators.

The onager's coat is thicker in winter

MIGRATOR
Also called the Asiatic wild ass, the onager can run away from enemies at speeds of 40 mph (65 km/h). It migrates to find fresh grass and water.

Some turn white in winter for camouflage in the snow.

Camels can close their nostrils to prevent sand getting in.

Even the soles of the feet are hairy.

HAIRY HAMSTER
As they forage for seeds and nuts, dwarf hamsters push food into their cheek pouches and then carry it underground for storage. Dwarf hamsters have very thick fur to help them survive the extreme climate. They also stay in their burrows much of the time.

*Large ears
and eyes
to sense
danger.*

*Back legs are
four times as
long as the
front legs.*

SERT JUMPER

the darkness of the desert night, jerboas emerge
m their burrows to feed on seeds, shoots, and
sects. Jerboas are like tiny kangaroos, able to jump
ay from enemies on their strong back legs. Their
ng tail helps them to balance when they jump
d supports their body when they rest.

WALKING WATER TANK

The thick fur of a two-humped
Bactrian camel holds in body heat
during the bitterly cold Asian
winters. These camels molt fur
in spring when the weather gets
warmer. Camels have long, thick
eyelashes to protect their eyes
from sharp grains of sand.

AMAZING CAMEL FACTS

• A camel can drink up
to 13 gallons (60 liters)
of water in minutes.

• Camels do not sweat
until their temperature
reaches 105°F
(40.5°C) – a high
fever in a human.

• A 1,100-lb (500-kg)
camel can store more
than 110 lb (50 kg)
of fat in its hump(s).

*Humps store fat,
which can be broken
down to provide
energy and water.*

*Fur is
molted
in spring.*

*Webbed feet with thick
pads prevent the camel
from sinking into the sand.*

MOUNTAINS AND POLAR

LONG, FRIGID WINTERS, fierce winds, intense sunlight, and cold air with little moisture typify the climate of mountain and polar regions. Mammals in these habitats rely on thick fur coats or layers of fat to keep warm. Some of these mammals' coats change color seasonally, for camouflage. To escape the extreme winter cold, many polar mammals migrate to warmer habitats.

Vicuñas have thick fur and can run at up to 29 mph (47 km/h).

VICUÑA

MOUNTAIN CLIMBERS

Large plant-eating mammals living on mountains have to keep moving to find food and avoid predators. These herbivores include wild mountain sheep and goats, as well as the vicuñas and alpacas of South America. Sure-footed and agile, these hearty mammals have sharp, pointed hooves that grip on steep, slippery slopes.

Abou 600–70(sensitive whiskers t(help find foo(

POLAR OCEANS

In polar regions, the sea is often warmer than the air. It is also very rich in food. Some mammals migrate to polar oceans for the summer months, while others live there all year round.

Fatty blubber more than 4 in (10 cm) thick.

ARCTIC FOX IN
SUMMER COAT

TUNDRA CAMOUFLAGE
In the Arctic tundra – the permanently frozen lands around the edge of the Arctic – mammals may change color with the seasons. The Arctic fox, snowshoe hare, and stoat, for example, turn white in winter for camouflage against the snow. In the summer, when the snow melts, their coats change to brown or gray to blend with the landscape.

*Chest and belly stay
a pale, grayish white.*

*Hollow hairs trap
warm air near
the body.*

*rry paws act
e snowshoes.*

*wo
yers of
ick fur keep
e bear warm.*

EEP NG WARM
hic layers of fur
d f t insulate
lar mammals
;ains the cold, and
ubber acts as a food
ore for hard times. In
inter, small mammals,
ch as marmots, hibernate
burrows, while
male polar bears
ve birth to their
bs in cozy dens dug in the snow.

*Nonslip soles
to grip the ice*

POLAR
BEAR

ARCTIC TUNDRA

AROUND THE EDGE of the icy Arctic ocean is a flat, treeless region called the tundra, where the sub-soil is always frozen. Some mammals, such as musk oxen, are hardy enough to live here all year round. Others, including caribou, or reindeer, cannot stand the harsh climate and migrate here only for the summer months.

Long, curved horns for defense against wolves

Two-layered coat keeps out the cold.

MUSK OX

ARCTIC WOLF

SHAGGY COAT
Musk oxen have long, woolly coats lined with underfur eight times warmer than sheep's wool. Some hairs in the outer coat are over 3 ft (1 m) long. Musk oxen have sharp hooves for digging through snow or ice to find food.

SIBERIAN
LEMMING

FAST BREEDERS
When food is plentiful, lemmings
nibble shoots and roots and breed
fast. In some summers, lemming
populations "explode," forcing
thousands to wander great
distances to find food.

BIG FEET
The wide hooves of the
caribou, or reindeer,
help it to walk on deep
snow without sinking
in. Caribou breed on
the tundra, moving
south for winter.

Thick,
waterproof
fur turns
gray-white
in winter.

Sensitive ears
track sounds
from 2 miles
(3 km)
away.

Big feet

CARIBOU

Long,
powerful legs
to run great
distances
after prey

CAMOUFLAGED PREDATOR
Arctic wolves have thick
fur, which turns white in
winter. This allows them to
blend into the background
and creep close to prey,
such as musk oxen. Pack
hunting enables wolves
to kill larger prey
than if they
hunted alone.

AMAZING FACTS
• Wolves can leap up
to 15 ft (4.5 m) and can
even jump backward!

• Musk oxen have the
longest fur of any
mammal.

• Adult caribou munch
their way through 10 lb
(4.5 kg) of food a day.

423

MOUNTAIN TOPS

MAMMALS ARE SCARCE on mountaintops. To cope with the cold and wind, many have adapted like Arctic mammals. They have thick, shaggy fur coats to keep warm and may move up and down the mountain with the seasons. Some small mammals, such as groundhogs, hibernate in winter after building up layers of fat in the summer. The internal organs of mammals on high mountains also may differ from those in the lowlands. Many have developed larger hearts and lungs to help them get enough oxygen from the thin air at high altitudes.

BATHING MACAQUE
To keep warm in winter, these monkeys from the mountains of northern Japan take hot baths in volcanic springs.

Thicker fur grows in winter.

RARE HUNTER
The snow leopard, or ounce, hunts wild sheep and goats at elevations of up to 18,000 ft (5,500 m) in the Himalayas. It roams its huge territory alone, and is rare as it has been hunted for its thick fur.

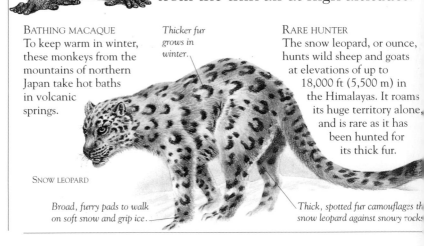

SNOW LEOPARD

Broad, furry pads to walk on soft snow and grip ice.

Thick, spotted fur camouflages the snow leopard against snowy rocks

FURRY CHINCHILLA

High up in the Andes mountains, chinchillas huddle
in rocky holes. Many have been hunted for
their coats, so they are rare
in the wild. Chinchillas
eat plants, holding
food in their paws.

*Bushy tail is 6 in
(15 cm) long*

*Soft,
dense fur
coat*

CHINCHILLA
*Summer coat is short and smooth;
winter coat is long and dense with
soft underfur.*

AMAZING FACTS

• The yak is the
highest-living large
mammal, grazing at
20,000 ft (6,000 m)
in the Himalayas.

• Chamois can live for
two weeks without food.

• According to legend,
yetis, or abominable
snowmen, live in the
Himalayas, but no one
has proved they exist.

CHAMOIS

*Both
sexes have
horns.*

SURE-FOOTED
CHAMOIS

The chamois has great
balance and can jump
nearly 30 ft (9 m) up
sheer rock faces in the
mountains of southern
Europe and western
Asia. Chamois browse
on plants, moving
down from the
peaks in winter.

*Hooves have a
hard, thin edge
for gripping rocks.*

*Shock-
absorbing legs
and spongy
hoof pads for
extra grip
on steep or
slippery
slopes*

425

OCEANS AND SEAS

LIVING NEAR THE SURFACE of the world's oceans and seas are a variety of marine mammals that come to the surface regularly to breathe. Some, such as whales and dolphins, never leave the water; others, such as seals, return to land to mate and have their pups. Sea mammals are streamlined, with modified limbs and tails for swimming and thick fat, or blubber, to keep them warm.

FURRY WARMTH

Unlike other sea mammals, the sea otter has no blubber for insulation. Instead it relies on thick, waterproof fur for warmth. An adult may have as many as 800 million hairs, which help provide buoyancy in the water.

SEAL GROUP

Seals fall into three main groups. True seals, like the one below, swim with their back flippers and have no visible ear flaps. Eared seals, like the sea lion on the right, swim with front flippers. Walruses are the third group.

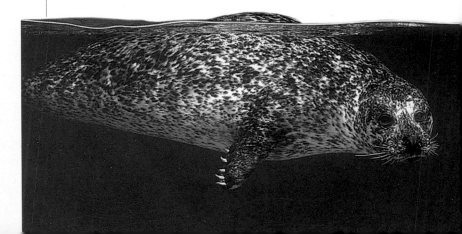

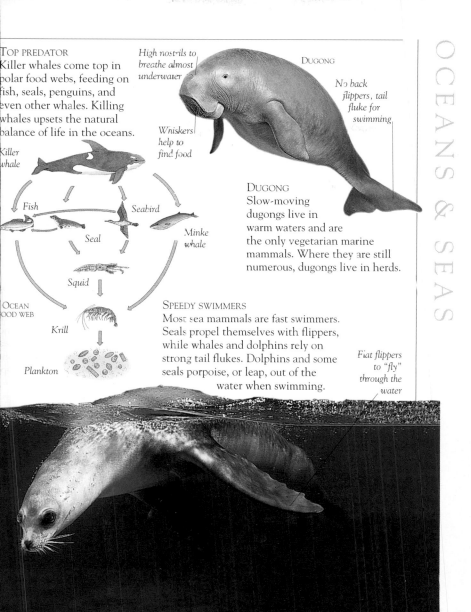

TOP PREDATOR
Killer whales come top in polar food webs, feeding on fish, seals, penguins, and even other whales. Killing whales upsets the natural balance of life in the oceans.

High nostrils to breathe almost underwater

Whiskers help to find food

DUGONG

No back flippers, tail fluke for swimming

Killer whale

Fish

Seabird

Seal

Minke whale

Squid

DUGONG
Slow-moving dugongs live in warm waters and are the only vegetarian marine mammals. Where they are still numerous, dugongs live in herds.

Ocean food web

Krill

SPEEDY SWIMMERS
Most sea mammals are fast swimmers. Seals propel themselves with flippers, while whales and dolphins rely on strong tail flukes. Dolphins and some seals porpoise, or leap, out of the water when swimming.

Plankton

Flat flippers to "fly" through the water

POLAR OCEANS

HARDY WHALES AND SEALS, such as beluga whales and ringed seals, survive in polar oceans all year round. Many other sea mammals migrate to these cold waters in summer, when food is plentiful. This surge in sea life is fueled by the vast numbers of tiny creatures called plankton, which form the basis of food webs that include fish, whales, squid, seals, and seabirds.

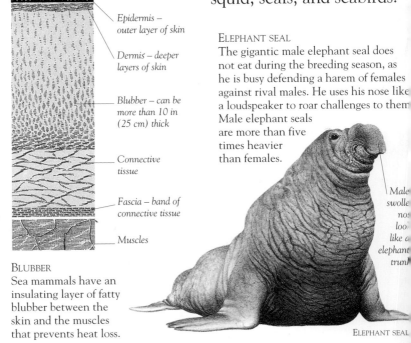

Epidermis – outer layer of skin

Dermis – deeper layers of skin

Blubber – can be more than 10 in (25 cm) thick

Connective tissue

Fascia – band of connective tissue

Muscles

BLUBBER
Sea mammals have an insulating layer of fatty blubber between the skin and the muscles that prevents heat loss.

ELEPHANT SEAL
The gigantic male elephant seal does not eat during the breeding season, as he is busy defending a harem of females against rival males. He uses his nose like a loudspeaker to roar challenges to them. Male elephant seals are more than five times heavier than females.

Male swollen nose looks like an elephant trunk

ELEPHANT SEAL

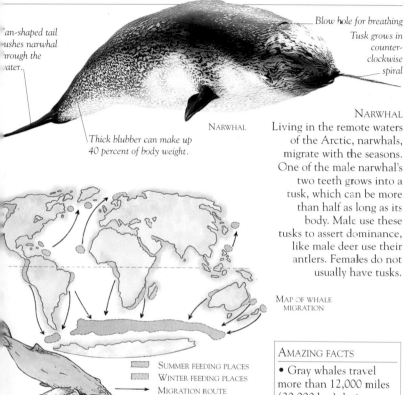

Fan-shaped tail pushes narwhal through the water.

Blow hole for breathing

Tusk grows in counter-clockwise spiral

NARWHAL

Thick blubber can make up 40 percent of body weight.

NARWHAL

Living in the remote waters of the Arctic, narwhals, migrate with the seasons. One of the male narwhal's two teeth grows into a tusk, which can be more than half as long as its body. Male use these tusks to assert dominance, like male deer use their antlers. Females do not usually have tusks.

MAP OF WHALE MIGRATION

▨ SUMMER FEEDING PLACES
▨ WINTER FEEDING PLACES
→ MIGRATION ROUTE

WHALE MIGRATION

In summer, many whales travel to the cold polar waters of the Arctic and the Antarctic to feed. In winter, when the sea freezes over, the whales swim back to warmer waters in the tropics to mate and have their young. They eat little in the winter, using up the energy stored as body fat from the summer feast at the poles. Migrant whales include gray, blue, and humpback whales.

AMAZING FACTS

• Gray whales travel more than 12,000 miles (20,000 km) during migration.

• The elephant seal can survive without food for about 100 days.

• Male humpback whales sing the longest and most complex songs in the animal kingdom.

WHALES AND DOLPHINS

GIANT WHALES and smaller dolphins travel the world's oceans, mating and giving birth in the water. They dive deep into the ocean, surfacing frequently to breathe air through a blowhole on the top of their head. Whales and dolphins have large, complex brains, live in groups, and communicate over vast distances using sound, which travels well through water. There are at least 80 species of whale, which fall into two main groups: toothed whales and baleen whales.

GRAY WHALE

Scratches from fights with other whales or from collisions with boats

The gray whale is half the size of the gigantic blue whale.

BALEEN WHALE
Blue, fin, gray, and humpback whales are all kinds of baleen whale, which are larger than toothed whales. They feed by straining fish and plankton from the water, using fringed plates of horny baleen, which hang from their great arched jaws like curtains.

BLUE WHALE

An elephant could stand on a blue whale's tongue!

Grooves allow throat to stretch s whale can gulp hug amounts of water

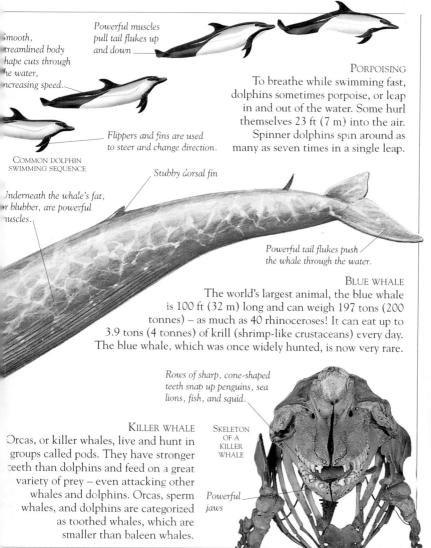

Smooth, streamlined body shape cuts through the water, increasing speed.

Powerful muscles pull tail flukes up and down

Flippers and fins are used to steer and change direction.

COMMON DOLPHIN SWIMMING SEQUENCE

PORPOISING
To breathe while swimming fast, dolphins sometimes porpoise, or leap in and out of the water. Some hurl themselves 23 ft (7 m) into the air. Spinner dolphins spin around as many as seven times in a single leap.

Stubby dorsal fin

Underneath the whale's fat, or blubber, are powerful muscles.

Powerful tail flukes push the whale through the water.

BLUE WHALE
The world's largest animal, the blue whale is 100 ft (32 m) long and can weigh 197 tons (200 tonnes) – as much as 40 rhinoceroses! It can eat up to 3.9 tons (4 tonnes) of krill (shrimp-like crustaceans) every day. The blue whale, which was once widely hunted, is now very rare.

Rows of sharp, cone-shaped teeth snap up penguins, sea lions, fish, and squid.

SKELETON OF A KILLER WHALE

KILLER WHALE
Orcas, or killer whales, live and hunt in groups called pods. They have stronger teeth than dolphins and feed on a great variety of prey – even attacking other whales and dolphins. Orcas, sperm whales, and dolphins are categorized as toothed whales, which are smaller than baleen whales.

Powerful jaws

RIVERS, LAKES, AND SWAMPS

RIVERS, LAKES, AND SWAMPS provide inviting environments, rich in food and nesting places, that attract a wide range of mammals. These water-loving mammals are strong swimmers, gliding through the water to find food or escape danger. Some, like otters or river dolphins, spend most or all of their time in the water. Others, like raccoons, visit freshwater habitats to feed. These ecosystems are often threatened by drainage or pollution from industry, towns, or agriculture.

BAIKAL SEAL

FRESHWATER SEAL
Living in and named after Siberia's largest lake, the Baikal seal is the only seal that lives in fresh water. About 70,000 seals live in the lake, feeding on fish and resting on lake shores and islands. Ancestors of Baikal seals may have migrated to the lake from the Arctic along a river during one of the ice ages.

UNDERWATER LIFE
Otters are well adapted for swimming underwater. They have waterproof fur, webbed toes, and a long tail that acts as a rudder. Cubs are taught to enter the water but instinctively know how to swim.

Ears and nostrils can be closed under the water.

Otters swim b undulating their bod and tail and pushir with their back fee

Thick, flesh muscula ta

Front legs steer.

FISHING FOR FOOD

Fish are an important source of food for water mammals. The fishing cat of southern and southeastern Asian marshes and swamps can flip fish out of the water with its slightly webbed paws. It also dives into the water after fish and catches them in its sharp teeth.

Open mouth that shows off huge teeth is a display of threat.

Eyes, nose, and ears stay above the surface when hippo is underwater.

HIPPOPOTAMUS

RARE MAMMALS

Large mammals are not common in watery habitats. The hippos and antelope of African lakes and swamps are an exception, as are the manatees of western Africa, the Amazon, and the Everglades. More commonly found smaller mammals include mink, muskrats, and beavers.

RIVERS AND LAKES

MANY MAMMALS MAKE their homes in safe freshwater lakes, ponds, and rivers. Homes can be hidden away in riverbanks or lakesides, and beavers have even learned to build their homes in the middle of lakes where predators find it hard to reach them. Some mammals use sound or electric fields to find food in muddy water.

PLATYPUS

BOTTOM FEEDER
Feeding mainly along the bottom of lakes and rivers, the platypus probes the mud with its sensitive bill for small aquatic animals such as worms, insects, and crayfish. Platypuses, which have no teeth, crush food between horny, ridged plates inside their bill. They nest in burrows.

Webbed feet with claws for burrowing

Underwater, the platypus can shut its eyes and ears to keep water out.

AMAZING FACTS

• The platypus can detect electric fields given off by its prey.

• Strong enough to hold a horse with a rider on its back, the largest beaver dam measured 2,300 ft (700 m) long!

• Using its sharp front teeth, a beaver can fell a small tree in ten minutes.

EXCELLENT SWIMMERS
Muscrats have webbed hind feet and long, flattened tails, which they use as a rudder. They feed mainly on water plants, but also eat fish and frogs. Muscrats dig burrows or construct homes from plants.

Waterproof fur

MUSKRAT

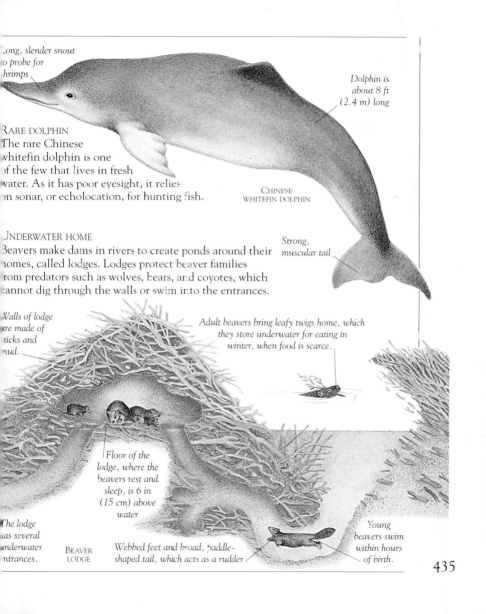

Long, slender snout to probe for shrimps

Dolphin is about 8 ft (2.4 m) long

RARE DOLPHIN

The rare Chinese whitefin dolphin is one of the few that lives in fresh water. As it has poor eyesight, it relies on sonar, or echolocation, for hunting fish.

CHINESE
WHITEFIN DOLPHIN

Strong, muscular tail

UNDERWATER HOME

Beavers make dams in rivers to create ponds around their homes, called lodges. Lodges protect beaver families from predators such as wolves, bears, and coyotes, which cannot dig through the walls or swim into the entrances.

Walls of lodge are made of sticks and mud.

Adult beavers bring leafy twigs home, which they store underwater for eating in winter, when food is scarce.

Floor of the lodge, where the beavers rest and sleep, is 6 in (15 cm) above water

The lodge has several underwater entrances.

BEAVER LODGE

Webbed feet and broad, paddle-shaped tail, which acts as a rudder

Young beavers swim within hours of birth.

435

SWAMPS

WATERLOGGED FORESTED AREAS, swamps can be fresh- or saltwater and are more extensive in tropical than in temperate areas. At different times of year, the water level in swamps may rise and fall, affecting the lives of the mammals who live there. These mammal inhabitants may swim through the water, wade through the mud, or live high up in the trees. For the few that can survive the variable water level and muddy conditions, food and shelter are plentiful.

Nose goes red if monkey is angry or excited

BIG NOSE

The agile proboscis monkey leaps through the branches of mangrove trees in the swamps of Borneo. The male, which is much larger than the female, has a long nose that makes his honking danger calls strikingly loud.

Long 2½-ft (76-cm) tail for balance

PROBOSCIS MONKEY

UNSINKABLE ANTELOPE

The long hooves and flexible ankles of the sitatunga antelope allow its feet to splay, preventing it from sinking into mud. The sitatunga swims well and often hides underwater.

WINGED HUNTER
The graceful fisherman bat detects its prey by echolocation, then uses its huge, powerful wings to swoop down into the water and catch it.

Sharp claws snatch fish and insects.

Large, rounded tail pushes manatee through the water at speeds of 15 mph (25 km/h).

When breathing, only the tip of the manatee's snout is above the surface.

SHY PLANT EATER
Manatees, often called sea cows, are shy, rare animals that feed at night mainly on sea grasses. Florida manatees, of the Everglades, reach a maximum size of almost 13 ft (3.9 m) and weight of 3,650 lb (1,660 kg).

MANATEE

DOMESTIC MAMMALS

WHAT IS A CAT?

CATS ARE NATURE'S most efficiently designed hunting carnivores. They have powerful bodies, superb vision, and razor-sharp teeth and claws. Most cats are self-reliant, stalking their prey alone in dusk or darkness. One species has also succeeded in living with people and is now kept as a pet around the world.

AFRICAN LION

ANCIENT EGYPTIAN CAT

Short, rounded head

Sandy-brown coat for camouflage

Cats lived near settlements, where they could easily find food.

Strong front legs and muscular neck for catching prey

Sharp claws are kept sheathed when not in use.

HISTORY OF THE DOMESTIC CAT
Wall paintings show that cats were being tamed in ancient Egypt before 2500 B.C. Although the Egyptians forbade the export of their cats, they still spread to ancient Greece by 500 B.C. They were also recorded in India before 100 B.C.

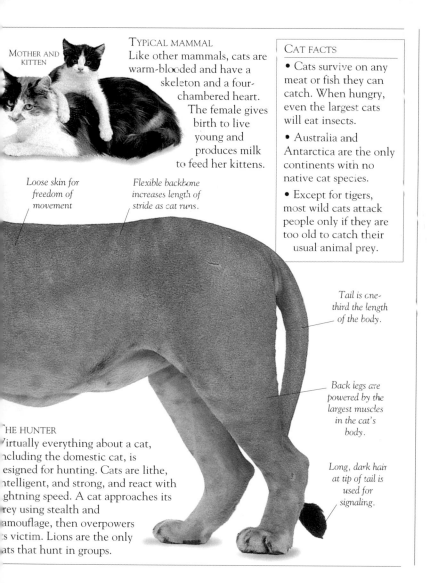

MOTHER AND KITTEN

TYPICAL MAMMAL

Like other mammals, cats are warm-blooded and have a skeleton and a four-chambered heart. The female gives birth to live young and produces milk to feed her kittens.

Loose skin for freedom of movement

Flexible backbone increases length of stride as cat runs.

CAT FACTS

• Cats survive on any meat or fish they can catch. When hungry, even the largest cats will eat insects.

• Australia and Antarctica are the only continents with no native cat species.

• Except for tigers, most wild cats attack people only if they are too old to catch their usual animal prey.

Tail is one-third the length of the body.

Back legs are powered by the largest muscles in the cat's body.

Long, dark hair at tip of tail is used for signaling.

THE HUNTER

Virtually everything about a cat, including the domestic cat, is designed for hunting. Cats are lithe, intelligent, and strong, and react with lightning speed. A cat approaches its prey using stealth and camouflage, then overpowers its victim. Lions are the only cats that hunt in groups.

441

CAT ANATOMY

ALL CATS ARE AGILE and athletic predators. Their bodies are powerful and flexible, specially designed for running, jumping, and climbing. Some types of cat even excel at swimming. Superb hunters, cats first swiftly chase and then overpower prey with their strength. Sharp teeth are used to finish off the catch.

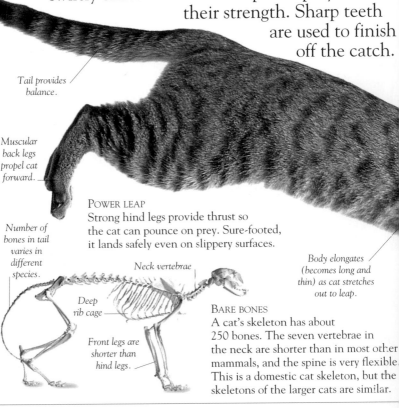

Tail provides balance.

Muscular back legs propel cat forward.

POWER LEAP
Strong hind legs provide thrust so the cat can pounce on prey. Sure-footed, it lands safely even on slippery surfaces.

Number of bones in tail varies in different species.

Neck vertebrae

Deep rib cage

Front legs are shorter than hind legs.

Body elongates (becomes long and thin) as cat stretches out to leap.

BARE BONES
A cat's skeleton has about 250 bones. The seven vertebrae in the neck are shorter than in most other mammals, and the spine is very flexible. This is a domestic cat skeleton, but the skeletons of the larger cats are similar.

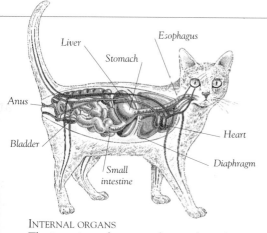

Esophagus

Liver

Stomach

Anus

Bladder

Heart

Diaphragm

Small
intestine

ANATOMY FACTS

• A cat breathes four
times faster than a
human, and its heart
beats twice as fast.

• Cats do not chew
their food, but swallow
it in large chunks.

• The back muscles of
a cat are very flexible.

• The record body
length of a domestic
cat is 41.5 in (105 cm).

INTERNAL ORGANS

The intestines of a cat are short and simple
since they need to digest only meat and not
plants. Most of the nutrients from the food are
absorbed in the small intestine.

Powerful jaw
muscles attach to
side of skull.

Incisor, or
biting, teeth

Canine
teeth to kill prey

Carnassial teeth
tear prey apart.

Front legs take
most of the
impact of
landing.

Pads on the feet
help cushion the
cat as it lands.

CAT SKULL

A cat's skull is large compared to
the size of its body. The eye
sockets are big to allow for broad
range of vision. The jaws are short
and strong. All of a cat's teeth are
sharp and scissorlike for tearing
and cutting, rather than flat, like
a human's, for crushing.

Eyes and ears

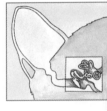

As predators, cats depend on their highly developed senses of sight and hearing to find prey. The majority of cats hunt at night, so they need to be able to see in near darkness. A cat can see about six times better than a person can at night. However, a cat's color vision is not as developed as ours. Cats also rely on their acute hearing to pinpoint the exact location of prey. Sounds inaudible to humans, or even dogs, can be detected by cats.

SOUND DETECTORS
The serval, a cat from the African savannah, has large, mobile ears. It can pick up the high-pitched calls of rodents hidden in the grass.

THE OUTER EAR
A cat's outer ear acts like a funnel, channeling sounds to the eardrum. Each ear can rotate to locate sounds precisely.

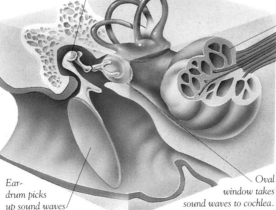

Ossicles (ear bones) send sound into inner ear.

Semicircular canals are filled with fluid.

Cochlea changes vibrations into nerve impulses.

Auditory nerve takes signals to brain.

THE INNER EAR
Sound waves vibrate the eardrum, which then moves the ossicles. The vibrations change to electrical impulses and travel down the auditory nerve to the brain. Here they are deciphered into meaningful sounds.

Eardrum picks up sound waves

Oval window takes sound waves to cochlea.

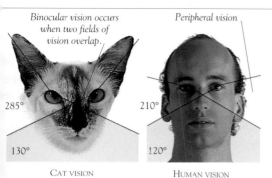

Binocular vision occurs when two fields of vision overlap.

Peripheral vision

285°

130°

CAT VISION

210°

120°

HUMAN VISION

THROUGH A CAT'S EYES
Cats can see at a wider
angle around their heads
than people can. This
allows them to be alert to
movements to the side or
slightly behind them.
Binocular vision allows
them to see images as
three-dimensional, as well
as to judge distance and
depth very accurately.

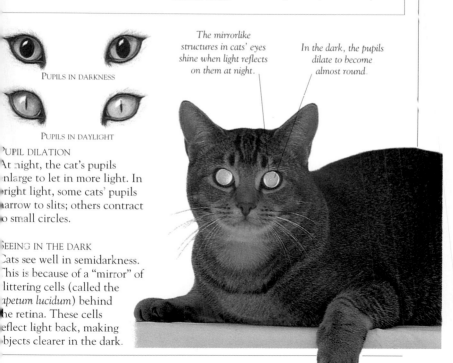

PUPILS IN DARKNESS

PUPILS IN DAYLIGHT

PUPIL DILATION
At night, the cat's pupils
enlarge to let in more light. In
bright light, some cats' pupils
narrow to slits; others contract
to small circles.

SEEING IN THE DARK
Cats see well in semidarkness.
This is because of a "mirror" of
glittering cells (called the
tapetum lucidum) behind
the retina. These cells
reflect light back, making
objects clearer in the dark.

*The mirrorlike
structures in cats' eyes
shine when light reflects
on them at night.*

*In the dark, the pupils
dilate to become
almost round.*

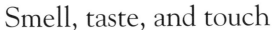

Smell, taste, and touch

Cats have extremely acute senses. They rely on smell to identify the things around them, and on touch to feel their way around, particularly in the dark. Another sensory device cats possess is the Jacobsen's organ, located in the roof of the mouth. This structure seems to respond to both smell and taste, and helps the cat to detect scents that their nose cannot – for example, when a female is ready to mate.

The senses of smell and taste tell the cat if this toad is edible.

Cats never eat anything without carefully sniffing it first.

SENSE OF SMELL

A cat's nose contains some 19 million smelling nerves, compared to a human's 5 million. Cats are especially sensitive to rancid odors, such as meat that has gone off. They normally seek out fresh meat rather than scavenge dead animals.

ENTICING CATNIP

Many cats, especially tomcats, find the smell of catnip irresistible. This garden herb contains a chemical that relaxes cats, or can make them roll around. About 50 percent of cats do not react to catnip at all.

TOUCH-SENSITIVE HAIRS

Whiskers are specialized, stiff hairs with highly sensitive nerves in their roots. They help a cat like this leopard to familiarize itself with its surroundings. A cat uses its whiskers to gauge if it can fit through a gap.

The cat's saliva leaves its scent.

Cats groom each other to spread their scent, and also to show affection.

CAT COMMUNICATION

Cats use smell to communicate far more than people do. They recognize the familiar scents of their companions. Because their skin is covered in touch-sensitive nerves, cats also communicate by grooming each other.

Characteristic lip-curling known as flehmening

FLEHMENING

The curious way that a cat curls its upper lip is called flehmening. It does this to draw smells into the Jacobsen's organ in its mouth. Male cats flehmen to detect the scent of nearby females. The Jacobsen's organs of the lion and tiger are more sensitive than those of domestic cats.

Paws and claws

A cat uses its paws for everything from gentle grooming to fierce fighting. To aid a cat in one of its most important skills, running, the bones of the feet have evolved so that a cat permanently walks on its toes. In the wild, injuries to the paws can prove fatal, since these can prevent a cat from hunting successfully.

CLAWS FOR CLIMBING

Most cats are masterly climbers, and can make even a vertical ascent with ease. Coming back down is more problematic, since the claws curve the wrong way to grip when descending. Cats awkwardly make their way down a tree backward.

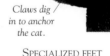

Claws are made of keratin, like human nails.

Dewclaw on front leg is placed like a thumb and helps grip.

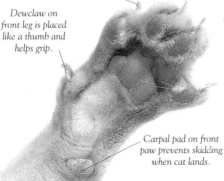

Claws dig in to anchor the cat.

Carpal pad on front paw prevents skidding when cat lands.

SPECIALIZED FEET

A cat has furless pads of tough leather on the underside of its paws. These pads enable the animal to stalk silently, and they cushion the impact of landings. Pads also help the cat to "brake" suddenly in mid-run. The cheetah has unique grooved pads to improve its control when running.

SCRATCHING ITS MARK

This jaguar, like other cats, scratches trees to keep its claws clean and sharp. Scratching also marks a cat's territory. A cat leaves behind its scent from glands between its toes, while the scratches themselves show the cat has been in the area.

Claws extended to grasp toy

HUNTING WEAPONS

Watching a cat play will reveal many of its hunting techniques. Cats use their front paws to swipe at, scoop up, rake, or grip their catch. Playing with toys is one way domestic cats practice these moves. Pets tend not to use their claws ferociously against their owners.

This 3-week-old kitten is already beginning to develop its hunting skills.

RETRACTABLE CLAWS

When a cat rests, ligaments keep its claws protected under extensions of the toe bones. The claws are only extended when needed. A cheetah, however, has its claws out permanently so it can grip the ground when it runs.

CLAWS
RETRACTED

CLAWS
EXTENDED

Relaxed cat with claws retracted out of sight

Ligaments slacken to unveil claws when necessary.

449

CAT MOVEMENT

NORMALLY GRACEFUL and controlled, cats can also react with a sudden burst of energy. Balance, strength, speed, and quick judgment help cats to chase and seize elusive prey. The only physical quality cats lack is endurance. The cat is a particularly talented leaper, able to jump four and a half times its body length and land on a chosen spot with great accuracy.

JUMPING
Cats can leap vertically when necessary. The caracal and lynx are expert jumpers, leaping up into the air to swipe a bird as it takes off. With one paw, they can knock their catch to the ground.

A kitten extends its paws and claws to prepare for landing.

Head outstretched as cheetah accelerates to its full speed.

CHEETAH

Claws help a cat climb and maintain its balance.

Looking before leaping, to judge its distance from the ground

TERRITORIAL MOVEMENTS
One of a cat's main daily movements is to patrol and mark its territory. It will roam around looking out for other cats or potential prey. Cats climb both to survey their area and because a higher position gives them an advantage over competitors.

LEAPING

A cat's most characteristic movement is its leap, demonstrated here by a lioness. The back muscles flex and relax as the cat leaps, with the tail extended for balance. The powerful back legs lift the cat and are the last part of the body to leave the ground.

The lioness stretches her body forward as she takes off.

Tail is turned up for balance.

Slender, light body and long legs enable the cheetah to reach high speeds.

The tail is more than half the length of the body. It swings to counterbalance the body during sharp turns.

RUNNING

Most cats can leap better than they run, but the cheetah is built for speed. Its backbone is extremely flexible, so when the front legs touch the ground, the back end springs forward. In midstride the body stretches full out and all four legs leave the ground. At full sprint the cheetah can reach 60 mph (96 km/h).

When running, the front paws never touch the ground at the same time as the back paws.

451

Balancing and falling

Some types of cat spend a significant part of their lives in trees, moving confidently along even the narrowest branches. However, if it does fall, the cat has evolved a unique method of protecting itself. Its eyes, brain, and sensitive balance organs in the inner ear ensure that the cat always lands on its feet.

The head rotates first to align with the ground.

1 INSTANT REACTION
The inner ear instantly reacts if the cat is off balance. This warns the brain that it needs to begin to respond to the fall.

2 ROTATING RAPIDLY
The front of the body receives signals from the brain and twists to follow the head. The backbone is so supple that it can rotate 180°.

Front legs pull around to upright position.

GEOFFROY'S CAT

LIVING THE HIGH LIFE
Many of the small wild cats hunt and sleep in trees. The Geoffroy's cat from South America uses its sharp claws, powerful vision, good reflexes and superb sense of balance to stalk mammals and birds in the treetops.

This cat lives in the mountainous forests of southern South America.

PERFECT BALANCE
This leopard looks precariously balanced, but it will easily secure its kill off the ground and away from scavengers. The leopard is one of the biggest members of the cat family that spends a lot of time in the trees. It is strong enough to drag up a carcass heavier than its own body weight.

Back end still recovering

Eyes checking where it will be landing.

The back legs will help to absorb the force of impact.

3 READY FOR IMPACT
As the cat's front legs begin to stretch out to make contact with the ground, the back of the body is still swiveling around. The collarbones at the top of the front legs will act as shock absorbers when the cat lands.

Legs prepared to run when cat touches ground

4 LANDING ON ITS FEET
Only seconds after losing its balance, the cat is well positioned to land safely. The head and soft underparts are protected from injury. The cat instinctively relaxes its body before impact, which prevents it from tearing its muscles or jarring its joints.

Front legs take most of the shock of the landing.

HUNTING

VIRTUALLY ALL CATS hunt on their own, so they must attack with surprise and speed. They stealthily approach their unsuspecting prey using any available cover. When they are close enough they suddenly pounce, seizing their quarry in a deadly grip.

HOUSEHOLD HUNTER
The domestic cat is famed for its prowess as a mouser. Some cats also excel at catching lizards, birds, or insects. However, hunting is a learned behavior, so not all pet cats make efficient hunters.

GROUP CHASE
Unlike most cats, lions hunt in groups. This means they can kill animals larger than themselves. The lionesses of the pride do nearly all of the hunting. To improve their chances of a kill, they single out a weak-looking animal, surround it, and then chase it down.

Cat holds its body and tail close to the ground.

FATAL BITE

This leopard pins down its victim to stop it from escaping. Then it bites through the neck of its catch to sever the spinal cord. If a cat cannot eat its kill all at once it will drag the carcass under cover to protect it from scavengers.

FRUSTRATED KILLER

Domestic cats will play with a toy as if it were a prey animal. They creep up on the object, then bite and shake it. Wild cats sometimes play with their quarry before killing it.

Spotted coat pattern keeps the animal camouflaged.

Mature cats play occasionally, but not as often as kittens.

ASIAN LEOPARD CAT

SILENT STALKER

Except for the cheetah, cats can manage only short bursts of speed. They must steal quite close to an animal before they bound forward. Approaching slowly and silently, the stalking cat is alert to every movement. When it is within striking distance it springs on its prey without warning.

The cat runs forward in this position, then stops and crouches down.

455

FUR TYPES

SLEEK AND FINE, or long and luxurious, a cat's fur is its finest feature. The coat insulates a cat in hot or cold weather, carries its scent, and is sensitive to touch. Fur type is often suited to where a cat lives, although the wide variation of coats in domestic breeds is due to selective breeding by people.

Awn hairs

Down hairs | *Guard hairs*

BRITISH SHORTHAIR
This breed is typical of short-coated cats. It has a short, dense, crisp coat. The thick, plush fur stands out from the body like a rug.

Coat is about 2 in (5 cm) thick.

A CAT'S COAT
There are three kinds of hair in a cat's coat, although not every breed has all three. The longest are the coarse outer guard hairs. In wild and domestic cats, these carry the pattern. Slightly shorter awn hairs lie beneath. Short, soft down provides insulation.

PERSIAN
Persian cats have the longest and densest fur of any cat breed. The hairs are silky and fine, giving the cat a very fluffy appearance – even the paws are tufted. In warm summer months the cat molts, which makes its coat look shorter.

Persians have thick down and up to 4-in-long (10 cm) guard hairs.

Fur is especially curly on back and tail.

CORNISH REX

The unusual fur of the Rex breeds is wavy and crimped. All of the hairs in a Cornish Rex's coat are short and curly. The coat is made up solely of down and awn hairs, both of which are very soft to the touch. The fur is fine, so Rexes can be susceptible to the cold.

AMERICAN WIREHAIR

This cat's fur is distinctively wiry and springy. Every hair, including those in the ears and on the tail, is crimped, or even coiled. The Wirehair's fur is of medium length and very frizzy. It feels like lamb's wool to the touch.

Wiry coat makes pattern look raised.

WILD CAT FUR

Wild cats have coats of two layers: warm down hair underneath and a resilient outer coat. In cold climates, cats have thicker fur. The Pallas's cat from Asia has the longest coat of any wild cat. It was once mistakenly believed to be the ancestor of domestic cats with long hair.

Longer fur on underside for warmth when lying on cold ground

PALLAS'S CAT

"HAIRLESS" SPHYNX

Although the Sphynx looks bald, it has traces of fur on its tail and a light covering of down on its body. It also has very short eyebrows and whiskers. This breed's lack of hair means that it is vulnerable to sunburn.

Coat is like suede.

457

Colors and patterns

Cats come in a huge variety of colors and patterns.
Many have distinctive markings that originally
evolved to help cats in the wild stay hidden
from their prey. Domestic cats often come in
more conspicuous colors because they
have little need for camouflage.
Breeders have achieved
some very striking color
and pattern combinations.

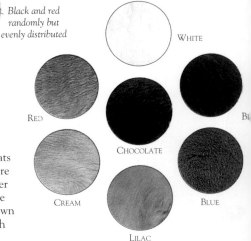

SEAL TORTIE
POINT SIAMESE

CORNISH REX
TORTOISESHELL

CHARACTERISTIC MARKINGS
Siamese cats have a characteristic pattern of
darker areas on the tail, legs, ears, and face.
These markings are described as points. Young
kittens develop their points as they mature.

*Black and red
randomly but
evenly distributed*

WHITE

TORTOISESHELL
For genetic
reasons, tortoiseshell patterns
occur almost entirely in female
cats. Tortoiseshell fur is a
combination of black and red.

RED

BL

COLOR RANGE
Some cats have unpatterned coats
of one pure, solid color. There are
many varieties, some simply paler
versions of the basic colors. Here
the typical darker colors are shown
above their lighter variants, with
white shown on its own.

CHOCOLATE

CREAM

BLUE

LILAC

Tabby Markings

This cat's spotted coat exemplifies the dark markings typical of tabbies. In different tabby cats, the patterning might be stripes, spots, or patches. These patterns are left over from the natural camouflage markings of wild cats. Tabby patterning is very common in feral cats (domestic cats that live in the wild).

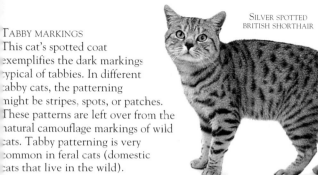

SILVER SPOTTED BRITISH SHORTHAIR

Black spots are striking against a silver background.

Wild Cat Patterns

The stripes or spots of a wild cat's coat are vital because they help the animal blend into its surroundings. Patterns camouflage a cat by breaking up the outline of its body shape. The markings of wild cats vary so considerably that the shape of the patterns is one way to distinguish the species. Individual cats of the same species also have slightly varying patterns.

Each individual ocelot has a different pattern.

Golden coat with black markings

OCELOT

Markings break up cat's outline in forests.

Bold, ringed black spots

JAGUAR

Unique striped markings

TIGER

Named after its cloudlike pattern

Gray-brown coat with marbled markings

CLOUDED LEOPARD

WHAT IS A DOG?

THE DOMESTIC DOG, called *Canis familiaris* in Latin (from the word *canis* meaning dog), is one of 35 existing species of canids – meat-eating animals that evolved for the pursuit of prey across open grassland. The dog family ranges from the tiny Fennec Fox to the large Gray Wolf.

Insulating fur

Excellent hearing

Strong jaws and large canine teeth to catch and hold prey

Powerful muscles for speed and endurance

GRAY WOLF

GRAY WOLF
The Gray Wolf, one of two existing wolf species (the other is the endangered Red Wolf of southeastern US), is the ancestor of the domestic dog. It was once the most widespread mammal, apart from humans, outside the tropics.

JACKAL
The jackals of Africa, southeastern Europe, and Asia, have an undeserved bad name. Jackals are good parents to their young and do not scavenge as much as is supposed. Their diet ranges from fruit to small gazelle.

JACKAL

RED FOX

RED FOX
The Red Fox, like all foxes, is a small canid with a slender skull, large ears, and a long, bushy tail. Its coat comes in three colors – a flame red, a blackish silver, and the intermediate, "Cross" fox.

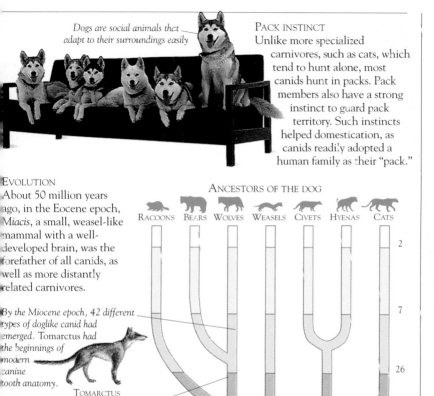

Dogs are social animals that adapt to their surroundings easily

PACK INSTINCT
Unlike more specialized carnivores, such as cats, which tend to hunt alone, most canids hunt in packs. Pack members also have a strong instinct to guard pack territory. Such instincts helped domestication, as canids readily adopted a human family as their "pack."

EVOLUTION
About 50 million years ago, in the Eocene epoch, *Miacis*, a small, weasel-like mammal with a well-developed brain, was the forefather of all canids, as well as more distantly related carnivores.

By the Miocene epoch, 42 different types of doglike canid had emerged. Tomarctus had the beginnings of modern canine tooth anatomy.

TOMARCTUS

Hesperocyon was a long-bodied, short-limbed canid living in the later Eocene epoch. Fossils have been found in North America.

HESPEROCYON

Miacis had the distinctive teeth of a canid, and also spreading paws, indicating adaptation to life in the trees.

ANCESTORS OF THE DOG

RACOONS   BEARS   WOLVES   WEASELS   CIVETS   HYENAS   CATS

2

7

26

38

MIACIS

54

MILLIONS OF YEARS AGO

DOMESTICATION

DOGS WERE FIRST DOMESTICATED from wolves over 10,000 years ago in the Middle East and accompanied people across the world. Contact between humans and dogs may have evolved as wolves scavenged around human settlements. The dog's great potential as a guard and hunting companion was soon realized.

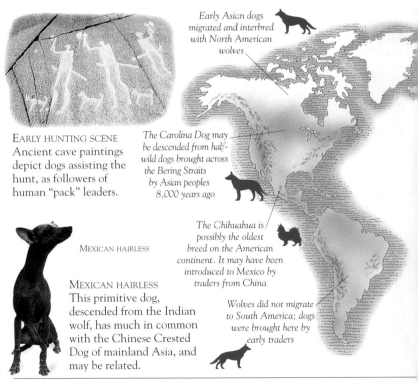

Early Asian dogs migrated and interbred with North American wolves

EARLY HUNTING SCENE
Ancient cave paintings depict dogs assisting the hunt, as followers of human "pack" leaders.

The Carolina Dog may be descended from half-wild dogs brought across the Bering Straits by Asian peoples 8,000 years ago

MEXICAN HAIRLESS

The Chihuahua is possibly the oldest breed on the American continent. It may have been introduced to Mexico by traders from China

MEXICAN HAIRLESS
This primitive dog, descended from the Indian wolf, has much in common with the Chinese Crested Dog of mainland Asia, and may be related.

Wolves did not migrate to South America; dogs were brought here by early traders

PHARAOH HOUND
This oldest-recorded breed graces the tombs of ancient Egyptian pharaohs. It was probably a descendant of the Phoenician hound – the Phoenicians traded dogs throughout the Mediterranean.

PHARAOH HOUND

DOG OWNERSHIP FACTS
• Worldwide, over 200 million dogs are kept as pets.

• North America has the largest number of pet dogs (60 million); next is France (10.8 million), followed by Russia (10 million). Japan and Britain each have around 7 million dogs.

Sheepdogs originated in Europe more than 1,000 years ago

Mastiff-type dogs were domesticated in the Stone Age and later used in battle by the Greeks

The Greyhound is portrayed on 8,000-year-old Mesopotamian pottery

Wolflike dogs similar to spitzes, such as the Elkhound and the Siberian Husky, originated in Arctic regions

DINGO
The Dingo was brought to Australia 4,000 years ago. It is now a feral dog (a domesticated dog that has reverted to the wild).

BASENJI
The Basenji's roots lie lost in the mists of antiquity. This nonbarking African breed has remained more or less pure for thousands of years. It is depicted on Egyptian tombs.

BASENJI

DINGO

463

DOG ANATOMY

THE BASIC DESIGN of the dog is that of a highly developed carnivorous mammal of the hunt. Over the centuries, humans have modified dog anatomy to exploit particular talents, and for aesthetic appeal.

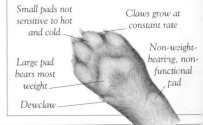

Insulating coat

Loin

Brush, or tail

Croup

Flank

Stifle

Lower thigh

Knee

Hock

Pastern

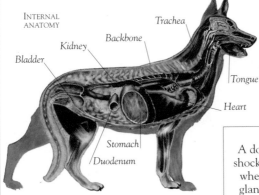

INTERNAL ANATOMY

Trachea

Kidney

Backbone

Bladder

Tongue

Heart

Stomach

Duodenum

INTERNAL ORGANS

The organs of the dog are essentially the same as those of humans, and function in the same way. Although its attitude toward food is that of a hunter-scavenger, the dog is not a pure carnivore, tending toward an omnivorous diet. Its digestive system can cope with anything from fruit and nuts to shellfish and raw meat.

PAWS

A dog's paws carry pads that act as shock absorbers, provide a good grip when running, and contain sweat glands. The claws, unlike those of most cats, cannot be retracted.

Small pads not sensitive to hot and cold

Claws grow at constant rate

Non-weight-bearing, non-functional pad

Large pad bears most weight

Dewclaw

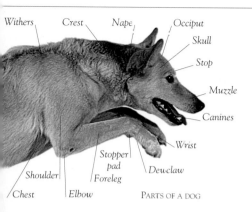

Withers Crest Nape Occiput

Skull

Stop

Muzzle

Canines

Wrist

Stopper
pad   Dewclaw
Shoulder   Foreleg

Chest Elbow   PARTS OF A DOG

CLASSIC DESIGN

The classic canine design is seen in most wild
or feral dogs and many domesticated
mongrels: a lithe body, long legs, a long tail
for balance and communication, efficient
prick ears, and excellent vision – all ideal
features for a resourceful hunting animal
with plenty of stamina.

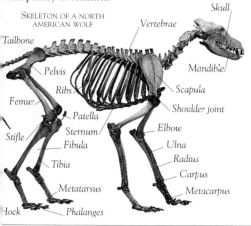

SKELETON OF A NORTH
AMERICAN WOLF

Skull

Vertebrae

Tailbone

Pelvis

Ribs

Femur

Patella

Stifle

Sternum

Fibula

Tibia

Metatarsus

Hock   Phalanges

Mandible

Scapula

Shoulder joint

Elbow

Ulna

Radius

Carpus

Metacarpus

TEETH

An adult dog has 42 teeth,
including four stabbing,
canine or "dog" teeth and
four molar teeth called
carnassials that are
designed to shear through
tough flesh.

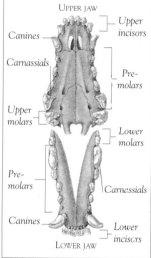

UPPER JAW

Canines

Carnassials

Upper
molars

Premolars

Canines

Upper
incisors

Premolars

Lower
molars

Carnassials

Lower
incisors

LOWER JAW

THE SKELETON

The basic dog framework
provides strength, flexibility,
and speed. However, selective
breeding has resulted in some
breeds possessing weak areas.
Extra-long spines can lead to
"slipped-discs"; flattened skulls
to breathing troubles; and short
legs may result in knee injuries.

465

More on anatomy

All predatory animals depend on their sight, hearing, and sense of smell to catch prey. A dog's sense organs are some of the most sophisticated in the animal kingdom. Dogs' reproductive systems follow the basic mammalian pattern, but with some distinct features in the male.

Cerebral cortex
Frontal sinus
Nasal membranes
Vomeronasal organ
Tongue
Soft palate
Windpipe

CROSS SECTION
OF THE HEAD

SMELL AND TASTE

Dogs are marvelous smellers, in fact about one million times better than humans. Their long noses contain "smelling membranes" about 40 times larger than ours. Taste is not as important, as dogs "gobble" rather than "savor" food.

SIGHT

Dogs' eyes are more sensitive to light and movement than ours but they can often "miss" creatures that stand very still. Yet shepherds claim their working dogs will react to hand signals at a distance of 0.6 miles (1 km). Dogs are not totally color-blind, but see mainly in black, white, and shades of gray. The anatomy of a dog's eye is very similar to ours.

Lacrimal gland
Pupil
Cornea
Iris covers anterior chamber
Lower eyelid
Third eyelid
Lens
Sclera
Retina
Optic nerve

CROSS SECTION
OF THE EYE

DOG'S EYE VIEW 250°–290°

HUMAN'S EYE VIEW 210°

VISION

A dog has a wider field of vision than a human because its eyes are set toward the sides of its head. Its carnivorous, hunter ancestors needed lateral vision.

HEARING

Dogs have excellent hearing. Equipped with large external ears served by 17 muscles, they can prick and swivel these sound receivers to focus on the source of noise. They can register high-pitched sounds of 35,000 Hz (vibrations per second), compared to humans' 20,000 Hz. This greater hearing range assists in tracking down quarry.

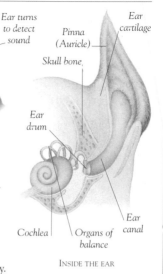

Ear turns to detect sound

Pinna (Auricle)

Ear cartilage

Skull bone

Ear drum

Cochlea

Organs of balance

Ear canal

INSIDE THE EAR

EAR TYPES

Hanging ears protect the ear when hounds hunt through vegetation. Erect ears trap sound waves most effectively.

HANGING EARS

POINTED EARS

REPRODUCTIVE ORGANS

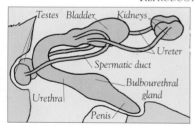

Testes Bladder Kidneys

Ureter

Spermatic duct

Bulbourethral gland

Urethra

Penis

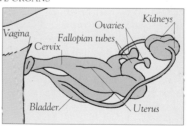

Vagina

Ovaries Kidneys

Fallopian tubes

Cervix

Bladder Uterus

MALE

The dog's penis contains a bone, through which the urethra passes, and a bulbourethral gland that swells up, thereby "tying" the dog and bitch together during sexual intercourse.

FEMALE

The female has a typical mammalian arrangement: vagina, cervix, uterus, fallopian tubes, and ovaries. When a bitch is neutered, the ovaries, fallopian tubes, and uterus are surgically removed.

LIFE CYCLE OF DOGS

ON AVERAGE, a dog's life span is about 12 years, though some breeds live a lot longer than others. In terms of aging, the first year of a dog's life equals 15 human years, the second equals nine years, and thereafter, each dog year counts for four human years.

GETTING ACQUAINTED

Exploratory sniffing before mating begins

THE "HEAT" PERIOD
The female is called the bitch. She becomes sexually mature at 8–12 months old. Twice a year, she goes into "heat," usually for 18–21 days. This is when ovulation occurs.

MATING

Female remains willing but passive

MATING
The male is sexually active all year and is attracted to the scent of a female in "heat." When a female is ready to mate, she draws her tail to one side. The transmission of sperm is completed within a minute but the couple remain "locked" together for half an hour.

DEVELOPMENT OF A PUPPY

7 DAYS
At this age the puppy only sleeps or nurses. Its eyes and ear canals are closed, but it responds to its mother's touch.

14 DAYS
The eyes are opening but they cannot focus properly for another 7 days. Between 13 and 17 days the puppy begins to hear.

3 WEEKS
At 3 weeks the puppy can focus its eyes and move around. Its nails should be trimmed to prevent it from scratching the mother.

1. The yolk sac provides nourishment to the embryo for the first few days

Yolk sac

Embryo

Most puppies will emerge head first in diving position

2. By the third week of pregnancy, the embryo has a developing head, eyes, and limbs

3. By midpregnancy, all the internal organs are developed

4. At six weeks, the skeleton has developed

PREGNANCY

Pregnancy in the bitch lasts an average of 63 days. The swelling of her tummy is noticeable from the fifth week onward. The breasts and nipples become bigger, and milk can often be produced 5–6 days before labor begins.

Mother sits contentedly while puppies nurse

Puppies huddle together for food and security

BONDING WITH MOTHER

BIRTH

When the puppies are almost ready to be born, the mother may stop eating and find a nest site. She gives birth to the first puppy soon afterward, and may rest for minutes or hours after each puppy is born. Each puppy's placenta usually comes out within 15 minutes.

30 DAYS

The puppy begins to play. Teething starts at 3–5 weeks. It should receive its first worming dosage.

6 WEEKS

Milk teeth are present, but the puppy is still nursing, and it should not be separated from its mother.

8 WEEKS

Mother and pup can be separated now, and the puppy should receive vaccinations against major diseases.

DOG BEHAVIOR

DOGS EXHIBIT A BROAD RANGE of behavior patterns that spring from their origins as social, hunting animals. Ear and tail movements are obviously expressive, but all patterns are vital rituals that express a dog's relationship with its environment.

SCENT MARKING
A dog marks out territory via deposits of urine or feces, or by scratching the ground with its hind legs.

SCENT GLANDS
Distinctive scents are produced by sebaceous glands in the dog's anal sacs (anal glands) that are passed on to feces, and by sweat glands in the hind paws. These scents lay down sniffable information that only dogs can interpret.

Dog shows interest in a scent

HOWLING
Howling is an ancient form of dog communication. Wild dogs and wolves howl to let other pack members know where they are and, in some cases, to inform strangers that they are in possession of territory. It can also be a sign of distress or loneliness.

DIGGING
Dogs inherit their love of digging from their ancestors, who stored food in order to survive when hunting was poor. It leads well-fed dogs to bury bones and dig them up later.

AGGRESSION

Aggression can indicate possessiveness of prized objects, territory, or animals. It can be directed at outsiders who are not members of the home pack. Fear and pain also cause aggression.

SUBMISSION

Submissive individuals in the canine hierarchy reveal their position by their crouched postures, and by rolling onto their backs, looking away, and appearing meek and defenseless.

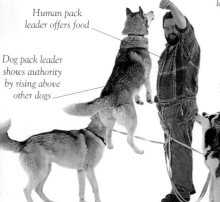

Human pack leader offers food

Dog pack leader shows authority by rising above other dogs

DOMINANCE

Dogs asserting their dominance make eye contact, with tail raised and ears erect, and often place their neck on the other dog's shoulder. Size, though helpful, does not necessarily affect dominance.

Tail carried high indicates boldness

PLAY BOW

The play bow, often exhibited by puppies, is a clear request to human or fellow dog to meet on friendly terms. Indicating total lack of aggressive intent, it is usually an invitation to play.

Body is lowered to ground

HIERARCHY

Packs of wild canines have leaders to exercise authority and coordinate activity. This is usually, but not always, a male. Gatherings of domestic dogs behave in the same way.

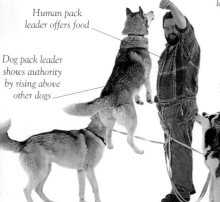

INTRODUCTION TO BREEDS

AMONG DOMESTICATED ANIMALS only the dog has been selectively bred to produce such a wide variety of types. Worldwide, there are over 500 different breeds. National kennel clubs differ in the way they group breeds so, for the purposes of this book, general categories have been used.

GUNDOGS

Gundogs were developed to pick up the air scents of game and also be good sporting companions. They are highly responsive and amenable workers. Field trials are held regularly to test working skills.

IRISH RED-AND-WHITE SETTER

BORDER COLLIES HERDING SHEEP

CHOW CHOW

SPECIAL DOGS

This is a miscellaneous collection of breeds. Many, such as the Chow Chow, are highly distinctive, and some have specialized in particular types of work. Most make good companions; many popular pets fall into this category.

HERDING DOGS AND GUARD DOGS

These dogs were bred to protect and herd livestock, work as guards, pull and carry loads, or assist police and armed forces. Most of these dogs are happiest when they have access to open spaces and a job to do

HOUNDS

These athletes with
sensitive noses and
sharp eyes were the
first dogs used by
humans. They helped
their (much slower)
masters by hunting
down animals, such
as deer, for food.

FOXHOUNDS

TERRIERS

Developed from hounds to tackle small,
burrowing animals, terriers are
generally small, short-legged,
stocky animals with
alert and spirited
temperaments. No
group of dogs is
more expert
at burrowing
than terriers.

NORFOLK
TERRIERS

TOY DOGS

These breeds' main function is to be loyal,
decorative, and friendly companions. Many
are useful for raising the alarm and nipping
intruders' ankles. Small and dainty, they
play a vital role in people's lives.

PEKINGESE

MONGRELS

Most dogs in the world are
mongrels or "crossbreed"
dogs that have interbred at
random. Apart from their
individual endearing
qualities, they are often
better-tempered, less
disease-prone, and more
adaptable than purebreds.

DOMESTIC MAMMALS

WHAT IS A HORSE?

SOME 60 MILLION YEARS AGO the first horses ran on the plains of North America. The modern horse has single-hooved feet and a greater length of leg than its earlier ancestors. Like all mammals, horses suckle their young, and as herbivores, their natural food is grass. They are social creatures, and prefer to live in groups.

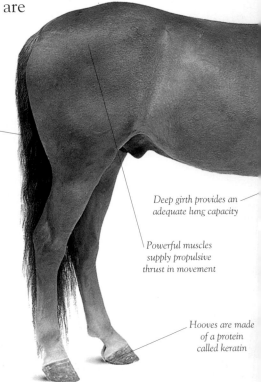

Long tail helps to keep flies off the body

Deep girth provides an adequate lung capacity

Powerful muscles supply propulsive thrust in movement

Hooves are made of a protein called keratin

HORSE FACTS

• Horses are measured from the ground up to the withers, which is the highest point of the shoulders.

• In 1910, North America had about 20 million domestic horses.

• There are over 150 officially recognized horse and pony breeds.

• Most modern horse breeds have been deliberately created to do a specific task.

Long hair on the back of the neck is called a mane

Horses have an excellent sense of hearing

Withers

Long head and neck allow horse to graze while standing

It takes over two years for a horse foal to take on adult proportions

Long legs developed to run from danger

HORSES AND HUMANS

As this cave painting shows, early humans hunted horses for their meat and skin. By keeping horses in herds, these essential items became more readily available. Eventually, horses were used for riding and pulling carts, and later they were bred to perform all kinds of work.

BORN TO RUN

Both wild and domestic horses give birth to fully developed offspring. This is because in the wild the young foal must keep up with its mother and the herd, as well as escaping from predators.

475

MAIN HORSE TYPES

MOST MODERN HORSES are thought to be descended from four types that inhabited Europe and Asia over 6,000 years ago. Their features can still be seen in some breeds today. Domestication led to the variety of modern breeds and their spread across the world.

Broad forehead with straight profile

PONY TYPE 1
This hardy pony looked similar to today's Exmoor breed of Great Britain. It lived in northwestern Europe.

Lean with narrow body

HORSE TYPE 1
Originating from central Asia, this horse lived in dry, arid conditions and resembled the modern Akhal-Teke.

PONY TYPE 2
Similar to Przewalski's horse, the Type 2 was powerfully built with a heavy head. The breed roamed over northern Eurasia.

Small head

HORSE TYPE 2
Living in the hot deserts of western Asia, this slim horse was possibly the ancestor of the Arab and Caspian.

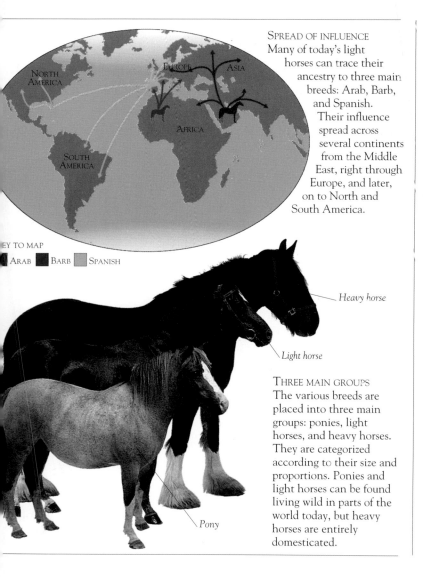

SPREAD OF INFLUENCE
Many of today's light horses can trace their ancestry to three main breeds: Arab, Barb, and Spanish. Their influence spread across several continents from the Middle East, right through Europe, and later, on to North and South America.

NORTH AMERICA

EUROPE   ASIA

AFRICA

SOUTH AMERICA

KEY TO MAP
ARAB   BARB   SPANISH

Heavy horse

Light horse

Pony

THREE MAIN GROUPS
The various breeds are placed into three main groups: ponies, light horses, and heavy horses. They are categorized according to their size and proportions. Ponies and light horses can be found living wild in parts of the world today, but heavy horses are entirely domesticated.

477

BODY AND CONFORMATION

A HORSE'S BODY IS perfectly designed for its way of life. The neck is long so it can stoop to graze, and long, muscular legs allow it to run away from danger. The proportions of a horse's body, or conformation, may vary according to the group or breed.

Points

The external features of a horse are called the points. Each point has a different name and together they make up the horse's conformation.

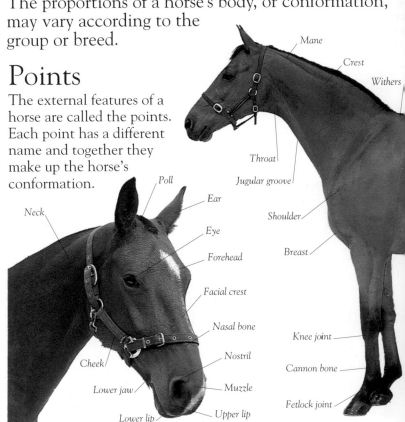

Mane

Crest

Withers

Throat

Jugular groove

Shoulder

Breast

Poll

Ear

Neck

Eye

Forehead

Facial crest

Nasal bone

Knee joint

Cheek

Nostril

Cannon bone

Lower jaw

Muzzle

Fetlock joint

Lower lip

Upper lip

PROPORTION
In a perfectly
proportioned
horse, certain
measurements
of the body should
all be equal. Those
shown in blue should
correspond to each other,
as should the lines drawn
in both red and gray.

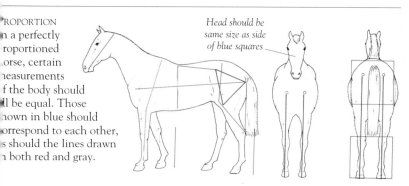

Head should be same size as side of blue squares

Point of hip

Croup

Back

Dock

Hindquarters

Tail

Gaskin

Flank

Stifle joint

Point of hock

Tarsal joint

Cannon bone

Hoof

Coronet

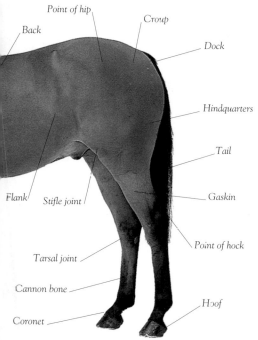

FRONT AND REAR LIMBS
When viewed from the
front, a line from the
shoulder should pass
through the center of the
knees, fetlock, and foot. A
straight line should also
pass through the rear legs.

ANATOMICAL FACTS

• The body and head of
a horse are streamlined
and this helps to reduce
wind resistance.

• A long neck and
well-sloped shoulders
may indicate that the
horse is fast and good
for riding.

• Large eyes usually
show not only that the
horse has good vision,
but also a calm nature
and intelligence.

Skeleton and muscles

The framework of the horse consists of a skeleton, made up of a number of connected bones that are moved by muscles. Along the spinal, or vertebral, column, which runs from the head to the tail, is the spinal cord – the connection between the horse's brain and body. When a horse wants to move, it sends a message from its brain down the cord via nerves to signal the appropriate muscle.

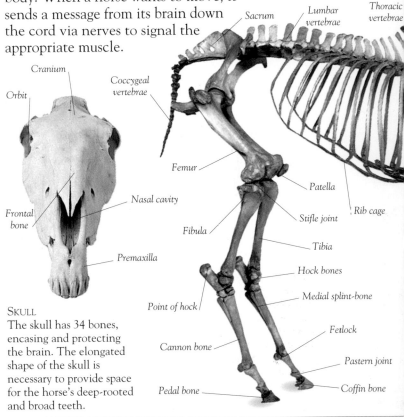

Sacrum

Lumbar vertebrae

Thoracic vertebrae

Cranium

Coccygeal vertebrae

Orbit

Femur

Patella

Nasal cavity

Stifle joint

Rib cage

Frontal bone

Fibula

Tibia

Premaxilla

Hock bones

Medial splint-bone

Point of hock

Fetlock

SKULL
The skull has 34 bones, encasing and protecting the brain. The elongated shape of the skull is necessary to provide space for the horse's deep-rooted and broad teeth.

Cannon bone

Pastern joint

Pedal bone

Coffin bone

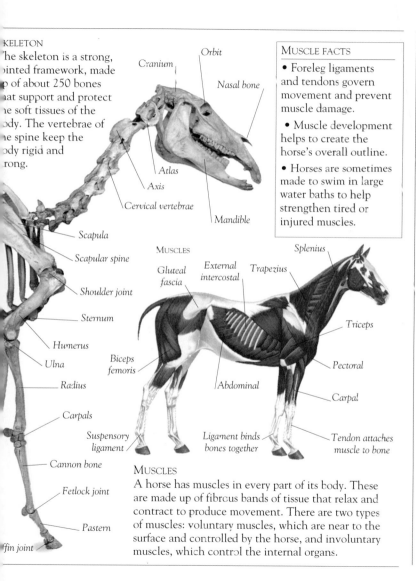

SKELETON

The skeleton is a strong, jointed framework, made up of about 250 bones that support and protect the soft tissues of the body. The vertebrae of the spine keep the body rigid and strong.

Cranium

Orbit

Nasal bone

Atlas

Axis

Cervical vertebrae

Mandible

Scapula

Scapular spine

Shoulder joint

Sternum

Humerus

Ulna

Radius

Carpals

Suspensory ligament

Cannon bone

Fetlock joint

Pastern

ffin joint

MUSCLE FACTS

• Foreleg ligaments and tendons govern movement and prevent muscle damage.

• Muscle development helps to create the horse's overall outline.

• Horses are sometimes made to swim in large water baths to help strengthen tired or injured muscles.

MUSCLES

Gluteal fascia

External intercostal

Trapezius

Splenius

Triceps

Biceps femoris

Abdominal

Pectoral

Carpal

Ligament binds bones together

Tendon attaches muscle to bone

MUSCLES

A horse has muscles in every part of its body. These are made up of fibrous bands of tissue that relax and contract to produce movement. There are two types of muscles: voluntary muscles, which are near to the surface and controlled by the horse, and involuntary muscles, which control the internal organs.

481

Patterns and markings

Individual horses can be identified by body markings, which can be either natural or acquired. Natural markings are often areas of white hair on the head, legs, and hooves. Acquired markings are the result of branding or injury. Branding has been done for more than 2,000 years and can help to identify the horse if it is stolen.

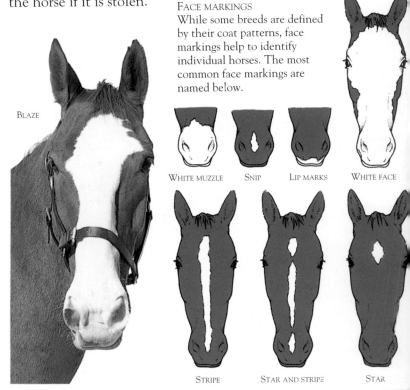

FACE MARKINGS
While some breeds are defined by their coat patterns, face markings help to identify individual horses. The most common face markings are named below.

BLAZE

WHITE MUZZLE   SNIP   LIP MARKS   WHITE FACE

STRIPE   STAR AND STRIPE   STAR

ERMINE   SOCK   STOCKING   ZEBRA

LEG MARKINGS
These markings are often white. They are called ermine if they are just above the hoof, a sock if they extend below the knee, and a stocking when extending above the knee. Zebra markings are dark rings.

HOOF MARKINGS
The blue hoof is made of hard blue horn and is most often associated with ponies. Hooves of black and white vertical stripes are seen on the Appaloosa and other spotted horse breeds.

BLUE HOOF   STRIPED HOOF

DORSAL STRIPE
This mark extends from the tail to the withers. It is found on primitive horses such as the Tarpan, and is associated with dun-colored coats.

IDENTITY MARKINGS
Artificial markings help identify ownership and sometimes breed. Brand marks are applied by a hot iron rod which stops the hair from growing back. Freeze marks are frozen on in a similar way.

BRAND MARK   FREEZE MARK

FOOD AND DIET

LIKE ANY ANIMAL, horses get their energy from food. They are herbivores, which means they do not eat meat. In the wild, horses can survive on grass and herbs as long as their grazing area is large enough. In the winter, when it is cold and there is less food, wild horses get out of condition, while in the summer they put on weight.

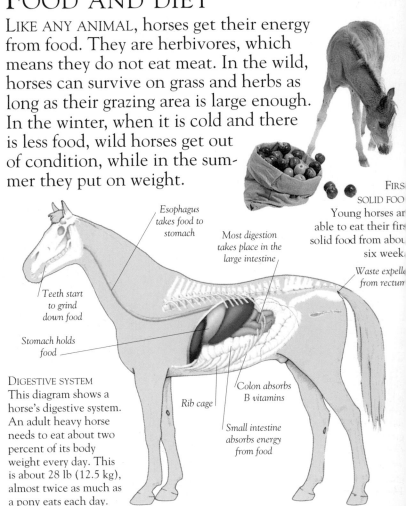

FIRST
SOLID FOOD
Young horses are
able to eat their first
solid food from about
six weeks

*Esophagus
takes food to
stomach*

*Most digestion
takes place in the
large intestine*

*Waste expelled
from rectum*

*Teeth start
to grind
down food*

*Stomach holds
food*

DIGESTIVE SYSTEM
This diagram shows a
horse's digestive system.
An adult heavy horse
needs to eat about two
percent of its body
weight every day. This
is about 28 lb (12.5 kg),
almost twice as much as
a pony eats each day.

Rib cage

*Colon absorbs
B vitamins*

*Small intestine
absorbs energy
from food*

TEETH AND JAWS

Grazing wears down the foal's milk teeth and by the time the horse is five, these are replaced by a set of 36 adult teeth. The incisors cut the food into small pieces, and the molars grind it down, ready for digestion.

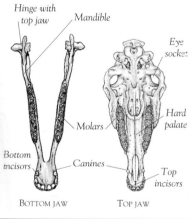

Hinge with top jaw

Mandible

Eye socket

Molars

Hard palate

Bottom incisors

Canines

Top incisors

BOTTOM JAW   TOP JAW

BALANCED DIET

Horses need a balanced diet, with enough vitamins and minerals to help them stay healthy and in condition. Horses should be fed little and often, and allowed constant access to fresh water.

Fruit and root vegetables must be chopped up lengthwise so the horse does not choke

Feed bowl holds carrots, corn, linseed, nuts, chaff, and a slice of apple

Hay is grass that has been cut and dried

Bucket of clean, fresh water

FOOD DANGERS

• Plants like deadly nightshade, bracken, and ragwort may poison a horse if it eats them in any quantity. Pastures where horses are left to graze must be cleared of these plants.

• Horses should not graze in an area within 14 days of any spraying.

BEHAVIOR

TODAY'S DOMESTIC HORSES show the same patterns of behavior as their wild ancestors. The herd instinct still dominates, and horses prefer to be kept in groups rather than on their own. Much of their behavior is linked to the way they communicate with other horses.

Horses sleep for only short periods at a time

SLEEPING
Horses are able to sleep standing up. In the wild, this increases their chances of escaping from predators.

EARS
The position of a horse's ears is an important indicator of its mood. If the ears point forward, this shows curiosity. When the horse is uncertain, it keeps one ear forward and the other backward.

SHIRE HORSE

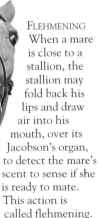

FLEHMENING
When a mare is close to a stallion, the stallion may fold back his lips and draw air into his mouth, over its Jacobson's organ, to detect the mare's scent to sense if she is ready to mate. This action is called flehmening.

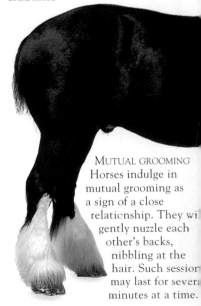

MUTUAL GROOMING
Horses indulge in mutual grooming as a sign of a close relationship. They will gently nuzzle each other's backs, nibbling at the hair. Such session may last for several minutes at a time.

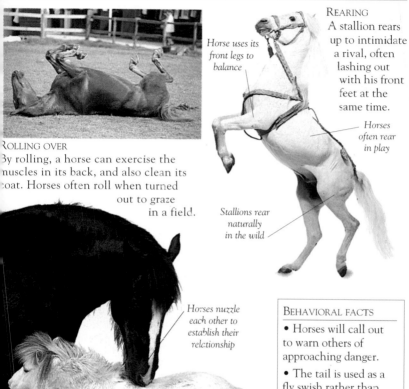

REARING
A stallion rears up to intimidate a rival, often lashing out with his front feet at the same time.

Horse uses its front legs to balance

Horses often rear in play

Stallions rear naturally in the wild

ROLLING OVER
By rolling, a horse can exercise the muscles in its back, and also clean its coat. Horses often roll when turned out to graze in a field.

Horses nuzzle each other to establish their relationship

SHETLAND PONY

BEHAVIORAL FACTS
• Horses will call out to warn others of approaching danger.

• The tail is used as a fly swish rather than for communication.

• Repeated pawing at the ground with the hooves is often a sign of nervousness.

• A horse's ears are very mobile and can rotate independently 180° forward and back.

USES OF THE HORSE

IN SPITE OF THE SPREAD of mechanization, the horse still has a place in society. Today, horses can be found hard at work in cities, forests, and farmland. While traditional horse sports like racing and steeple-chasing remain popular, they are now being joined by activities such as trail riding.

Working horses

Horses work in forests because they cause less damage than tractors. Farmers in developing countries also find horses easy to keep, as they can live off the land. Though no longer used in war, horses are retained in many countries for ceremonial duties and the police horse has so far proved to be irreplaceable.

MULE TRAINS
Even in the late 20th century, it has been hard to find anything to replace the mule to transport goods over uneven ground. Mules are still used in many parts of the world.

London police horses undergo about 40 weeks of training

488

ROYAL
ARTILLERY
HORSE AND
RIDER

CEREMONIAL DUTIES
Many countries still use horses for ceremonial duties. This dates from wars where horses were used as cavalry and to haul artillery.

POLICE HORSES
Mounted police can be seen in many cities today. Horses offer the rider a good view and mobility, and can move through crowds more easily than either motorcycles or cars.

Working cow ponies in the US tend to average 15 hh

Average working life of a police horse is about 14 years

BRITISH POLICE
HORSES AND
RIDERS IN
CEREMONIAL
DRESS

QUARTER
HORSE

HERDING CATTLE
Horses are still used to herd cattle and sheep in the Americas, the former USSR, Australia, and New Zealand.

Horses for sport and leisure

Since the end of World War II, there has been a tremendous increase in the use of the horse for pleasure. Sports such as horse racing remain as popular as ever, and interest in such competition as show jumping and dressage has been heightened by television. Riding vacations are now a popular and relaxing pastime for many people.

POLO
Probably originating in Persia, polo has been played for 2,500 years. Modern polo is played by two teams of four using long mallets to hit the ball into the opposition's goal.

DRESSAGE
The American Morgan Horse, once favored by the US cavalry, is shown in ridden and harnessed classes. It is also used for Western and pleasure riding, and jumping.

Rider sits on the horse's center of balance

A hard hat protects the rider's head in case of a fall

Pony will cover 3–6 miles (4.8–6.4 km) in an hour

The use of plain snaffle bridles for recreational riding is almost universal

RACEHORSES

Horse racing has become a huge international industry. This statue in the Kentucky Horse Park in the US, is of the famous racehorse *Man. O' War*, or *Big Red*, who was beaten only once in 21 races. When he died in 1947, more than 1,000 people attended his funeral.

HORSE SPORTS FACTS

• The longest-running horse race is the Palio in Siena, Italy, begun in the 1200s and still run today. The winning horse attends a special banquet afterward.

• The word polo comes from the Tibetan *pulu*, meaning ball.

• The first steeplechase was held in 1830 at St. Albans, England.

Riders learn to use aids such as the reins

Each rider keeps a pony-length away from the next

A novice rider is given a quiet, reliable horse

Riding school ponies are frequently cross-bred animals

RIDING VACATIONS

Those who want to ride occasionally or just for pleasure, can take a riding vacation. These rides can last from a single day to a whole week. The distance covered in each day varies between 10–25 miles (16–40 km). Trips are always supervised and provide an opportunity to reach beautiful and inaccessible areas of a country.

491

Index

Acknowledgments

Contributors to this title include:
Editors: Elise Bradbury, Laura Buller, Alan Burrows, Bernadette Crowley, Alastair Dougall, John Mapps, Susan McKeever, Miranda Smith, Leo Vita-Finzi, Selina Wood, Sarah Watson.

Designers: Alexandra Brown, Sarah Crouch, Janet Allis, Tanya Tween.

DK India Team:
Managing Editor: Punita Singh
Managing Art Editor: Rachana Bhattacharya
Senior Editor: Sheema Mookherjee
Senior Designer: Sabyasachi Kundu
Designer: Sukanto Bhattacharjya
DTP Coordinator: Jacob Joshua
DTP Designers: Sunil Sharma, Umesh Aggarwal

PAGEOne: Melanie McDowell, Chris Stewart, Suzanne Tuhrim, Sophie Williams.

Dorling Kindersley would like to thank: Hilary Bird and Mark Lambert for indexing, Robert Graham for research and editorial support, Caroline Potts for picture library services, Natural History Museum, University Museum of Zoology, Cambridge, Thurston Watson for model making.

Photographs by:
Julie Anderson, Dennis Avon, Akhil Bakhshi, Simon Battensby, Geoff Brightling, Jane Burton, Peter Chadwick, Gordon Clayton, Geoff Dann, Philip Dowell, Mike Dunning, Neil Fletcher, Steve Gorton, Frank Greenaway, Steve Gorton, Marc Henrie, Kit Houghton, Colin Keates, Dave King, Bob Langrish, Cyril Laubscher, Ranald Mackechnie, Andrew McRobb, Ray Moller, Tracy Morgan, Stephen Oliver, Oxford Scientific Films, Nick Parfit, Tim Ridley, Bill Sands, Karl Shone, Steve Shott, Harry Taylor, Kim Taylor, Michael Ward, Jerry Young.

Illustrations by:
Graham Allen, Janet Allis, Stephen Biesty, Joanna Cameron, Rowan Clifford, Karen Cochrane, John Davis, Ted Dewan, Gill Ellsbury, Samantha Elmhurst, Angelica Elsebach, Giuliano Fornari, Chris Forsey, Will Giles, Craig Gosling (Indiana University Medical Illustration Department), Tony Graham, Nick Hall, Nick Hewetson, John Hutchinson, Mark Iley, Stanley Cephas

Johnson, Aziz Khan, Richard Lewington, Kenneth Lilly, Ruth Lindsay, Mick Loates, Janos Marffy, Malcolm McGregor, Sean Milne, Richard Orr, Maurice Pledger, Sandra Pond, Bryan Poole, Sally Alane Reason, Colin Salmon, Tommy Swahn, John Temperton, Simon Thomas, Kevin Toy, David Webb, Amanda Williams, Ann Winterbotham, John Woodcock, Debra Woodward, Colin Woolf, Dan Wright.

Picture credits:

t=top b=bottom c=center l=left r=right

The publisher would like to thank the following for their kind permission to reproduce their photographs:
Dennis Avon 286b, 323bl; 346bl; Professor Edmund D. Brodie Jr. 165cr; Lester Cheeseman 251c; Dr. Barry Clarke 23tr; John Holmes 175cl; Colin Keates 27cl; Dave King 25cr; Bob Langrish 487tl; Leszczynski 157cl **Ardea/**M Krishnan 257bl; Eric Lingren 238tl
BBC Natural History Unit/Galleria Degli Uffizi, Florence 168tl
Bridgeman Art Library/210tl, 233br
Centaur Studios/175bl
Bruce Coleman/231bc; Jen and Des Bartlett 258-259, 279tl; Erwin & Peggy Bauer 216tl; Fred Bruemmer 203bl; John Cancalosi 236tl, 342bl; Eric Crichton 80cl; Gerald Cubitt 81br; Geoff Doré 81bc; M.P.L Fogden 154-

155; P.A. Hinchcliffe 60tr; Dr. M. T. Kahl 344tr; Jan van de Kam 338br; Stephen J. Krasemann 379tl; Gordon Langsbury 354-355b; 355r; Cyril Laubscher 290br; Werner Layer 366-367; Luiz Claudio Mango 307tr; George Mcarthy 287b;351tl; Michael McCoy 237tl; Rinie van Meurs 338 tr; Charlie Off 330bl; Dr. Eckart Pott 30-31, 133tc; Dr Sandro Prato 139tr; Hans Reinhard 99tl, 352cl, 361b, 365bc, 438-439; Hector Rivarola 349bl; Kevin Rushby 63tl; Dr Frieder Sauer 79br; Pacific Stock 142-143; Kim Taylor 51tr, 88cr, 94cr, 133tl, 272-273b, 302cr; 276c, 305b; 313cl; Norman Tomalin 106c
Mary Evans Picture Library/69ac, 151tr
FLPA/L Chance 237bl
Robert Harding/300cl; 301cr; 302cr; 353b; 475tr
Musée Nationale d'Histoire Naturelle/158tr 159tc
Naturhistoriska Riksmuseet/158c
Natural History Museum/Frank Greenaway 98cr; 99br, 16cr, 170cl, 170bl, 170br, 171tl, 172t, 172b, 173t, 173c, 173br, 177c, 179tl, 212bl, 212cl, 215cl, 216bl, 217t, 218b, 219t, 221tl, 223cr, 223br, 224tl, 225b, 226t, 226bl, 227br, 228b, 229t, 230–231, 230cr, 230b, 231c, 231t, 233t, 237tl, 241cr, 243br, 248r, 252bl, 256b, 437br
Nature Photographers/289tr; E.Lemon 300br; H. Miles 358bl; Paul Sterry 337br; 341r; 337br

Natural Science Photos/C Banks 221cr, 256tr, 256cl; M. Boulard 131bc; P. Bowman 92cl; M. Chinery 135cl; C Dani & I Jeske 209br, 221bl; Carol Farneti 106bl; Adrian Hoskins 95cr; G Kinns 246cl; JG Lilley 204c, 204b; Chris Mattison 227t, 246br; Jim Merli 176cr, 180bc, 188cl, 193tr, 255tl, 253t, 257tr; Pete Oxford 203tl, 205bl; Queensland Museum 253c; Richard Revels 92tr, 132cr, 252tr; C & T Stuart 249bl. P.H. & S.L. Ward 61cr, 137c; David Yendall 101tr

N.H.P.A/Stephen Dalton 437tl; Melvin Grey 271cl; Peter Johnson 362 bl; R & D Keller 373tl; Peter Parks 153br, 282tr; Philippa Scott 301tl; John Shaw 301br; 348r

Frank Lane Picture Agency/ E&D Hosking 281t; 303tr; 355tl; 362-363; 365cr;/ T&P Gardner; F.Polking 304br; Silvestris 328tr;/Roger Tidma 353t;/ Roger Wimshurst 307tr;/ W.Wisniewski 359br

Oxford Scientific Films/Doug Allen 364l; Larus Argentatus 274-275, 301bl; Kathie Atkinson 57tr; G.I. Bernard 101cl; Raymond Blythe 130bl; Densey Clyne 127tr; C.M. Collins 68bl; J.A.L. Cooke 79c, 134tl; David B. Fleetham 387tr; Michael Fogden 125tl; Peter Gathercole 67tr; Howard Hall 153t; 387cr; Stan Osolinski 166-167; Papilio

296br; Alan Root/Okapia 371cr

Mantis Wildlife Films/32cl; Peter O'Toole 68cr; James Robinson 76cr, 99br; Harold Taylor 83c; Steve Turner 81cr, 125tr; P & W Ward 124cr

Museum der Bildenden Kuenste, Leipzig/24cl

Planet Earth/K & K Ammann 387br; Andre Barttschi 321 bc; John R. Bracegirdle 386cl; Richard Coomber 436bl; Carol Farneti-Foster 449tr, 459tr, 386br; Daniel Heuclin 245bl; Gerard Lacz 217cr; John Lythgou 308b, 347tr; Mark Mattock 336cl; E Hanumantha Rao 244cl; Brian Kenney 232t, 236bl, 238bl, 255bl; Jonathan Scott 387bl, 387tl; Anup and Manoj Shah 451tr; Yuri Shibbnev 311tl; Martin Wendler 239c

Premaphotos/K.G. Preston-Mafham 59tr, 67br, 71br, 73cl, 74br, 80br, 106bl, 110bl, 123t, 123cr. Dr Bill Sands 70cr

Science Photo Library/Mark Deeble & Victoria Stone 213cr; John Downer 214br; Michael Fogden 215tr, 249tr; J.C. Revy 114cr; Tui de Roy 186cr; Alastair Shay 247cr

Tony Stone Images/Mike Surowiak 101bc; 196cl; Maurice Tibbles 189c

Werner Forman Archive/14cl

Wild Images/Romulus Whitaker 193br; 214tr; Howard Hall 153 cl

Jerry Young/12c, bl, br

Zefa/J. Schupe 7tr; 447tr, 455t.